MAKING IS CONNECTING

MAKING IS CONNECTING

The social meaning of creativity, from DIY and knitting to YouTube and Web 2.0

DAVID GAUNTLETT

polity

First published in 2011 by Polity Press
Reprinted in 2013
Polity Press
65 Bridge Street
Cambridge CB2 1UR, UK

Polity Press
350 Main Street
Malden, MA 02148, USA

ISBN-13: 978-0-7456-5001-2
ISBN-13: 978-0-7456-5002-9(pb)

A catalogue record for this book is available from the British Library.

Typeset in 10.75 on 14 pt Adobe Janson
by Servis Filmsetting Ltd, Stockport, Cheshire
Printed and bound in the United States by Edwards Brothers Malloy

For further information on Polity, visit our website:
www.politybooks.com

For Finn

CONTENTS

ACKNOWLEDGEMENTS

I am very grateful to my colleagues in the Communication and Media Research Institute (CAMRI), University of Westminster, for useful conversations and support, especially Pete Goodwin, Colin Sparks, Sally Feldman, Geoffrey Davies, Fatimah Awan, Jeanette Steemers, Anastasia Kavada, Tim Riley, Caroline Dover, Charles Brown, Anthony McNicholas, and David Hendy.

I am glad to acknowledge the UK's Arts and Humanities Research Council (AHRC), and the Research Council's UK Digital Economy programme, for research awards which, although not specifically supporting this project, did fund related work and gave me time to think about these things. These include four projects which commenced between 2007 and 2010, with the reference numbers AH/H038736/1, AH/F009682/1, AH/F006756/1, and EP/H032568/1. And I am grateful to Fatimah Awan and Anna Piela, for working hard on these projects when I wasn't.

Many thanks to Jenny Gauntlett, Pete Goodwin, and

Andrea Drugan, who took the trouble to read the whole manuscript, and made invaluable suggestions. Polity's anonymous reviewer, who later revealed himself to be Andrew Dubber, also provided excellent comments. Nick Couldry and Dougald Hine helped to spark ideas in general, and provided useful suggestions on the conclusion in particular. Thank you to Andrea Drugan at Polity for being such a supportive editor. Lauren Mulholland, Clare Ansell, and the copy-editor, Jane Fricker, have also been very helpful.

Tessy Britton, always full of examples of exciting community projects and other creative things, deserves special mention, and Cecilia Weckström at Lego was another inspiring source of things to think about. For general encouragement and support, and/or useful discussions, I am also grateful to Annette Hill, Knut Lundby, Paul Sweetman, Sonia Livingstone, Peter Lunt, Amanda Blake Soule, Jesper Just Jensen, Anna-Sophie Trolle Terkelsen, David Brake, Lizzie Jackson, Edith Ackermann, Thomas Wolbers, David Whitebread, and the super people at the School of Everything 'Unplugged' meetups, including David Jennings, Tony Hall, and Alison Powell.

Thanks also to the students who took my new and untested 'Creativity' module at the University of Westminster in spring 2010.

As ever, love and thanks to Jenny and Finn for supporting and inspiring me every day. And as always, the responsibility for any errors, weird arguments, sentimentality, and unreasonable optimism that you may find here remains my own.

1

INTRODUCTION

This is a book about what happens when people make things. I hope it will add to the conversation about the power of the internet and the World Wide Web – a place where we have seen everyday creativity flourish in recent years. But people have been making things – and thinking about the meaning of making things – for a very long time. And the power of making, and connecting through creating, extends well beyond the online world to all kinds of activities in everyday life.

I hope to pull some of these things together, in ways which are hopefully not too obvious as we start. You may reasonably wonder, for instance, how a commentary by Victorian art critic John Ruskin on medieval cathedrals can have affected my understanding of YouTube videos. And you may be surprised when the nineteenth-century socialist and tapestry-weaver William Morris dispenses a blueprint for the making and sharing ethos of Web 2.0 in general, and Wikipedia in particular, 120 years early. We will note how the former Catholic

priest and radical philosopher Ivan Illich outlined the necessary terms of human happiness, 40 years ago, see how it lines
up with the latest studies by economists and social scientists
today, and then connect it with knitting, guerrilla gardening, and creative social networks. But not necessarily in that
order. We will encounter the 1970s feminist Rozsika Parker,
explaining embroidery as a 'weapon of resistance', and several
knitters, badge-makers, and bloggers, and they will help us to
think about how making things for ourselves gives us a sense
of wonder, agency, and possibilities in the world.

MAKING IS CONNECTING

This brings us to the title of the book: 'Making is connecting'. It's a perfectly simple phrase, of course. But having spent
some time thinking about people making things, and people
connecting with others – making *and* connecting – I realized
that it was meaningful, and more pleasing, to note that these
are one and the same process: making *is* connecting.

I mean this in three principal ways:

- Making is connecting because you have to connect things
  together (materials, ideas, or both) to make something new;
- Making is connecting because acts of creativity usually
  involve, at some point, a social dimension and connect us
  with other people;
- And making is connecting because through making
  things and sharing them in the world, we increase our
  engagement and connection with our social and physical
  environments.

Of course, there will be objections and exceptions to each of
these, which we may consider along the way. But that's my
basic set of propositions.

THREE REASONS WHY I WANTED
TO WRITE THIS BOOK

This book came about because of a number of things I had been thinking about, which I hope are worth listing briefly here.

First, I started out as a sociologist interested in the place of media in people's lives. That was OK for a while, but 15 and even 10 years ago, the main media that people were usually dealing with was produced by big professional organizations, and it seemed somewhat subservient to be exploring what people were doing with their products. Some of the activity was quite active, thoughtful, and imaginative, some of it was mundane, and none of it could score very highly on a scale of creativity because it was all about creative works made by *other people*. Thankfully, the World Wide Web soared in popularity, becoming mainstream in itself, and opened up a world of diversity and imagination where the content itself is created by everyday users (as well as a growing number of professionals). This opportunity to make media and, in particular, share it easily, making connections with others, was unprecedented in both character and scale, and therefore a much more exciting thing to study.

Second, this exciting world of participation was, therefore, an exciting thing to participate in *myself*. I've always liked making things, but they didn't have an audience. With the Web, making writings, photographs, drawings – and indeed websites themselves – available to the world was so easy. It was also rewarding, as people would see your stuff and then send nice comments and links to their own. So I experienced the feeling that making is connecting for myself.

Third, and stemming from the academic interests mentioned in the first point, I was meant to be doing research about what people did, and why, but had always been uncomfortable with the idea of just speaking to them, taking them through an 'interview' for my own purposes, without giving them anything very interesting to *do*. Therefore, for several years, I have been developing 'creative research methods' where people are asked to *make* something as part of the process. The idea is that going through the thoughtful, physical process of making something – such as a video, a drawing, a decorated box, or a Lego model – an individual is given the opportunity to reflect, and to make their thoughts, feelings or experiences manifest and tangible. This unusual experience gets the brain firing in different ways, and can generate insights which would most likely not have emerged through directed conversation. I have found that the process is especially revealing and effective when people are asked to express themselves using metaphors. All of this was discussed in my previous book *Creative Explorations*.[1] In these studies it was clear that thinking and making are aspects of the same process. Typically, people mess around with materials, select things, experimentally put parts together, rearrange, play, throw bits away, and generally manipulate the thing in question until it approaches something that seems to communicate meanings in a satisfying manner. This rarely seems to be a matter of 'making what I thought at the start', but rather a process of discovery and having ideas *through* the process of making. In particular, taking *time* to make something, using the hands, gave people the opportunity to clarify thoughts or feelings, and to see the subject-matter in a new light. And having an image or physical object to present and discuss enabled them to communicate and connect with other people more directly.

Maybe in the end that's more than three, but for all these reasons I wanted to explore the idea that making is connecting.

WEB 2.0 AS AN IDEA AND A METAPHOR

This book does not suppose that creative activities have suddenly appeared in the story of human life because someone invented the World Wide Web. However, the Web has certainly made it easier for everyday people to share the fruits of their creativity with others, and to collaboratively make interesting, informative, and entertaining cultural spaces. This process has been boosted by the emergence of 'Web 2.0', a term which I'll be using quite a bit in this book. So we should pause here to clarify what 'Web 2.0' means. It's not simply a particular kind of technology, or a business model, and it certainly isn't a sequel to the Web as previously known. Web 2.0 describes a particular kind of ethos and approach.

I normally explain it using a PowerPoint slide showing gardens and an allotment that I made using Lego (see figure 1). In the first decade or so of the Web's existence (from the 1990s to the early to mid-2000s), websites tended to be like separate gardens. So, for example, the NASA website was one garden, and my Theory.org.uk website was another garden, and a little-known poet had made her own poetry website, which was another garden. You could visit them, and each of them might be complex plots of creative and beautiful content, but basically they were separate, with a fence between each one. There's nothing *wrong* with this model, as such; it works perfectly well as a platform for all kinds of individuals, groups, or organizations, big and small, to make stuff available online. But this model is what we might now call 'Web 1.0'. By contrast, Web 2.0 is like a collective allotment. Instead of individuals tending their own gardens, they come together to work collaboratively in a shared space.

This is actually what Tim Berners-Lee had meant his World Wide Web to be like, when he invented it in 1990.

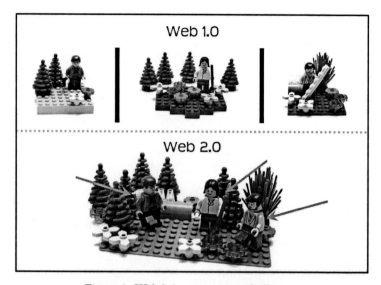

Figure 1. Web 2.0 as a communal allotment

He imagined that browsing the Web would be a matter of writing and editing, not just searching and reading. The first years of the Web, then, were an aberration, and it has only more recently blossomed in the way its creator intended. As an illustration of this, I clearly remember that when I read about this read/write model in Berners-Lee's book, *Weaving the Web*, when it was published in 1999, it seemed like a nice idea, but naïve, and bonkers. How could it possibly work? I didn't want to spend hours crafting my lovely webpages only for some visitor to come along and mess them up. But of course, my problem – shared with most other people at the time – was that I had not learned to recognize the power of the network. We still thought of everybody 'out there' as basically 'audience'.

At the heart of Web 2.0 is the idea that online sites and services become more powerful the more that they *embrace* this network of potential collaborators. Rather than just seeing the internet as a broadcast channel, which brings an audience to a website (the '1.0' model), Web 2.0 invites users in to play. Sites such as YouTube, eBay, Facebook, Flickr, Craigslist, and Wikipedia only exist and have value because people use and contribute to them, and they are clearly *better* the more people are using and contributing to them. This is the essence of Web 2.0. The man who coined the term, Tim O'Reilly, has drawn up four levels of 'Web 2.0-ness' to illustrate this.[2] In this hierarchy, a 'level three' application could 'only exist on the net, and draws its essential power from the network and the connections it makes possible between people or applications', whereas a 'level zero' application is the kind of thing that you could distribute on a CD without losing anything. (Levels one and two are mid-points in between.)

So Web 2.0, as an approach to the Web, is about harnessing the collective abilities of the members of an online network, to make an especially powerful resource or service. But, thinking beyond the Web, it may also be valuable to consider Web 2.0 as a metaphor, for any collective activity which is enabled by people's passions and becomes something greater than the sum of its parts.

In the books *We Think* by Charles Leadbeater, and both *Here Comes Everybody* and *Cognitive Surplus* by Clay Shirky, the authors discuss the example of Wikipedia, noting the impressive way in which it has brought together enthusiasts and experts, online, to collaboratively produce a vast encyclopaedia which simply would not exist without their millions of contributions.[3] These contributions, of course, are given freely, and without any reward (apart, of course, from the warm glow of participation, and the very minor recognition of having your username listed somewhere in an article's history logs). Both authors then go on to consider whether the Wikipedia model of encyclopaedia-making can be translated across to – well, everything else. In these cases, Wikipedia becomes a metaphor for highly participatory and industrious collaboration. However, most of the time they're not *really* thinking of 'everything else' – it's 'everything else online'. Wikipedia becomes a model of highly participatory and industrious *online* collaboration. But the really powerful metaphorical leap would be to go from Web 2.0 to real life – the social world and all its complexities, not just from Wikipedia to other internet services.[4]

So, in this book we will, in part, be taking the message of making, sharing, and collaboration, which has become familiar to the people who enthuse about Web 2.0, and seeing if it works in a broader context – in relation to both offline and online activities – and with bigger issues: real social problems rather than virtual online socializing. This connects with the argument – or the hope – that we are seeing a shift away from a 'sit back and be told' culture towards more of a 'making and doing' culture. The 'sit back and be told' position is forcefully introduced in schools, and then gently reinforced by television and the magic of the glossy, shiny, and new in consumer culture; the 'making and doing' is what this book is all about.

THE 'SIT BACK AND BE TOLD' CULTURE

Since the historical point at which education became institutionalized in a system of schools, learning has become a process directed by a teacher, whose task it is to transfer nuggets of knowledge into young people's minds. It has not always been this formulaic, of course, and some teachers have always sought to inspire their students to produce their own perspectives on art, poetry, or science. Nevertheless, and in spite of some innovative pedagogical thinking in the 1960s and 1970s, school education has tended to settle around a model where a body of knowledge is input into students, who are tested on their grasp of it at a later point.

In the UK, for example, this became especially embedded through the introduction of a National Curriculum (from 1988), with tests for children aged 7, 11, and 14, as well as the qualifications examined at 16 and advanced levels up to age 18, intended to record student performance across the country and therefore to enable the production of school 'league tables'. Teachers would therefore support their students best by preparing them for tests and stuffing them full of the 'right' answers. The limitations of this approach to learning were, thankfully, not lost on teachers, journalists, and others – even though conservative newspapers seemed to be both delighted that 'standards' could finally be monitored and compared, but also appalled by the falling quality of education which seemed to accompany the introduction of these tests and tables, even though the test scores seemed to get better and better. (The tests for 14-year-olds were scrapped in 2009 – but more to reduce the administrative burden on the examinations system, rather than the burden on students.[5]) In the United States, the 'No Child Left Behind' legislation introduced in 2001–2, despite its pleasant-sounding title, similarly made regular testing mandatory in US schools, with similar results: test scores might seem to rise, but many critical groups argue that the quality of *learning* sinks.[6] In 2010, an overhaul of the system proposed by President Obama appeared to include significant changes to funding formulas, but no change at all to the system of regular student testing, which would remain at the heart of what *The New York Times* described as a renewed 'drive to impose accountability for students' standardized test results'.[7]

Meanwhile, the twentieth century was emphatically the era of 'sit back and be told' media: especially in the second half of that century, leisure time became about staying in, not

going out, and remaining pretty much in the same spot for
long chunks of time, looking at a screen. This isn't a gloomy
view, it's the facts: in 2010, Americans watched on average
over four and a half hours of television per day, much as they
had done for several decades.[8] In the UK, it's just under four
hours per day.[9] This is, of course, a lot, and since it's an average, you know that for everybody watching less than this,
there are as many other people watching more.

Marshall McLuhan's famous statement that 'the medium
is the message' can be taken in various ways, but fundamentally it points to the way in which the arrival of a medium,
such as television, in our lives, can affect the way we live –
not really because of the content of the messages it carries,
but from the generally less noticed ways in which it causes us
to rearrange our affairs. This is a very good insight. Media
'effects', when we are talking about media *content*, are notori-
ously hard to measure, generally inconsequential, and mixed
up with other influences.[10] But the overall 'effect' of the
introduction of television – assuming that the broadcasters
offer some reasonably enjoyable or informative programmes
– is clearly *massive* in terms of how people spend their lives.

Four hours of viewing, as an *average*, and *every day*, is an
astonishing transformation in how human beings spend time,
compared with the pre-television era. This doesn't mean
that television is full of rubbish or that people are idiots for
watching it. It's not hard to find four hours of informative
and entertaining things on telly every day. But it would be
difficult to argue that this was a highly creative or sociable
way for people to spend their time, or that this is not an
extraordinary change in the way that human beings spend
their non-working hours, compared with the preceding few
thousand years.

This relatively passive orientation to time outside work is
further reinforced, as mentioned above, by consumer culture.

As Theodor Adorno and Max Horkheimer observed in the 1940s, and as many critics have noted since, modern capitalism succeeds not by menacing us, or dramatically crushing our will on the industrial wheel, but by encouraging us to enjoy a flow of convenient, cheerful stuff, purchased from shops, which gives us a feeling of satisfaction, if not happiness.[11] Few of us are immune to the appeal of attractively packaged items, with the sheen and smell of newness, which help us to forget our troubles, at least for a moment.

The notion of the *fetish* might be useful in understanding this. The fetish has sexual connotations, but these are not (necessarily) crucial here. In Freud, a fetish is basically about unconsciously overcoming anxiety through attachment to particular objects.[12] In Marx, the fetish describes the way in which we forget that the value of a commodity is a social value, and come to think of it as independent and real.[13] Somewhere between these two related ideas, we might see the fetish as the common, everyday way in which we find pleasure in the purchase of consumer goods, and acknowledge that it may be silly or irrational, but still a pleasure; and then consistently forget how temporary this diversion is. Between them, television and consumerism draw people into a dully 'satisfied' reverie in which – as we will see later – it may not be especially surprising that environmental pollution and other societal problems are generally seen as troubling, but distant, and basically 'somebody else's problem'.

TOWARDS A 'MAKING AND DOING' CULTURE

More optimistically, however, we can see a growing engagement with a 'making and doing' culture. This orientation rejects the passivity of the 'sit back' model, and seeks opportunities for creativity, social connections, and personal growth. Guy Claxton's 2008 discussion of education, *What's the Point of School*, highlights ways in which some teachers are beginning to reject the 'sit back and be told' school culture described above, and instead are setting their students challenges which are much more about making and doing.[14] Students are encouraged to work together to ask questions, explore different strategies of investigation, and create their own solutions. This approach is open about the fact that learning is an ongoing process that everyone is engaged in – teachers themselves might show that they are engaged in a learning project, such as starting to keep bees, or learning a musical instrument. Rather than displaying laminated examples of the 'best answer' on the walls, these classrooms show works in progress, experiments, even things that have gone wrong. They encourage a 'hands-on' approach to learning, and a spirit of enquiry and questioning.

In the case of the media, there is obviously the shift towards internet-based interactivity, which has had a genuine impact on the way that people spend time and on the ways in which they can connect with each other. Today, at least three-quarters of the population of the UK and USA are regular internet users, with almost all young people using it regularly.[15] A large-scale study of young people across the USA, published by the Kaiser Family Foundation in 2010, found that 74 per cent of 12- to 18-year-olds had created a profile on a social networking website, 49 per cent had read blogs, 28 per cent had written a blog, and 25 per cent had posted a video.[16] In the UK, online social networks are just as popular, with more than a third of the whole population having an account on Facebook, for example.[17] Every year, more and more people are writing blogs, participating in online discussions, sharing information, music and photos, and uploading video that they have made themselves.[18] The desire to communicate and share via social networks such as Facebook has also been the key driver in the growth of internet access on mobile phones.[19] The popularity of Web 2.0 is especially significant here, as easy-to-use online tools which enable people to learn about, and from, each other, and to collaborate and share resources, have made a real difference to what people do with, and can get from, their electronic media. The *range* of collaborative things that people do online is extraordinary. Academics, to some extent, have tended to focus on the more 'serious' uses, such as political activism, and the ubiquitous Wikipedia. But of course there are online communities about absolutely everything.

In the non-virtual world, there is a resurgence of interest in craft activities, clubs, and fairs,[20] and their DIY technology equivalents involving machines and robotics, as celebrated in *Make* magazine.[21] Environmental concerns have encouraged people to reduce the amount of stuff they consume, and to find new ways to re-use and recycle. The Transition Towns movement has encouraged communities to work together to find sustainable ways of living.[22] And as we will see, the Web has played an important role in offline real-world activities, as a tool for communication, networks, and organization.

DEFINING CREATIVITY

I will use the word 'creativity' – and the phrase 'everyday creativity' – quite freely in this book, in relation to the activities of making which are rewarding to oneself and to others. Attempting to produce a clear-cut and simple definition of creativity can be a diverting and sometimes frustrating task, but we'll start thinking about it here and then come back to it later.

Let's start by looking at how other people define 'creativity'. Mihaly Csikszentmihalyi is perhaps the best-known of today's creativity researchers. His *Creativity* study was based on interviews with people who were at the highest end of observed creativity – famous creative names, several of whom had won Nobel prizes for their inventions or creations. This seems to put him at the old-fashioned, or at least the elite, end of the scale, but there are perfectly good reasons for this. Csikszentmihalyi has pioneered a sociological approach to creativity, which is actually not at all old-fashioned or traditional: it rejects the classical notion of the creative 'genius' and instead observes how the thing we call creativity emerges from a particular supportive environment. Rather than being a lightning-bolt of unexpected inspiration, he argues, creative outputs appear from individuals who have worked hard over many years to master a particular 'symbolic domain' (physics, poetry, architecture, or whatever) and are encouraged by other supportive individuals, groups, and organizations. Csikszentmihalyi is interested in the sociological question of how these things come about – surges of creativity which make a difference to culture, science, or society. He writes:

> Creativity, at least as I define it in this book, is a process by which a symbolic domain in the culture is changed. New songs, new ideas, new machines are what creativity is all about.[23]

This is high-impact creativity, and importantly, it is creativity which is noticed and appreciated by other people:

> According to this view, creativity results from the interaction of a system composed of three elements: a culture that contains symbolic rules, a person who brings novelty into the symbolic domain, and a field of experts who recognise and validate the innovation.[24]

So the inventive individual is only one part of this triad. Creativity in Csikszentmihalyi's formulation needs a particu-

lar established context in which to happen, and also needs to
be recognized as something significant by other key people
working in that domain. As he puts it:

> Just as the sound of a tree crashing in the forest is unheard
> if nobody is there to hear it, so creative ideas vanish unless
> there is a receptive audience to record and implement
> them.[25]

This approach to creativity sets the bar very high, of course.
First you have to produce something brilliantly original, that
has never been seen before in the world. Then, as if that
wasn't hard enough already, it has to be recognized as a brilliantly original thing by other people. Furthermore, they
can't be just *any* people, but have to be the movers and shak-
ers, the well-known thought leaders, in the field where you
hope to make an impact. (This makes life especially difficult
since the established people in any particular area are often
very attached to their own high status, and are not necessarily likely to give a warm reception to promising newcomers.)

That's one way of looking at creativity, and it is the
right lens for Csikszentmihalyi's analysis of the social conditions which enable recognized, significant innovations
to emerge. Other writers on creativity have also followed
Csikszentmihalyi's definitions and approach, sometimes
in a bid to illuminate 'lower level' creativity. But the lens
which is helpful for asking 'How do major cultural or scientific innovations emerge?' is not necessarily the right lens
for studying the much more everyday instances of creativity
which concern us in this book.

After all, we do typically think of creativity as something
which can happen quite routinely, whenever any of us does
something in an unexpected but striking and inventive way.
We don't *only* say that something is 'creative' when it has

been recognized with a Nobel prize, nor do we limit the label to the kind of thing that each of us only does once or twice in a lifetime. Because we are inventive human beings, creativity is something we do rather a lot, and understood in this broad sense it includes everyday ideas we have about how to do things, many of the things we write and produce, acts of management or self-presentation, and even, of course, witty or insightful speech.

When taken down to this everyday level, the edges of what we might call creativity become rather fuzzy, of course. If I managed to bake and decorate a birthday cake which looked like a dinosaur, for instance, I would feel really 'creative'. And you might agree. But if you had been told that I was a professional birthday-cake maker who had been producing the same dinosaur cake for ten years, you definitely wouldn't. Between these two poles, my creativity rating might also be affected by, say, whether or not you thought it was 'cheating' to use shop-bought sweets to represent the eyes and scales, and whether or not you suspected I'd looked at pictures of other dinosaur cakes on the internet. It's easy to get bogged down in this kind of thing. But as I said in *Creative Explorations*:

> You could argue endlessly, if you wanted to be rather trivial, about whether one thing 'is' and another thing 'is not' creative. But that's not really the point. The point is that creativity is widely dispersed and, more importantly, is one of the most central aspects of being human.[26]

Most of the research literature *about* creativity, however, does not really take this view. A reasonable summary is provided by Charles Lumsden, who considered a range of definitions from leading figures, and found that 'the "definitions" of creativity I have seen in the literature . . . carry the unique imprint of their progenitors while suggesting some mild degree of consensus: creativity as a kind of capacity to think up something new that people find significant'.[27] The trouble with this approach, though – as I'll go on to say in chapter 3 – is the strong emphasis on the end product, and the judgement of others. Creativity might be better understood as a *process*, and a *feeling*. In this way of looking at it, creativity is about breaking new ground, but internally: the sense of going somewhere, doing something that you've not done before. This might lead to fruits which others can appreciate, but those may be secondary to the process of creativity itself, which is best identified from within.

Hold onto these thoughts for now. In a section at the end of chapter 3 I'll be wheeling out a gleaming new definition of creativity which hopefully overcomes these problems.

WHAT THIS BOOK IS AND WHAT IT IS NOT

This book is a discussion about the value of everyday creativity, taking in handmade physical objects and real-life experiences as well as the recent explosion of online creativity. Indeed, it seeks to make connections from one sphere to the other, in the hope that we can learn about recent Web 2.0 creativity by looking at what people have said about the values, ethics, and benefits of more traditional craft and DIY activities, and perhaps also vice versa. This is generally done through the use of some relevant theories and philosophies – quite grounded and earthy ones, nothing very abstract – and knitted, I hope, into the reality and experience of particular creative activities.

This is *not*, though, a set of case studies about particular craftspeople, artisans, bloggers, and YouTube-makers. That wasn't meant to be the point of this book – you can get such material elsewhere, and I didn't want the discussion to be based around a sequence of meetings and anecdotes. Nor is it one of those books which weaves together autobiography with more general insight – although if you want that kind of thing, happily I can now recommend two very good books which came out around the time I was finishing writing this one: *The Case for Working with Your Hands: or Why Office Work is Bad for Us and Fixing Things Feels Good* by the philosopher and motorcycle mechanic Matthew Crawford (published in the USA with the slightly shorter title, *Shop Class as Soulcraft: An Inquiry into the Value of Work*), and *Made by Hand: Searching for Meaning in a Throwaway World* by Mark Frauenfelder, the editor-in-chief of *Make* magazine.[28] Those two books, along with Richard Sennett's excellent *The Craftsman* – which I also recommend – primarily concern the values, applied intelligence, and feelings associated with making things *by hand*, as well as the need to understand how our material world works so that we can engage with it, fix it, or transform it.[29]

This book is about those things too, to some extent, and includes a few autobiographical bits, but it's more about the value of making stuff more generally. In particular, it's about making and sharing our own *media* culture – I mean, via lo-fi YouTube videos, eccentric blogs, and homemade websites, rather than by having to take over the traditional media of television stations and printing presses – which isn't quite 'by hand' in the literal pottery-making, woodcarving sense, but which I feel is still basically a handicraft which connects us with others through its characterful, personality-imprinted, individual nature, as well as because it's a form of communication.

AND THE *REAL* POINT OF THE BOOK IS . . .

The other reason why the book mostly doesn't pick over lots of examples of creativity, one by one, is because I wanted to address the broader question of *'Why* is everyday creativity important?' Because I feel that it's incredibly important – important for society – and therefore *political.* And, to be frank about my motives, people don't seem to get this. Presenting this kind of thing in front of academics who see themselves as 'critical' and 'political' scholars, I get the definite feeling that they think that what I'm doing is, at best, a sweet kind of sideshow. Whilst they struggle with 'real' issues such as government regulation of broadcasting, or something to do with political parties, I am enthusing about everyday people making nice objects or clever little videos, which may be pleasant but is an irrelevance in terms of political or social concerns. If it's any kind of issue at all, it's a 'cultural' one: and who cares really if people watch silly entertainment on television, or if they make their own silly entertainment; if they grow their own flowers, make their own toys or gloves, or buy them from a supermarket; or if people write their own songs, or buy someone else's.

But I think it's absolutely *crucial.* Even if each of the things made seems, to a grumpy observer, rather trivial. You may note that my examples just above are not the absolute essentials of life – people can survive without silly entertainment, flowers, gloves, or songs, if they have to. But it is the fact that people have made a *choice* – to make something themselves rather than just consume what's given by the big suppliers – that is significant. Amplified slightly, it leads to a whole new way of looking at things, and potentially to a real political shift in how we deal with the world.

One example of how the idea of everyday creativity can be scaled up into something significant, political, and vitally important, is the Transition movement. The Transition movement stems from the idea that – although we are likely to face really huge challenges as climate change grows, and as the oil that we rely on so much runs out – human beings are *creative* and can work well together to do great things. And therefore, if we think imaginatively together, and make plans and ideas for a new enjoyable way of living which doesn't rely so much on the environmentally damaging things, or things we're running out of, then we might be OK. This is an approach based on optimism and creativity, and it could actually work. The movement is taking off, and you can read about it in the books *The Transition Handbook* by Rob Hopkins and *The Transition Timeline* by Shaun Chamberlin, or at the website, www.transitionnetwork.org.[30]

The Transition movement is a great illustration of what I'm talking about, then, but so is the less obviously 'political' content of online video and craft sites, and everyday home-made events, untrained attempts at art, humble efforts to make a knitted owl with solar-powered eyes, and anything else where people are rejecting the givens and are making their world anew. This helps us to build *resilience* – one of the key Transition words – and the *creative capacity* to deal with significant challenges.

OUTLINE OF THE BOOK

The book begins by forgetting about the internet at first, and exploring some philosophical, political, and practical explanations of the human drive to make things. In chapter 2 this is mostly centred around two Victorian makers and thinkers, John Ruskin and William Morris. In chapter 3, we look at more recent craft and DIY ideas, activities, and motivations. By chapter 4, we arrive at the internet again, and consider 'making is connecting' in online environments.

Then we turn to the value of having social connections, and collaborative projects, in everyday life: chapter 5 looks at recent research into happiness, and chapter 6 considers 'social capital' – the community glue made up of friendly connections with others. Chapter 7 is about having the tools for creative expression and making a difference, and features quite a bit of the philosopher Ivan Illich. Chapter 8 takes on some of the criticisms of Web 2.0 and its enthusiasts, and finds reason to disagree with some, but concur with others. Finally, chapter 9 pulls things together in a conclusion, where we set out five key principles of 'making is connecting', and consider their implications in terms of the media, education, work, politics, and the environment.

One note, before we begin: in the text I haven't included URLs, the addresses of websites, where this would be redundant. For example, when I mention YouTube, I don't then say '(www.youtube.com)' because it seems unnecessary, and such sites are so easy to search for anyway. And when I mention Freecycle, the Freecycle site that would be of most interest to you would depend which country you're in, so again I assume you can find it for yourself. (I do state URLs where there are important subtle differences – like when I am talking about www.landshare.net and not www.landshare.com.)

This book has a website at http://www.makingisconnecting.org. The site includes videos, additional material, relevant links, and other information.

2

THE MEANING OF MAKING I:

PHILOSOPHIES OF CRAFT

In this chapter, and the next one, we will begin our more detailed study of the idea that 'making is connecting', by looking (mostly) at the offline, non-digital world of people making things for themselves and others. This is the activity that we might call 'craft' – although that phrase is loaded with connotations which will vary between people and between places. Craft might suggest the careful work of a woodcarver or a ceramicist, a skilled practice of making beautiful objects. The term might be associated with traditional and rather twee items which you might have seen on sale at craft fairs in church halls – corn dollies and doilies at surprisingly high prices. Or it might suggest a newer, cool approach to making things yourself, as seen in the recent rise of knitting, 'craft guerrilla' fairs, DIY culture, and other trendy craft activities.

The term 'craft' is further complicated by its relationship with 'art'. Somehow the two concepts have become separated, so that 'art' tends to mean the truly creative transformation of ideas and emotions into visual objects (or texts, performances, music, or whatever), whilst 'craft' – having been shoved out of that space – ends up indicating the less prestigious production of carvings or pots, by less creative people who just like making carvings or pots. This view is, of course, most unfair. As Peter Dormer has observed:

> The separation of craft from art and design is one of the phenomena of late-twentieth-century Western culture. The consequences of this split have been quite startling. It has led to the separation of 'having ideas' from 'making objects'. It has also led to the idea that there exists some sort of mental attribute known as 'creativity' that precedes or can be divorced from a knowledge of how to make things.[1]

One way to avoid this trap is to reject the positioning of 'art' as superior, and instead to regard its stance as unnecessarily pretentious and exclusive, and therefore rather silly, in comparison to the more earthy, engaged spirit of craft. There is still, of course, the problem that this may not be the majority or dominant view.

In recent years the status of craft has been helped by Richard Sennett's excellent book *The Craftsman* – amongst readers and thinkers, I mean, rather than amongst doers and makers, who may not need such writings to persuade them. Sennett argues vigorously against the second-class status of craft, and is especially good on his core theme that thinking and making are aspects of one unified process. The craftsperson does not do the thinking and then move on to the mechanical act of making: on the contrary, making is part of thinking, and, he adds, feeling; and thinking and feeling are part of making.[2] Sennett emphasizes craft as a unity of body and mind – in particular, working with the hands as a central part of the process of thinking and making

– and craft as exploration, a process of 'problem solving and problem finding'.[3] More broadly, in Sennett's hands, craft becomes a process of making personal self-identity, and citizenship. Sennett treats craft with great seriousness, which is warranted, and welcome, and rather moving. But he perhaps misses some of the dimension of pleasure, even joy. As Ellen Dissanayake has written:

> There is an inherent pleasure in making. We might call this *joie de faire* (like *joie de vivre*) to indicate that there is something important, even urgent, to be said about the sheer enjoyment of making something exist that didn't exist before, of using one's own agency, dexterity, feelings and judgment to mold, form, touch, hold and craft physical materials, apart from anticipating the fact of its eventual beauty, uniqueness or usefulness.[4]

This urgent need to *make*, for the sake of the pleasure and understanding gained within the process of making itself, is identified by Dormer as one of the reasons why craft has been able to survive, and perhaps become stronger, in spite of its detachment from so-called fine art:

> Enough people have wanted to go on making things. Enough people believe they can expand their ideas and knowledge about the world through learning and practicing a craft. Some people believe that if you want to truly understand a thing you have to make a version of that thing – a model, representation, or piece of mimetic art.[5]

The two quotations above seem to sum up some essential dimensions of craft: the inherent satisfaction of making; the sense of being alive within the process; and the engagement with ideas, learning, and knowledge which come not before or after but *within* the practice of making. These engaging ideals are at the heart of all artistic and creative impulses, and make a mockery of the idea that craft is an inferior or second-class kind of activity. Whilst 'fine art' is more dependent on hierarchies and elites, upon which it relies to validate the work, craft is more about creativity and the process of making at a vibrant, grassroots level: proud of its grounded, everyday nature, and not insecurely waiting for an artworld critic, collector, or curator to one day say that it was all worthwhile. In particular, craft seems to be about a *drive* to make and share things, no matter what anyone says. In a different essay, Peter Dormer writes:

> Making – craft, skill, and the realisation of an object through craft labour – is not a trivial issue for craftspeople. Making is both the means through which the craftsperson explores their obsession or idea and an end in itself.[6]

In this sense, making and connecting is not an option – it is experienced as a necessity. It seems vital and contemporary, but woven into a vision of craft – a connection between humans and handmade objects and nature – which is as old as the hills. Actually, though, as we will see in the next chapter, the notion of 'craft' which today seems timeless is actually quite new. It began with two Victorian thinkers who hated Victorian times, John Ruskin and William Morris, whose work and ideas occupy the rest of this chapter. Why are we looking at these two long-dead men? The answer lies, as you will see, in their ideas about *creativity* as a part of everyday life, and as a binding force in 'fellowship' – which today we would call *community*. In their own ways, they were saying that 'making is connecting', and their works have much to offer today.

JOHN RUSKIN

Ruskin was born in 1819, making him 15 years older than Morris. Although we typically picture eminent Victorians as craggy prophets with lots of grey hair and beards, Ruskin got going early. At the point when he published the second volume of *The Stones of Venice*, a book which really impressed William Morris whilst a new undergraduate at Oxford – in 1853 – both were young men (at 34 and 19 respectively).

Ruskin was extremely prolific. He is remembered primarily as an artist and art critic, and as a social thinker, but he also produced poetry and fiction, and wrote about architecture, geology, literature, science, and the environment. It is his ideas about art and society, and his critique of the dehumanized model of industrial production which we will focus on here.

Ruskin's opposition to industrialism, and exploitative capitalism, and his care for the common worker, mean that today we would interpret his stance as 'obviously' a left-wing, socialist kind of position. However, Ruskin is often described as a 'conservative', and indeed he begins his autobiographical *Praeterita* with the declaration, 'I am, and my father was before me, a violent Tory of the old school.'[7]

To modern viewers, who tend to place political philosophies – at least as a starting-point – on a left-wing to right-wing spectrum, this can seem confusing – or it certainly does if you assume that the conservatives and Tories must go on the right. In fact, a Ruskin kind of conservatism, which yearns for the (rather distant and idealized) past because of an attachment to the values of communities, local-level organic production, care for the environment, and valuing all workers rather than treating them as parts in a machine, all sounds quite radical and progressive to modern ears – or it does if you see them as a programme for the future, rather than just the mourning of a lost past. That was certainly the attraction for William Morris. As Clive Wilmer notes:

> No political label quite fits Ruskin's politics. . . . His 'Toryism' was such that it could, in his own lifetime, inspire the socialism of William Morris and the founders of the Labour Party; and when he called himself a 'conservative', he usually meant as a preserver of the environment – what we should call a 'conservationist'.[8]

Ruskin's writing was often complex, and unpredictable – not necessarily in a good way. In one lecture he declared, 'For myself, I am never satisfied that I have handled a subject properly till I have contradicted myself at least three times.'[9] Nevertheless, within his massive output there are certain jewels of clarity and vision. One of these is *Unto This Last*, a set of four essays published as a book in 1862, in which the author brings together his ideas to form a powerful moral critique of *laissez-faire* economics – the newly established orthodoxy which maintained that unimpeded individual self-interest should be the driving force of social and economic organization. This, its proponents said, would enable the greatest amount of economic growth, which would be generally good for society even if an unlucky proportion of the population was condemned to inevitable poverty and/or the most menial, meaningless, and exhausting work.[10]

This ideology infuriated Ruskin, whose moral and romantic instincts would not allow any system where life was abused and exploited for any purpose.[11] But Ruskin was also making a rigorous, rational argument against the claims of the economists to have established a 'scientific' approach to the cultivation of wealth. The aim of developing a perfect economic system where material concerns are detached from moral ones, and where individual interests are detached from social context, was intellectually wrong as well as morally empty, he argued. This is captured most simply in the assertion, which appears near the end of *Unto This Last*, and is spelled out in capitals: 'THERE IS NO WEALTH BUT LIFE'.[12]

For Ruskin, financial wealth which does not contribute to the stock of human happiness is no wealth at all. He goes on to assert:

> That country is the richest which nourishes the greatest number of noble and happy human beings; that man is richest who, having perfected the functions of his own life to the utmost, has also the widest helpful influence, both personal, and by means of his possessions, over the lives of others.[13]

Ruskin was aware that his critics would try to dismiss him as old-fashioned, sentimental, and failing to take a 'realistic' approach to modern industrial society. *Unto This Last* is therefore a detailed demolition of the prevailing economic philosophies of the day, which ends up suggesting a necessary reorientation of values, even if it does not set out a full social and political programme.

Unto This Last seemed to Victorian society at the time to be a rather shocking and misguided outburst from one of its most celebrated art critics.[14] Ruskin himself notes in the preface that the essays, when published in the *Cornhill Magazine* a year earlier, 'were reprobated in a violent manner, as far as I could hear, by most of the readers they met with'. This was the famous gentleman who had already published five volumes of *Modern Painters*, as well as highly regarded books on architecture and drawing. Why was he suddenly upsetting the establishment with these radical ideas?

RUSKIN ON CREATIVITY AND IMPERFECTION

In fact, Ruskin's social-political views are well grounded in his previous writings on art and architecture, and, interestingly for us, stem from an emphasis on the primacy of human *creativity*. I introduced *Unto This Last*, above, as an instance of rather unusual clarity in Ruskin; another such burst of Ruskin insight and lucidity had appeared eight years earlier in an essay entitled 'The Nature of Gothic'. This was the sixth chapter of the second volume of *The Stones of Venice*, a typically sprawling three-volume discussion of Gothic architecture. This is the Ruskin that caught the attention of the undergraduate William Morris, as mentioned above. He read chunks of it excitedly to his Oxford friend Edward Burne-Jones in 1853, and, as a lifelong fan of this essay in particular, Morris would republish it as a beautiful book by his own Kelmscott Press in 1892, writing in the preface that 'in future days [this chapter] will be considered as one of the very few necessary and inevitable utterances of the century'.[15]

In 'The Nature of Gothic', Ruskin focuses his attention on the defining characteristics of Gothic architecture – finally getting round to specifying why it is special, and why he loves it so much. The reasons, it turns out, are good ones, and not simply a matter of aesthetic choice. Ruskin admires the 'savagery' and 'rudeness' of the Gothic style, not for a masculine tough reason, but because he sees it as the loving embrace of humanity's imperfections. The craftspeople who contribute to a Gothic building put in *thoughtful* work, even though it is imperfect. To force a craftsperson to make things to fixed specifications – 'with absolute precision by line and rule' – was to make them a 'slave', Ruskin asserted.[16] In the medieval Gothic style which he favoured, however, 'this slavery is done away with altogether; Christianity having recognised, in small things as well as great, the individual value of every soul'.[17] Ruskin therefore welcomes the collaborative mish-mash, the combined construction of individual quirks and talents, a celebration of imperfection, imagination, and 'do what you can'.

Yes, even the laid-back phrase 'do what you can' appears in Ruskin, as he suggests that Christianity says to every Gothic crafter, 'Do what you can, and confess frankly what you are unable to do; neither let your effort be shortened for fear of failure, nor your confession silenced for fear of shame.'[18] He sets this fine spirit of noble and creative imperfection against the ignoble desire to see the 'narrow accomplishment' of supposedly 'perfect' work done to a readymade pattern.[19] This brings out the moral choice to be made: 'You must either make a tool of the creature, or a man of him. You cannot make both.'[20] A human being can be forced to work as a 'tool', following the precise instructions of their masters, making things correctly, but they are dehumanized and their spirit is gagged. Or they can be allowed to 'begin to imagine, to think, to try to do anything worth doing' – and this might lead to roughness, failure, and shame, but also unleashes 'the whole majesty' of the individual.

This tips Ruskin into a fiery denunciation of England's new industrial landscape, where 'the animation of her multitudes is sent like fuel to feed the factory smoke', and where men's creativity and intelligence is suffocated by repetitive machine work – oh, he says, 'this is to be slave-masters indeed'.[21] But he continues with a gentler point of comparison:

> On the other hand, go forth again to gaze upon the old cathedral front, where you have smiled so often at the fantastic ignorance of the old sculptors: examine once more those ugly goblins, and formless monsters, and stern statues, anatomiless and rigid; but do not mock at them, for they are signs of the life and liberty of every workman who

struck the stone; a freedom of thought, and rank in scale of
being, such as no laws, no charters, no charities can secure;
but which it must be the first aim of all Europe at this day
to regain for her children.[22]

This contrast between medieval craftsmanship and Victorian
industrialism brings Ruskin to a critique of the division of
labour – the system of capitalist efficiency whereby complex
tasks are broken down into discrete stages, with each worker
being responsible for the repeated production of one bit,
rather than the whole. This form of organization had been
praised by Adam Smith in the very first sentence of his 1776
treatise, *An Inquiry into the Nature and Causes of the Wealth
of Nations*, where the process is said to have produced 'the
greatest improvements in the productive powers of labour'.[23]
Later in the same work, Smith worried that unstimulating
specialization may mean that the worker 'has no occasion
to exert his understanding, or to exercise his invention, in
finding out expedients for removing difficulties which never
occur . . . and generally becomes as stupid and ignorant
as it is possible for a human creature to become'.[24] These
concerns, buried deep in the text, were largely ignored by
Smith's disciples.

THE DIVISION OF LABOUR

Today, we recognize the argument against the division of
labour as a key element of the Marxist critique of capitalism. Karl Marx's argument that the division of labour led
to alienation would be considered fully in the first volume
of Marx's *Capital*, published 14 years after 'The Nature of
Gothic', in 1867. Earlier, in 1844, Marx was writing privately
of the alienating effect of machine-work upon the worker,
'Just as he is thus depressed spiritually and physically to the

condition of a machine, and from being a man becomes an abstract activity and a belly.'[25] But Ruskin would not have read Marx's work at this time,[26] and makes the same kind of argument in his own way.

Both Ruskin and Marx employ the notion that the male worker who is reduced to repetitive machine-work ceases to be 'a man'. But there are interesting differences in how the two thinkers make their similar argument. For Ruskin, the primary crime of the industrial system is that it steals from the worker the opportunity to create a whole object and to put his own creative mark upon it. Marx's critique is motivated by similar concerns, but the master economist uses somewhat different language and emphases; Marx's wage-slave worker is for Ruskin a creative spirit whose voice has been stolen. He writes:

> We have much studied and much perfected, of late, the great civilized invention of the division of labour; only we give it a false name. It is not, truly speaking, the labour that is divided; but the men: – Divided into mere segments of men – broken into small fragments and crumbs of life; so that all the little piece of intelligence that is left in a man is not enough to make a pin, or a nail, but exhausts itself in making the point of a pin, or the head of a nail.[27]

Ruskin anticipates an objection from his reader, that if any particular worker is a great artist who is unable to express himself, due to the division of labour, then he should be 'taken away and made a gentleman', and encouraged to produce beautiful designs which could then be executed by 'common workmen'. But he says:

> All ideas of this kind are founded upon two mistaken sup-positions: the first, that one man's thoughts can be, or

ought to be, executed by another man's hands; the second, that manual labour is a degradation, when it is governed by intellect.[28]

For Ruskin, the thought and the craft of making, the mental and the physical, were united in the same process. The division of labour was flawed, therefore, not only because it separated the stages of production into meaningless and tedious bits, but also because it separated the intellectual and the physical work which should be united in the process of making:

> We are always in these days endeavouring to separate the two; we want one man to be always thinking, and another to be always working, and we call one a gentleman, and the other an operative; whereas the workman ought often to be thinking, and the thinker often to be working, and both should be gentlemen, in the best sense.[29]

For Ruskin, as Peter Anthony observes, work was vital in terms that were moral and spiritual, connecting 'man' with nature and with God; whereas for Marx its significance was social and economic.[30] Marx's analysis is a critique of a kind of slavery, and Ruskin makes the same point, just as strongly, but it is embedded in a celebration of human creativity and craft, and the moral imperative that this should be freely expressed, individual, and unconstrained. Where Marx has a plan for how to fix this – the revolution which would replace the present system with a communist one – Ruskin's lament is less explicitly prescriptive, and can certainly seem unrealistically nostalgic – as in the wish, above, that we should simply elevate all workers to be 'gentlemen'. Nevertheless, even if Ruskin did not offer a simple manifesto for change, his great contribution was to establish individual autonomous creativity as a core value which society must nurture, not crush, if it is to retain any moral authority, or quality of life.

WILLIAM MORRIS RIDES IN

It was this emphasis on the power of individually crafted work which caught the attention of the young William Morris. As we have seen, this approach, suggested by Ruskin, is not (simply) a celebration of individualistic 'making things' but rather has profound social implications. It begins with an appreciation of the unconstrained joyfulness which Ruskin saw in the often bizarre, strange, and rough ornamentation which individual craftspeople had contributed to Gothic buildings – so this part of the argument could seem just to be an appreciation of individual talents. Or, indeed, could seem slightly patronizing, since much of the time Ruskin doesn't even seem to think that their work was of any great quality – he's just happy that these long-dead workers have done their best, and made their mark. But the argument shifts from the individual to the society – from the simple artist to the 'big picture' – by a logical route: individual self-expression is so vital that if a society creates supposedly rational systems (such as the capitalist division of labour) which do not allow a voice to people's individual creativity, then the whole system rapidly becomes sick and degraded, like a tree in barren soil.

Morris believed this passionately, and developed this emphasis on individual creative expression into a more expansive vision of happy, empowered creative communities. As Viscount Snowden put it in a Morris centenary pamphlet published in Walthamstow in 1934:

> He aimed at a community of fellowship in which all individuals would share in common the joys of creative art.[31]

Morris had been embroiled in medieval fantasies and Romantic literature from an early age. He had read Walter Scott's historical novels before he was seven, played games of knights, barons, and fairies, and visited old churches with his father.[32] But as he became a young man, medievalism took on a more developed meaning, in tandem with new research which was building knowledge about medieval life. As his excellent biographer E. P. Thompson puts it:

> For Morris, the most important result of the new scholar-ship was in the reconstruction of a picture of the Middle Ages, neither as a grotesque nor as a faery world, but as a real *community* of human beings – an organic pre-capitalist community with values and an art of its own, sharply contrasted with those of Victorian England.[33]

Although life in Medieval England had its share of difficulties and injustices, it was not systematically engineered to degrade the human spirit, or wedded to the notion of self-interest as the inevitable motive of all behaviour. Being able to evoke a clear picture of a way of living so very different to his current reality helped Morris to retain his genuine faith in the possibility of change.

And whilst Ruskin was something of an amateur artist as well as art critic, Morris combined theory and practice much more comprehensively. He mastered all kinds of creative techniques during the course of his lifetime, moving on from painting and drawing to embrace embroidery, woodcuts, calligraphy and book printing, tapestry weaving, and textile printing. He clearly felt that a hands-on engagement with a craft was the only way to truly understand it.

Morris decried the 'profit-grinding society' with its abysmal working conditions and 'shoddy' goods.[34] Like Ruskin, he felt that workers should be able to take pleasure from making beautiful things from the finest materials. Unlike Ruskin, though, Morris was a well-organized entrepreneur and avid multi-tasker, who didn't waste any time in creating a successful business in response to this need. Thus, in 1861, Morris, Marshall, Faulkner & Co. was founded – 'Fine Art Workmen in Painting, Carving, Furniture and the Metals' – producing handcrafted objects, wallpaper, and textiles for the home, as well as major commissions for the decoration of rooms at St James's Palace, and the South Kensington Museum (now the Victoria and Albert), as well as several churches. In 1875, the business came under Morris's sole ownership, as Morris & Co.

Later in life, in 1891, Morris also founded the Kelmscott Press, which used the approach and printing techniques of 400 years earlier in order – as Morris explained to a journalist in 1895 – to give 'a beautiful form' to 'the ideas we cherish'.[35] By this point Morris's craft work had become more of an all-consuming hobby than a commercial venture, and the Press only issued limited numbers of its expensively made volumes.

'TIME-TRAVELLERS FROM THE FUTURE'

Morris's dedication to the production of high-priced luxury objects, and the lavishly decorated Kelmscott Press books, can seem puzzling since their very high production costs meant they were necessarily only available to an elite. In an 1891 newspaper interview, Morris presented his vision of a socialist society where 'We should have a library on every street corner, where everybody should read all the best books, printed in the best and most beautiful type.'[36] But in his own time, Morris did not seek to begin a 'books for all' publishing revolution, as Allen Lane would do later with affordable Penguin paperbacks.[37] Instead he made exclusive handcrafted treasures.

A helpful explanation for this anomaly is offered by Tony Pinkney:

> From this standpoint, then, the Kelmscott Press books, however expensive and restricted in social circulation in their own day, are not evidences of medievalist nostalgia and political withdrawal, but are rather time-travellers from some far future we can barely imagine, showing how lovingly artefacts might be crafted in the socialist world that is to come.[38]

Although Morris did not articulate it quite in this manner, this seems an appropriate way of understanding what his high-class business was really meant to represent. Morris's battle was fought on two fronts: first, to prompt a transformation of society, via grand and revolutionary plans, this necessarily having to happen at a point in the future; but second, to modify and disrupt things, in the here and now, by inserting finely produced material objects, and ethical working practices, into a society accustomed to 'shoddy' products and exploitative factories.

Clive Wilmer, editor of the very good Penguin Classics selection of Morris's work, *News from Nowhere and Other Writings*, similarly defends the author by explaining, on his behalf, that 'the creation of beautiful furnishings and so on is part of a process of *public education*, providing a model of good production methods and pioneering a return to higher standards of design'.[39] The expensive Kelmscott Press books are therefore consistent with Morris's 'all-or-nothing politics' – he would rather show the world the true ideal book, rather than compromise with more affordable models of lower quality.

Once we see Morris's craft work in this light, we can see that his written works – poetry, fiction, and prose – are just other dimensions of the *same* project. So rather than thinking that William Morris was a man who ran a craft business, and who also happened to be a writer of poetry and novels, and who also found time to produce political critiques and pamphlets, we instead come to the realization that William Morris was a man who projected a vision – a vision of great fundamental hope and optimism – through a striking number of different channels. On the one hand it might be a utopian novel, such as *News from Nowhere*, which fast-forwards the reader to an ideal, pastoral world of the future, where Morris would like you to live, or on the other hand it might be a utopian sitting-room, which fast-forwards its inhabitant to a world of well-made, comfortable, and attractive domestic objects, which Morris would like you to live in. Along with the political non-fiction writings, they are all 'visionary accounts of an ideal world', as Wilmer puts it, reminding us of the possibility of alternatives: 'To dream of the impossible and disregard reality is to question the inevitability of existing circumstances.'[40]

HOPE AND FULFILMENT

In this way, Morris offers his readers – and customers – a helping hand into the possibility of a new world. The more common approach of Marxist writers tends to be a more hectoring tone of voice – reaching its nadir, perhaps, in Theodor Adorno's writings in the 1930s and 1940s, where the critic seems unable to *believe* that people would be so stupid as to apparently enjoy the appalling sentimental offerings of the popular culture industry. On the one hand, it's a well-meaning stance: Adorno passionately believes that people deserve better. But on the other hand, he just seems disgusted to observe that almost everybody is a moron.

William Morris takes a kinder approach to everyday life, recognizing that people have to 'make do' within a system which is not of their choosing. Like Adorno, he feared that industrial capitalism diverted people's desires away from the natural love of nature, creativity, and fresh air, into 'sham wants' which it could more easily satisfy. But instead of telling them how dumb their lives are, he offers stories, manifestos, songs, and objects from a better future, to feed the positive aspirations which he believes still reside in human hearts. It is one of Morris's undoubted strengths, that although he despises and sometimes despairs of modern society, he is unwilling to give up hope. As E. P. Thompson observes,

> 'Hope' was a key-word in Morris's vocabulary. By 'hope' he meant all that gives worth and continuity to human endeavour, all that makes man's finest aspirations seem possible of achievement in the real world.[41]

Morris was also well ahead of his time on the environment and sustainability: he decried the pollution of the industrial age, which he had seen come to swamp London within his own lifetime, and argued that a sustainable relationship with nature would be essential for the continued survival of humanity. He observed that science had become a servant of the capitalist system, in terms of exploitation and profiteering, but was not being tasked to help *alleviate* the impact of industrial processes:

> And Science – we have loved her well, and followed her diligently, what will she do? I fear she is so much in the pay of the counting-house, the counting-house and the drill-sergeant, that she is too busy, and will for the present do nothing. Yet there are matters which I should have thought easy for her; say for example teaching Manchester how to consume its own smoke, or Leeds how to get rid of its superfluous black dye without turning it into the river . . .[42]

The notion that one arm of science and technology should be used to fix the environmental degradation caused by the other arm remains controversial, but Morris was 140 years ahead of the current debates.

Having established some of Morris's core values, we will now look in a little more detail at his views on creative cultures.

MORRIS ON MAKING AND SHARING

The distinctive and special thing about today's Web 2.0 world is that, at its best, it offers users a reasonably equal platform on which to share creative artefacts – such as videos, images and writings – which they have made themselves and which express their own emotions or ideas. If we acknowledge the limits (notably the limitations of access in terms of equipment, and in terms of skills), we can reasonably suggest that this is an ideal which William Morris would have approved of.

For Morris, the sharing of art in a community was one of the fundamentals, part of a society's life-blood. In a lecture in 1877 he declared:

> I do not want art for a few, any more than education for a few, or freedom for a few.[43]

Without the opportunity to make their mark on the world, and in particular on the things around them in everyday life, people's relaxation time would be 'vacant and uninteresting', and their work 'mere endurance', Morris says.[44]

Making one's mark in this way requires some *effort*, of course, but Morris assumes that this work brings its own rewards and so is fuelled from within. He knows that working as a slave to the capitalist system, with no control over one's tasks and no freedom of personal expression, offers no fulfilment at all; but he is just as certain that self-initiated and expressive work is a joy, not a burden, and he assumes people will take to it with vigour.[45]

In 'Useful Work versus Useless Toil', a lecture from 1884, Morris explains that creative work, which he more or less equates with any work worth doing, offers 'hope' – that key word again – in three ways. First there is 'hope of rest' – the pleasurable buzz of a job well done, as one comes to relax after the event. Second, 'hope of product' – the achievement of having made something worthwhile. And third, 'hope of pleasure in the work itself' – a conscious pleasure in the activity, while it is being engaged in, and not 'mere habit'.[46] This point is amplified in the most spirited tones:

> I think that to all living things there is a pleasure in the exercise of their energies. . . . But a man at work, making something that he feels will exist because he is working at it and wills it, is exercising the energies of his mind and soul as well as of his body. Memory and imagination help him as he works. Not only his own thoughts, but the thoughts of the men of past ages guide his hands; and as a part of the human race, he creates. If we work thus we shall be men, and our days will be happy and eventful.[47]

(As in all cases with these Victorian quotes, I hope the reader will forgive the author for his masculine language and read the stuff about a 'manly' existence to mean a full and zesty engagement with the spirit of humanity – which, of course, is both female and male.)

Morris acknowledges that this joyful celebration of work may seem 'strange' to many of his readers, as he knows that in current everyday reality they are trapped on the wrong side of the fence, doing 'slave's work – mere toiling to live, that we may live to toil'. This doesn't change the fact that an alternative exists, and Morris is not easily put off listing desirable possibilities just because their realization in the present world may be difficult to imagine.

Later in the same lecture, Morris turns his attention to the 'rich non-producing classes' who have a taste for pointless objects which are merely intended to reflect and symbolize their wealth. But this is not wealth, the author asserts, it is 'waste'. Wealth is something else entirely:

> Wealth is what Nature gives us and what a reasonable man can make out of the gifts of Nature for his reasonable use. The sunlight, the fresh air, the unspoiled face of the earth, food, raiment and housing necessary and decent; the storing up of knowledge of all kinds, and the power of disseminating it; means of free communication between man and man; works of art, the beauty which man creates when he is most a man, most aspiring and thoughtful – all things which serve the pleasure of people, free, manly, and uncorrupted. This is wealth.[48]

This redefinition of the meaning of 'wealth' echoes Ruskin's 'There is no wealth but life', of course, but Morris's list is interesting – not least of all because, over 100 years before the rise of the World Wide Web, it highlights the collection and dissemination of knowledge, communication between people, and the ability to create and share expressive material, as the true route to pleasure and fulfilment.

EVERYDAY ARTS

Morris understood 'genuine art' to be 'the expression of man's pleasure in his handiwork',[49] and deplored the separation between the professional world of 'art' and the everyday things that people make. Historically he judged the arts to be 'healthy' when they were built upon an intimate weaving together of 'craft' abilities and artistic ideas, the practical and the emotional, and the stimulation of both pleasure and intellect.[50] The artist should be humble, engaged with the everyday, and willing to make things themselves – to get their hands dirty, as it were. As Morris puts it: 'The best artist was a workman still, the humblest workman was an artist.'[51]

Today, the category of 'artist' is even more sharply removed from everyday creative practices, and often seems to be based on having the 'right' kind of art education, the necessary fashionable artworld connections, and pretentious way of talking about things. Until quite recently, this used to be deeply frustrating for creative people who did not happen to be part of the artworld in-crowd, because they were therefore denied the ability to share their work with others. You could go down the mainstream populist route, and hope to find TV stardom, or at least get anonymous but paid work doing graphics for movies; or you could hope to become the next darling of the artworld, ideally by memorizing some French poststructuralism and applying it to your 'vision' somehow; or nothing. Today, the Web means that people don't have to worry so much about labels – art/craft/whatever – and have relatively unlimited channels for sharing stuff they have made. As Clay Shirky has observed, the relevant filters now operate *after*, not before, publication, so at least you can get your stuff out there.[52] It is not guaranteed that anyone will pay attention, but at least work can be shown and shared, and the likelihood of it being noticed is much less dependent on a small number of elite gatekeepers.

Morris may have had some concerns about the ways in which today's everyday-creative makers offer their work to be profited from, via advertising, by the owners of the big content-hosting websites such as YouTube – an issue which we will return to in chapter 8. But if we leave that dimension to one side for now, the level of free and spontaneous creative sharing would certainly have given him a warm glow. The only healthy art, he said, is 'an art which is to be made by the people and for the people, as a happiness to the maker and the user'.[53] I am confident in saying that this is much more clearly a description of daily activity on YouTube than it is an account of the interactions between the elite inhabitants of the contemporary artworld, such as the people named in *ArtReview* magazine's *Power 100* list.

Finally, a note on individualism. Later in this book, where as mentioned we will have to consider whether sites like YouTube are best understood as hateful 'profit-grinding' mills for user-generated content, we will also have to consider whether we prefer the aggregated 'wisdom of crowds' notion of Web 2.0, where many users collaborate and contribute to produce the best resources, or whether the individual voice is more important. E. P. Thompson explains Morris's view thus:

> In both *News from Nowhere* and the lectures, the emphasis is upon the communal life. But (as Morris never ceased to repeat) true individualism was only possible in a Communist society, which needed and valued the contribution of each individual to the common good; and, in a society which fostered true variety, he knew that different men would choose to live in different ways.[54]

So we do not have to choose between the individual *or* the collective: rather, a diverse *community* of *individual* voices offers a satisfying combined solution.

3

THE MEANING OF MAKING II:
CRAFT TODAY

This chapter continues to follow the development of thinking about craft activity and making things. We will look briefly at how the ideas of Ruskin and Morris fed into the Arts and Crafts movement, and an ethos which would appear later in the twentieth century as 'DIY culture'. We will consider how those values can then spread out into a more general philosophy of everyday life. But then we'll try to be rather more concrete again, and consider some of today's popular craft practices, and the recent 'rise' of craft, and look at *why* people in the present day still like to make things themselves. And then at the end of the chapter, we will return to the discussion of the meaning of creativity, which we started in chapter 1, and will propose a new definition of creativity which seems better suited to our purposes.

THE EMERGENCE OF CRAFT

As mentioned in the previous chapter, craft can seem like a timeless practice, rooted in ancient and traditional ways of engaging with the world and building communities. Indeed, those practices may well be ancient – but the word 'craft' itself is relatively new. In the eighteenth century, 'craft' referred primarily to political cunning and a sly, jocular, tricksy approach to social issues.[1] By the time of Samuel Johnson's *Dictionary of the English Language* in 1755, 'manual art; trade' is listed as one of the meanings, along with 'art; ability; dexterity', alongside the earlier usage as 'fraud; cunning; artifice'.[2] At that point, though, craft was not associated with any particular methods or objects, and could be applied to any cultural practices.[3] During the nineteenth century, the notion of 'craft' or a 'craftsman' appeared even less often, remaining pretty dormant until the last quarter of that century, when it sprang into action.[4]

Although dissecting the etymology of specific words is not always the most valuable exercise, Paul Greenhalgh – a former Head of Research at the Victoria and Albert Museum – uses the rather arbitrary gathering of ideas and orientations under the notion of craft to set out its different constituent dimensions. He writes:

> The ideological and intellectual underpinning of the craft constituency is not a consistent whole, but has several distinct threads to it, which have only become intertwined relatively recently. It is these threads, or elements, that I will deal with here. There are three. I will describe them as *decorative art*, the *vernacular*, and the *politics of work*.[5]

The first of these, decorative art, is a broad term which seems to encompass all the 'applied' forms of creativity which have in common the bruised, second-class feeling of being excluded from the category of 'fine art'. The second element, the vernacular, refers to the authentic, natural voice of a community, unselfconsciously communicated through everyday things that people have made. In the third element, the politics of work, the actual crafted objects become secondary to the broader ideals about the conditions in which they are made. This is the political message of Ruskin and Morris, that creative workers must be free to express themselves through the production of whole objects. They have control over their own labour, and contribute to a vibrant and dynamic culture through the creation of their own individual things.

THE ARTS AND CRAFTS MOVEMENT

It was the combination of these three threads that led to the Arts and Crafts movement. This loose grouping of idealistic thinkers and craftspeople built on the ideas of Ruskin and Morris in different ways, but central to the movement was the idea that all creative work was of equal status, and was the means by which human beings could connect with nature, with their own sense of self, and with other people. Making things expressed individual life through the work of the hands, and therefore could not be divided into machine-like steps or repetitive sameness.[6]

The phrase 'Arts and Crafts' was first used in this context in 1887, and the movement burned brightly until the First World War. Although rooted in Victorian Britain, it spread around the world, most notably in the USA, where it connected meaningfully with American notions of self-reliance, individualism, community, and romantic connection with nature. Greenhalgh summarizes its legacy as follows:

The Arts and Crafts movement, in retrospect, can be seen to be the most successful construction of a theory and practice of ethical art. . . . The *vernacular* was the model, unalienated *work* was the means and *art* was the goal. The larger ideal pulled the three elements into proximity. It was a brilliant formulation: humankind would be liberated through communal creativity.[7]

It is something very much like this vision which inspires contemporary craft enthusiasts today, as well as exponents of Web 2.0 and online creativity. Although rooted in a seemingly distant age, its message is practical, positive, and ethical. As Greenhalgh goes on to say:

Ultimately, for craft pioneers, the movement was centred on physical and mental freedom. By uniting the work process directly to the demand for a higher quality of life, they had regenerated the idea that craft was synonymous with power.[8]

The American inheritors of the Arts and Crafts movement added the democratic element which today we would call 'DIY culture'. As we have seen, dehumanizing industrial methods were rejected because of a concern for the individual worker, but the Arts and Crafts alternative led to beautiful handmade products that the typical worker could not afford. This terrible paradox is immediately dissolved in the simple phrase: 'do it yourself'.

This solution to the conundrum was helped along by Gustav Stickley, a furniture maker, craftsman, and architect, based in New York. From 1901 to 1916, Stickley published a magazine called *The Craftsman*, which began as a US-based expression of the British Arts and Crafts movement – launching with detailed discussions of the life and work of

Morris and Ruskin, in the first and second issues respectively – but over time came to represent a distinct American version of that philosophy. Stickley's belief in 'a simple, democratic art' that would provide Americans with 'material surroundings conducive to plain living and high thinking' was such that he included his designs and working plans for furniture, metalwork, and needlework in the magazine[9] – even though this, to some extent, undermined his own business, which was based on selling this stuff as unique finished products. In this sense, Stickley invented, or rather revived, the concept of 'open source' – the system by which software developers today share unprotected code in the belief that others should be freely able to use it and improve it.

This democratic approach is highly consistent with the ideals of the Arts and Crafts movement: craft skills were valued for their own careful, individual, handmade beauty, not because they were supposed to be the skills of an expert elite. William Morris made things to a very high standard, because that gave him pleasure, and because he thought the care and quality of their production would bring pleasure to others too. But he didn't make things to a very high standard because he thought that it made him better than everybody else. 'Do it yourself' is, therefore, part of the original Arts and Crafts message – but processed through American optimism, and communicated in a cheerful and unpretentious way.

DIY CULTURE

Today, the mainstream notion of 'DIY' is associated with everyday home improvement – putting up shelves, assembling flat-pack wardrobes, and fixing drainpipes oneself, without professional help. This is a commonplace, suburban kind of phenomenon, popularly seen as a bit boring, and nothing to do with any kind of radical political movement.

When this kind of DIY emerged in the 1960s, though, it was – at least for some – associated with the alternative counterculture. In particular, it was argued that the formal education system had filled students' heads with abstract information, supposedly of some background value for those who might enter the professions, but lacking real-world usefulness.

The philosopher Alan Watts put it like this:

> Our educational system, in its entirety, does nothing to give us any kind of material competence. In other words, we don't learn how to cook, how to make clothes, how to build houses, how to make love, or to do any of the absolutely fundamental things of life. The whole education that we get for our children in school is entirely in terms of abstractions. It trains you to be an insurance salesman or a bureaucrat, or some kind of cerebral character.[10]

This was said during a 1967 symposium, of sorts, which took place on Watts's houseboat moored in Sausalito, California, in which his interlocutors included the LSD enthusiast Timothy Leary, the beat poet Allen Ginsberg, and the poet and environmentalist Gary Snyder. I mention these details to give a flavour of the context in which these ideals developed. It's not the typical bunch of people you'd associate with 'DIY culture' if the phrase 'do it yourself' only reminds you of giant hardware stores.

This critical attitude to schooling, allied with the notion that people can do things better themselves without such institutions, was reflected in the work of John Holt, whose books *How Children Fail* and *How Children Learn* raised public awareness of these new ideas in the 1960s.[11] (Similar themes were also developed by Ivan Illich in the early 1970s, whose work is discussed in chapter 7.) Holt argued that learning was something that humans do naturally from the earliest age, and that any machinery designed to make 'learning' happen as a specific kind of activity, separate from the normal experience of everyday life – as schools intend to do – could only get in the way.[12] This gave considerable support to the emergent home-schooling movement – literally a DIY approach to education, in which learners are typically supported to follow their own interests and explore the world in whatever way they choose. Responding to critics' fears that children would not bother to learn anything if left to their own devices, Holt argued that children should be *trusted* to build their own understandings, and could make their own meaningful connections with knowledge, which would be much more useful and effective for them than the abstract pile of procedures and information that children are told that they will need by schools.

Another key figure in this everyday-life DIY movement was Stewart Brand, who in 1968 launched his homemade publication, *The Whole Earth Catalog*, which was highly successful and influential, and had several further editions up to 1985. Subtitled *Access to Tools*, it offered readers a (mostly mail-order) gateway to all kinds of resources, including information, technical books, and courses, as well as physical tools such as those for building, metalwork, gardening, and early electronics.

The phrase 'whole Earth', which appears in the title of many of Brand's projects, refers to a thought that he had in 1966, that when NASA released a photograph showing the whole of the planet from space, it would lead to a change of consciousness as people realized their place in a global system of limited resources. One week later, he was thrown off the University of California Berkeley campus for wearing a day-glo sandwich board and selling 25-cent badges which read: 'Why haven't we seen a photograph of the whole Earth yet?' This was reported in the *San Francisco Chronicle*, and picked up by other newspapers, which helped his nascent viral campaign enormously.[13]

The well-illustrated *Whole Earth Catalog*, published two years after that, was eclectic in the extreme, but the things and ideas that it featured shared a common spirit. As it said in its statement of purpose at the front:

> We are as gods and might as well get good at it. So far, remotely done power and glory – as via government, big business, formal education, church – has succeeded to the point where gross defects obscure actual gains. In response to this dilemma and to these gains a realm of intimate, personal power is developing power of the individual to conduct his own education, find his own inspiration, shape his own environment, and share his adventure with who-ever is interested. Tools that aid this process are sought and promoted by the Whole Earth Catalog.[14]

Later, Brand went on to be a pioneer of home computing and the internet, and co-founded the online community, the WELL – The Whole Earth 'Lectronic Link – which will be discussed in chapter 6, and later still a proponent of certain technological solutions to environmental problems (as in his 2009 book, *Whole Earth Discipline*).

Across all of Brand's work – with the possible exception of his recent (reluctant) enthusiasm for nuclear power and geoengineering – we see the values of self-reliance, do it yourself, and community. And, to be fair, humanity wouldn't be needing the nuclear power and geoengineering if it had stuck to the caring, convivial, small-scale ecological values which Brand has always supported. Significantly, Brand's work helps us trace a direct path from William Morris and the Arts and Crafts movement, to its heir, the countercultural DIY movement, and on to the internet and Web 2.0.

PUNK DIY

A similar but different version of the DIY ethos is the 'lo-fi' music and zine culture, influenced in part by the punk scene. This DIY culture is characterized by a rejection of the glossy, highly produced, celebrity-oriented mainstream of popular culture, and its replacement with a knowingly non-glossy, often messily produced alternative which is much less bothered about physical beauty, and declares an emphasis on content rather than style.

This ethos is discussed, for example, in Amy Spencer's book *DIY: The Rise of Lo-Fi Culture*. She's an enthusiastic guide. On the first page she says:

> In the face of the bland consumerist pop that dominates the airwaves and the bestselling celebrity biographies that fill the bookshops it is exciting to realize that there are an increasing amount of independent and creative minds who care enough to go against the grain and produce music, art, magazines and literature that is truly unique – whether it is likely to sell or not.[15]

Spencer does not believe that online culture is destined to replace these independently made objects, because of the excitement associated with creating alternative cultural items that you can hold in your own hands. This is a shift away from the strict meaning of 'homemade' or 'handmade', since the ideal here is to pay a small printer or disc-presser to make you a box of, say, 500 things to sell or give to friends and like-minded souls. Spencer says:

The internet has enabled DIY culture to become more accessible and less elitist, but, remarkably, it hasn't diminished the enduring appeal of the homemade zine or the 4-track demo.[16]

As a former zine maker myself, I have to agree that having a box of *actual things* that you have created is quite delightful, and trading in that culture, where you might swap your zine for someone else's self-published comic, which perhaps comes with a 'free gift' of a metal badge or a two-track flexidisc, that expresses the undiluted enthusiasm of one or two committed creators in the form of a physical object . . . well, to be honest, the internet isn't *quite* the same.

On the other hand, producing boxes full of new physical objects is often bad for the environment, and getting rid of those objects, even to people who want them, is hard work. In the book *Web Studies*, published more than a decade ago, in 2000, I gave my own experience with zines to show how convenient this new World Wide Web thing could be:

When I was a student, I published a fanzine (or 'small press magazine') with an anti-sexist theme, *Powercut*, which was reproduced by a professional printing company (in exchange for a significant chunk of my humble student finances). Producing and printing the thing was the (relatively) easy part: it was the *distribution* which would eat up my life. I spent hundreds of hours visiting and writing to bookshops, and getting magazines and newspapers to write about it – with ordering details – so that I could spend yet more hours responding to mail order requests. I published two issues, and for each one, it took me a year to shift 800 copies. This was regarded as a considerable success in small press circles.

Today, like many people, I can write a review or article, stick it on the Web, then sit back and relax. 800 or so
people can have read it – well, *seen* it – within a week. I
largely enjoyed the *Powercut* experience, back in 1991–93,
but think how much simpler my life would have been –
and how much more of a life I would have had! – if Tim
Berners-Lee had bothered to invent the World Wide Web
just a few years earlier than he actually did.[17]

Amy Spencer notes that zines are more like gifts than commercial products, since they are done for love not money,
and argues that unlike mainstream media, the mode of their
production is inspiring for readers – showing that you don't
have to accept the given culture, and can create your own
instead.[18] She highlights the role of 'riot grrrl' zines as central to establishing the principles of 'third wave' feminism,
which rejected the victim stance and instead went on the
front foot. Rather than just complaining about offensive
popular culture, they created its replacement:

Here women redefined feminism for the 90s and recognised
each other as manufacturers of culture, as opposed to participants in a culture that they were encouraged to accept.
They were encouraged to reclaim the media and produce
their own cultural forms.[19]

They formed bands, and produced zines, which often paro-
died the conventions of mainstream culture with fake fashion
features, and ironic, angry versions of 'agony aunt' columns,
alongside more serious material on sexism, domestic violence, and body image. The alternative zine movement also
led to 'mama zines', offering an alternative to young parents
who did not wish to swallow the commercialized vision of
parenthood.

Betsy Greer, who coined the term 'craftivism' (meaning – as you would expect – the confluence of craft and activism), makes the point that today it is easy to buy stuff – clothing, music, reading-matter, children's toys, food, or whatever: cheap or expensive versions of any of these things are readily available. But, she argues, there is a resistance, a *political choice*, in not buying those things and choosing to make your own instead.[20] (Or, similarly, to buy or exchange a locally homemade thing from someone you know.) It is in this way that traditional crafts such as knitting, cooking, weaving, sewing, and gardening have come to take on a gentle revolutionary dimension.

We've only scratched the surface of DIY approaches and practices here, but the central idea at the heart of them all is a rejection of the idea that you overcome problems by paying somebody else to provide a solution. We've got used to experts, professionals, and businesses telling us that the way to do things – whether building a wall, or learning about a subject, or getting entertainment – is to pay other people, who know what they're doing, to do the task for us, because we couldn't really manage it ourselves. DIY culture says that's rubbish: you can do it yourself, and you can do it with more creativity, character, and relevance than if you got a generic or 'expert' solution. And, importantly, it *feels good* to do it yourself: it's really good for self-esteem – a crucial dimension of personal psychology – whereas getting it done for you is disempowering, and often frustrating, and less meaningful.

Of course, our time and our skills are usually far from unlimited, so it is often convenient to get experienced people to help us – that's fine, of course, and it keeps the economy going, as people can sell their time and expertise to others. But the DIY point that for many tasks you *can* do it for yourself, and would feel pride and pleasure if you did so, remains true.

CRAFTING AS AN ATTITUDE TO EVERYDAY LIFE

The DIY ethos, and a passion for craft, are not just about isolated projects, but spill over into everyday life more generally. Suggesting that people can make, fix, and repair things for themselves has much in common with sustainability and environmentalism. It also obviously connects with anticonsumerism – the rejection of the idea that the answer to all of our needs and problems can be purchased from shops. This doesn't mean that the crafty person rejects all 'stuff' – on the contrary, having interesting things in our lives, things that we enjoy and which we look after, is enriching. The problem, as John Naish argues in his book *Enough*, is that we keep on wanting to acquire things rather than finding pleasure in the ones we've got. When the basic human brain evolved, gathering stuff continuously was good for survival. Naish quotes Robert Trivers, an evolutionary biologist, who says: 'We've evolved to be maximising machines. There isn't necessarily a stop mechanism in us that says, "Relax, you've got enough".'[21]

So although most people now have some awareness of environmental issues, and may even suspect that having more and more things isn't going to make us happier, we don't tend to think 'I've got enough now'. Instead, we continue to acquire new stuff, rather than making or reusing things, if only for the temporary frisson of opening a glossy new item, or the novelty of an unfamiliar gadget. Even hearing about, for instance, the Great Pacific Garbage Patch – a mass of plastic waste floating in the ocean, covering an area at least the size of Texas[22] – makes us sad for humanity, but doesn't seem to affect individual behaviour.

Perhaps the warm values of craft and creativity can help here, offering a positive vision of making and reusing, rather than the more austere and negative-sounding 'stop that!' message suggested by anti-consumerism arguments and shocking pollution news. Since making and sharing things can make a positive contribution to well-being and a sense of connectedness – as argued throughout this book – then there is much to be gained from shopping less, and creating and recycling more. The human brain doesn't always think like that, however, so we need to make a conscious effort to reprogram ourselves.

This is not just about 'things' of course. The corresponding argument in the field of media and entertainment is that we can gain pleasure, and a sense of connectedness, from the homemade stories, films, animations, and reports made by everyday amateur people, on a domestic level, and shared online. There is already more than 'enough' professional material being generated every day. There is a strong argument for having well-resourced and independent news and current affairs programmes, and quality drama and entertainment on film, television, and online. But in a healthy society there should be just as much cheerfully unfinanced non-professional material made by all kinds of people, just because they want to, or have something to say, all around the world. (Ideally, though, we'd also be spending less time looking at screens, as indicated in chapters 1 and 9.)

Meanwhile, the notion of craft has been extended into spheres of life which are not really to do with making things – or making media – at all. A notable example is the concept of 'crafting gentleness', developed by Anthony McCann, a musician and former journalist, who is now lecturer of Contemporary Folk Culture at the University of Ulster. In his online invitation to consider 'crafting gentleness', he explains:

> The notion of crafting is often associated with activities like pottery, knitting, woodwork, quiltmaking and so on.

Engaging in these sorts of crafting can be a great way to remind ourselves that we can make a difference, to remind ourselves that we can learn to listen more carefully to how we make the differences that we make. Crafting materials can be a way to align ourselves to think more in terms of the consequences and effects of what we do, to consider that helpfulness and appropriateness might be friendlier values to live by than rigid rules of right and wrong. By sculpting, shaping, moulding, guiding, building, and by listening and responding as we go, we can become more aware of how we make a difference. Crafting can be a reclamation of the power of life.[23]

The hands-on engagement of crafting and making, then, connects us with broader values, but the crafting orientation becomes one which can be a continuous part of everyday life, regardless of whether or not we happen to have a hands-on craft project. Rather, the gentle crafting spirit comes, ideally, to occupy all interactions with people and with nature:

Here, crafting activities are understood as reminders that we can become aware of how we always-already make a difference, at any time, in any situation. We are *always-already* sculpting, shaping, moulding, guiding, building. We *always-already* have an influence on how we and others experience life. We can become more aware of how we *always-already* matter. . . . There is nothing more personal, political, or relevant than attending to the . . . character of our own attitude as we engage in crafting our experience and our relationships.[24]

The understanding that we make our own experiences, as well as shaping our material surroundings, is an important one to emerge from craft activity. This idea also arises from the 'slow' movement – the growing feeling that the world is becoming too fast, crazy, and driven by demands and targets and pointless aspirations, and that we have to reclaim a gentler pace.

In Carl Honoré's excellent 2004 book, *In Praise of Slow*, which introduced the slow movement to a general audience, the author shows how the modern impetus to cram as much stuff as possible into our days has a negative effect on our well-being, and also means that we gain less pleasure, and knowledge, from the things that we do.[25] He argues that a 'slower' approach to work, leisure, education, child development, and other areas of life can dramatically increase the quality of the experiences, even if they are fewer in number. He emphasizes that notions such as 'slow work' or 'slow education' do not represent a shift towards laziness, but are rather about taking a more measured pace, to do things properly, and to appreciate and enjoy them, without a constant sense of rush and the background panic that one isn't getting through things fast enough. So in some ways it is about working harder, and doing things better, by making decisions to reduce the rush.

The link with craft and making is that when one is not just a consumer, guzzling thing after thing, but also a producer, going through the necessarily slower and more thoughtful process of making something, one becomes more aware of the details and decisions which underpin everyday things and experiences, and therefore more able to gain pleasure and inspiration from the appreciation of things.[26]

CRAFT PRACTICES AND THE 'RISE' OF CRAFT

Having discussed craft as a general approach and ethos, we will now look, in a more direct and concrete way, at some of today's craft activities, and why people do them. In the first chapter I mentioned the apparent surge of interest in craft clubs and fairs, as well as DIY technology. Such trends may often seem to rise or subside, and to some extent are generated in the imagination of the mainstream media, whilst the reality is probably that the human appetite for making things may be reasonably stable across time. Human beings have obviously made things for their own use for thousands of years. The broad recent history seems to be that during World War II, in the USA, the UK, and elsewhere, the make it yourself and 'make do and mend' ethos was especially strong, encouraged by governments and embraced by the people, as a domestic tactic showing the kind of initiative that might help to win the war.[27] But after that period of self-help and austerity, through the second half of the twentieth century, people tended to be more delighted with manufactured goods, and were less impressed by homemade clothing, tools, or furniture, which could be seen as cheap and embarrassing.[28] But since the start of the present century – and obviously these are rough and blurred movements, not clear-cut phases – enthusiasm and respect for homemade things have risen again. This is, I think, partly because of the growth in awareness of environmental issues – people are increasingly aware that the manufacturing of endless stuff is not simply a proud sign of humanity's superior powers, but rather has troubling implications – and also because of the rise of the Web as a frequently homemade phenomenon, which can, additionally, connect and support crafters around the world.

Although heavily connected with traditions of craft and making which go back decades, and indeed centuries, this resurgence of activity is often explained – and, to be fair, genuinely *experienced* – as a 'new' phenomenon. For instance, in the 2008 book *Handmade Nation: The Rise of DIY, Art, Craft and Design*, one of the co-editors, Faythe Levine, writes

breathlessly about her excitement at setting up a stall at the
Renegade Craft Fair in Chicago, in 2003:

> A lot of us had no clue what we were doing, but there was
> this exhilarating energy throughout Wicker Park . . . I knew
> something big was happening. . . . We were redefining
> what craft was and making it our own. . . . Without really
> being conscious of it, we were creating an independent
> economy free from corporate ties. I quickly realised I was
> a part of a burgeoning art community based on creativity,
> determination, and networking.[29]

This exhilaration at being part of an apparently new craft
movement may also have been felt by some individuals 10,
20, or 100 years earlier, but no matter. *Handmade Nation*
certainly does seem to document a newly empowered and
organized movement – helped, as I've said, by the new visibility of their activities via the internet, which enables the
excited enthusiasts in one corner of the world to inspire and
encourage similarly energized individuals elsewhere, with
a depth and speed that was not previously possible. Special
mention must go here to Etsy, a vast and lovely platform
where people can buy and sell, but also admire and be
inspired by, a massive array of crafted things from around
the world. Ravelry, the superb social network for knitters,
has also been very influential.[30] As Garth Johnson, who
produces the blog extremecraft.com, says:

> It may sound strange that a bunch of people who are trying
> to reclaim handicraft are using technology to do so, but it's
> undeniably true. . . . It's the internet that holds the craft
> world together. Show me a crafter without a website and I'll
> show you a crafter who will probably have a website within
> six months. The handmade nation wields the internet just

as effectively as it does a knitting needle or a roll of duct tape.[31]

For these crafters, the internet is not the new place where craft itself happens – that's what we will be discussing in the next chapter – but is the new vehicle for communicating about (real-world) craft, for showing projects and connecting with others. It means that they have been able to collectively develop a firm and positive sense of shared meaning, and mission, which was probably more difficult to establish when craft activity was more fragmented and isolated.

One such expression of the personal and political meanings of this recent movement are expressed, for instance, in the 'Craftifesto', written by Amy Carlton and Cinnamon Cooper, founders of the DIY Trunk Show, an annual craft event in Chicago:

> *Craftifesto: The Power is in Your Hands!*
> We believe:
> *Craft is powerful.* We want to show the depth and breadth of the crafting world. Anything you want you can probably get from a person in your own community.
> *Craft is personal.* To know that something was made by hand, by someone who cares that you like it, makes that object much more enjoyable.
> *Craft is political.* We're trying to change the world. We want everyone to rethink corporate culture and consumerism.
> *Craft is possible.* Everybody can create something![32]

These statements show how craft has become more than just individuals making nice things: there is now a sense of community and shared purpose. *Handmade Nation* – which is not only a book but also a 2009 documentary film of the same name – showcases a rich array of craft activity from the USA, including people making clothes, dolls, books, bags, jewellery, prints, footwear, and other things, using a huge variety of techniques and styles. *Make* magazine, and the associated Maker Faire events, similarly showcase a huge range of DIY projects, which are often more to do with engineering and technology, but are driven by the same ethos, and often have an ecological dimension, by reusing former junk, or by producing or saving power.

CRAFT MOTIVATIONS

So what explains the activity, and the rise, of crafting? Part of the explanation appears above, in that crafting is now a community and a movement with appealing values, that people want to be a part of. But there are further personal reasons why people choose to be *making things* rather than joining other kinds of friendly-sounding communities. Sabrina Gschwandtner, a knitter who has published both a series of journals and a book called *KnitKnit*, says that she is frequently asked 'Why is handcraft so popular right now?' She suggests that it is 'a reaction against a whole slew of things, including our hyperfast culture, increasing reliance on digital technology, [and] the proliferation of consumer culture'.[33] She notes that sustainability is often a motivating factor. And she says that often,

> people want to see a project through from beginning to end, something they don't get to do in their daily lives. In their jobs, they do one part of producing something and they don't do the other parts. In producing a handcraft project, people can see something from start to finish and then have a material product that they can use themselves or give away.[34]

This is an argument that can apply to a range of crafts: the same point is made by Matthew Crawford to explain why fixing a motorbike is so satisfying, compared with office work, in his book *The Case for Working With Your Hands*.[35]

Other crafters interviewed for *Handmade Nation* provide further explanations. Deb Dormody, who makes and binds her own books, says that homemade things are special because they carry the 'authentic and personal' touch of the person who has made them[36] (which reflects the point made by Ruskin in the previous chapter). Christy Petterson, who makes earrings, postcards, and other things, tells of how she always liked being creative but had been put off doing 'art' because the education system had framed it as 'serious' and 'analytical'. It was only when she happened to find websites such as Getcrafty.com that she felt able and inspired to do whatever she wanted – 'I realised that I had found my people', as she puts it.[37]

Alena Hennessy, who makes clothes and tiles, had previously been an artist working through galleries, but found it limiting and boring. When she tried to break away from that world, the open and sharing community of craft people took her by surprise: 'In the craft community, I feel very connected to people whom I have never met in person. I didn't expect to be so inspired by what everyone else was doing. . . . It is very different from a typical gallery art scene: it is a really wonderful sort of collaborative, supportive, noncompetitive network', she says.[38] At a more individual level, Jenny Hart talks about how she had thought that embroidery looked 'tedious' and stressful – 'like it would make me want to pull my hair out' – but she discovered that it was a great way to relax and curb anxiety. She launched Sublimestitching.com to show others that embroidery did not have to be about following complex diagrams, but could simply be enjoyed:

I don't think our generation really likes to be told what to do. . . . We really like to have a lot of wiggle room for experimenting and being creative, and we like to have our mark on it. Embroidery leaves a lot of room for that.[39]

These motivations, then, all tend to combine personal satisfactions with the pleasure and inspiration of being part of a craft community.

CRAFTING TOGETHERNESS

The crafters featured in *Handmade Nation* are generally those who have become visible, and inspiring to others, through the online and offline networks of craft enthusiasts. And, of course, their views are no less significant for that. But the craftworld – unlike the artworld – is a place where fame, and comparative status amongst peers, is meant to be unimportant. In line with this reasoning, a number of books and websites about craft today emphasize the essentially intimate and personal nature of the experience of making. Here, making is still connecting – with materials, other people, and the world – but in gentle and quiet ways, with no need for grand celebratory announcements. One example is the book *The Creative Family*, by Amanda Blake Soule, which offers a powerful and democratic argument for widespread, unspecialized, everyday craft activity. The end products of craft activities here are not widely circulated on websites, are not sold for money, and seek no external recognition, but are hugely important for the reason given in the subtitle, *How to Encourage Imagination and Nurture Family Connections*. Soule does actually have a level of online fame, as the creator of the popular SouleMama blog, but this book emphasizes the personal and family benefits of everyday creative projects (which is one of the things that her 'adventures in thrifting, crafting and parenting' blog is about).

Despite the 'How to' subtitle – a formula favoured by publishers – the book is far from prescriptive. Instead, it encourages any activities which help families to bond, and appreciate each other, through creative work and play:

> Living a creative life can encompass all areas of our family life – from our hobbies, to the way we connect with nature, to the ways we connect in our community, to the ways we celebrate our days together, and to the ways we celebrate each other.[40]

Soule emphasizes the *process* of creativity, which helps people to learn and bond together. She emphasizes the value of all family members being engaged in creative projects – not just encouraging a child to do a painting (although that's good and fine), but everyone actively having one or two projects on the go:

> I see both my personal creative efforts and the act of engaging creatively with my children as being on the same continuum of creative living – they feed into each other. Being creative (in whatever capacity) is important: important to me, because I feel myself to be a more complete person when my creativity is expressed; important to my children, who witness adults growing, sharing and learning creatively; and important to my family, who grow and connect by creating together.[41]

Actively seeking out opportunities to be creative together is presented here as one of the most important things that families can do. Soule argues that this is good for the well-being of parents, who can continue to explore their own

interests and maintain a distinct identity, and for bonding
the family together, as well as for the creative development
of children. She also highlights the ways in which 'creative
living' can play a positive role in local and global communities – whether through direct engagement with particular
campaigns, such as those making clothes and blankets for
homeless or displaced people (like Afghans for Afghans, or
the Dulaan Project[42]), or through being mindful of the ways
in which creative activities could help or impact local groups,
or the environment.

A PROCESS WITH POWER

I read about lots of different kinds of craft activities for this
book, including volumes on knitting, embroidery, guerrilla
gardening, sustainable technology, homemade electronics,
and other things. As it turns out, it may not be the best use
of the available space to go through them one by one here,
but I can draw out a theme which connects them all: the
meaningful and rewarding *process* of making.

In *The Subversive Stitch*, Rozsika Parker writes about
embroidery as a craft practice which is two contrasting
things at once: on the one hand, it is, and has been, a marker
of femininity, but on the other hand, it is, and has been, a
'weapon of resistance' to the constraints associated with
the idea of femininity, enabling women to actively produce
things in the world – transforming materials into meaningful
objects – and to carve out a place for personal thought and
self-expression.[43] She argues:

> The processes of creativity – the finding of form for
> thought – have a transformative impact on the sense of
> self. The embroiderer holds in her hands a coherent object
> which exists both outside in the world and inside her

head. Winnicott's theory of mirroring helps us understand how the experience of embroidering and the embroidery affirms the self as a being with agency, acceptability and potency. . . . The embroiderer sees a positive reflection of herself in her work and, importantly, in the reception of her work by others.[44]

Similarly, in the conclusion to her study *The Culture of Knitting*, Joanne Turney writes that knitting 'offers a means of creativity, of confidence in one's own ability to "do", as well as occupying a space in which one can just "be"'.[45] The process of knitting is rewarding because something both pleasing and useful is produced, and for some because it represents an ethical and political choice – to make some clothing oneself rather than purchase it from the clothing industry, with its often very badly paid workers. Perhaps surprisingly, however, the outcome of the process is relatively unimportant. From her interviews with amateur knitters, Turney finds that:

> The emphasis of the personal, emotional and subjective testimonies of the respondents intimated that knitting was a journey, in which frequently the travelling (knitting) was more important or emotionally significant than the arrival at the destination (knitted object).[46]

A study of quilting by Marybeth C. Stalp reaches similar conclusions. Indeed, she finds a significant tension between the views of quilters' family and friends, and the quilters themselves. For her research, Stalp intensively interviewed 70 middle-aged women who identified themselves as 'quilters', and spoke to many more quilting guilds and groups. She reports that quilters' family members typically found the amount of time spent on quilting to be rather frustrating and difficult to understand, but tried to find value in the activity by praising the usefulness and the number of quilts made. For quilters themselves, however, this approach could just be annoying. They rarely knew how many quilts they had produced – this was of little interest to them – and found most of their pleasure in the *process*, not the product.[47] They were drawn to quilting as an expressive, creative activity, sometimes to continue or to 'recover' a family tradition of quilting; and as an activity which would give them space to think, to make, and 'to see themselves as part of a larger culture, a community of culture creators with a past and a future'.[48]

These pleasures and connections are not limited to knitting and sewing. The motivations of guerrilla gardeners, to take one more example, can be surprisingly similar. Guerrilla gardening refers to 'the illicit cultivation of someone else's land', as Richard Reynolds puts it, although the land in question has usually not been much cared for by its owner.[49] Guerrilla gardeners plant tulips on roundabouts, vegetables on roadside verges, and daffodils in neglected parks. These non-confrontational activists take pleasure in the secret and anonymous process of their work; their ongoing efforts to make the world a nicer place through small but beautiful interventions; and their sense of connection with the illicit planting community in particular, gardeners and environmental activists in general, and with nature itself. They gain pleasure from what they have done, but it is the *doing it* which really counts.[50]

AN UNEXPECTED DETOUR: THINKING ABOUT CREATIVITY WITH *STAR WARS*

Whilst I was working on all this, I was starting to teach a new module at the University of Westminster, entitled, simply,

'Creativity'. Some taught courses can start off by defining their terms in the first lecture, and move quickly on to consider the issues at stake in more detail. With 'creativity' I didn't think that the basic definition could be that simple, and so instead tried to take the students on a journey where we would modify and tweak our interpretation of 'creativity' as we went along.

In the first week I showed images of various things – a more or less 'random' selection of things for discussion, from the moon landings to a potato masher – and asked the students whether they considered each item to be 'creative' or not. When they said yes or no, a discussion of 'why' or 'why not' meant that we were able to pin down some of the key features of creativity – or at least, a kind of 'gut reaction' to what creativity might look like. This included many of the points that we mentioned in chapter 1: something new, original, or surprising; putting established elements together in a new way; and deliberate and thoughtful (rather than accidental) action. We also tentatively added 'handmade' and 'homemade', the product of individual physical activity, although this seemed rather unstable as a defining aspect.

One of the items I used for discussion was a poster for *Star Wars*, representing the original 1977 movie, and also one for *Star Wars Episode IV: A New Hope: Special Edition*, representing the 1997 reworked version of the film with added computer-generated (CGI) effects. I had correctly assumed that the students would be happy to recognize the original *Star Wars* as a creative product. Even if we acknowledge that it drew upon a number of existing genres and traditions – such as the Western, Samurai, romantic epic, and World War II movies – and then used them in a new way, it still qualifies easily. The more curious issue was whether George Lucas's tinkering – adding reasonably pointless and not entirely convincing CGI alien creatures, and establishing shots, with much time and expense, 20 years later – would count as creative. We were split: on the one hand, it would be churlish and absurd to decide that this technically cutting-edge and previously unheard-of level of movie reworking was 'not creative'. But on the other hand, it would be easy to argue that making *Star Wars* originally, from nothing, in a couple of years, was far more creative than spending several more years fiddling with details which made almost no difference to the emotional experience of the story.

This connected again with the 'handmade' debate. The computer-generated elements of the *Star Wars* Special Editions, and the vast amounts of CGI in the three prequel films, *The Phantom Menace* (1999), *Attack of the Clones* (2002), and *Revenge of the Sith* (2005), seemed to lack the charm and tangible appeal of the physical models constructed for the earlier films. Even though the newer films featured very complex digital vistas, with many moving vehicles and details, painstakingly created in a time-consuming process of computer craftwork by talented digital artists, viewers were still left with a feeling that this was unlovely digital overkill.

Although this judgement may be unfair, this move away from the more obvious 'handmade' feel, towards a level of glossy wizardry which we find it more difficult to relate to, seemed to contribute to a general feeling that 'creativity' was not really taking place. Of course, adding three less-good films onto the front of a much-loved trilogy didn't really help either.

This, then, added up to a strong vote in favour of loving but not overcomplicated craftwork, at a human level, designed to create a response of emotional engagement rather than mere appreciation of technological achievement. These thoughts fed into our ongoing conversation about the meaning of creativity.

Another item I showed to the students for considera-

tion was *Star Wars Uncut* (www.starwarsuncut.com) – a fan
project to remake *Star Wars* in a patchwork of 15-second
chunks. As the site explains:

> You and 472 other people have the chance to recreate *Star
> Wars: A New Hope*. Below is the entire movie split up into
> 15 second clips. Click on one of the scenes to claim it, film
> it, and upload it. When we're all done, we'll stitch it all
> together and watch the magic happen.

The 15-second clips have been made in a wide variety of
styles: animation using drawings, cardboard, and toys, and
live-action video with homemade costumes and props, puppets, and pets. The level of 'creativity' on show is quite
delightful.

But surely a low-quality, homemade, shot-for-shot remake
of an *existing* hit movie can't count as an especially 'creative'
activity, can it? This is the derivative work of fans – which
would be nothing if it were not for the original *genuinely*
creative effort of George Lucas and his colleagues, 33 years
earlier. Nevertheless, the work of the 473 *Star Wars Uncut*
contributors *does* seem to be a remarkable array of creativity.
Particular details, such as an Obi-Wan Kenobi whose beard
and hair are entirely rendered in masking tape, or an R2-D2
which is clearly someone's little brother in a dustbin, mean
that the viewer cannot help but smile in appreciation.

This brings us back to the problem with the standard definitions of creativity, as mentioned in chapter 1. There, you
may recall, we saw that creativity is usually identified by its
outcomes: things or ideas which haven't been seen before, and
which make a *difference* in the context in which they appear.
This is the essence of the well-known definition offered by
Mihaly Csikszentmihalyi, and is common to others.

But this standard notion of creativity, that it necessarily

involves producing something that hasn't been done before – whether we mean in that particular context, or in *any* context – contains the odd problem that you can't identify creativity just by seeing it – or feeling it. In fact, even odder than that, it means you can't identify creativity without having a detailed historical overview of everything that's been created already. So it is possible to do something that you feel is genuinely creative, and which really impresses your friends and colleagues, but which could still be discounted from being labelled 'creative' when an old sage turns up and observes that the same brilliant thing was done in 1826.

To be fair, Csikszentmihalyi insists that fully 'creative' creations should have been noticed and appreciated by influential people in the relevant field, and this means that such inventions should, by definition, have entered the historical record. But again, this brings us to an approach where creativity is something that can be confirmed or denied by taking a trip to the library. As Csikszentmihalyi is primarily conducting a sociological study of how a particular phenomenon can arise – where that phenomenon is an achievement or innovation which is widely hailed as a creative breakthrough – it makes sense to have this verifiable external view of creativity.

But outside of that particular context, it might be considered strange that we are unable to say if creativity has happened or not, without turning to subject experts. The Csikszentmihalyi approach denies that creativity is an experience, a feeling, or a process. Instead, it's all about certified outcomes, produced by people who have probably been hailed as a 'creative genius' in the newspapers. (Csikszentmihalyi himself, being sociological about it, wouldn't agree with the 'genius' line, but would say that they were talented individuals who benefited from being in the right place at the right time.)

CREATIVITY REFRAMED

The focus on celebrated outcomes is especially strange when we consider that Csikszentmihalyi is otherwise famous for the concept of 'flow'.[51] 'Flow' describes the experience where a person is wholly engaged in a task, to the extent that time passes unnoticed, and they forget about demands external to the task, such as the need to eat or make phone calls. Their work is challenging, in a satisfying way – not so much that it causes stress and anxiety, and not so little that boredom appears, but just at the right level, prompting absorbed fascination and the hope of discovery. Csikszentmihalyi reports that this experience is common to all of the super-creative people whom he has interviewed – but it is not exclusive to them. The 'flow' experience is presented as being desirable for, and attainable by, anybody, as they go about their work.

With this device – I am not sure how deliberately – Csikszentmihalyi separates the *feelings* and *experiences* associated with creativity, from the definable hard reality of 'actual' high-powered creativity. Although this is fine for his needs, I would like to suggest that – for the purposes of this book at least – we should reject the 'certified public genius' model of creativity and instead embrace a rather fuzzier understanding which is, perhaps, closer to the 'common sense' notion of creativity that we might use to describe a friend or colleague who seems to like making things or solving problems in everyday life. This doesn't necessarily mean the kind of people who like to knit or make pottery vases – they might enjoy making the household plumbing work effectively, fixing the car, devising innovative business strategies, or making websites. And, incidentally, being 'common sense' doesn't mean that something is necessarily correct, but it's not necessarily wrong either, and there must be some value in speaking to common experience.

We saw above that the meaning of everyday craft and creative activities was to be found within the *process*, not so much in its outcomes, and so it is important that our definition should reflect this as well. We could put it like this:

Everyday creativity refers to a process which brings together at least one active human mind, and the material or digital world, in the activity of making something. The activity has not been done in this way by this person (or these people) before. The process may arouse various emotions, such as excitement and frustration, but most especially a feeling of joy. When witnessing and appreciating the output, people may sense the presence of the maker, and recognize those feelings.

I'm afraid this is not a compact dictionary definition. That's because it is an attempt to describe something which, by its nature, is difficult to define concisely.

A one-sentence version might be:

Everyday creativity refers to a process which brings together at least one active human mind, and the material or digital world, in the activity of making something which is novel in that context, and is a process which evokes a feeling of joy.

This is slightly less satisfactory, because I had to cut some bits off, but reasonable.

In the longer version, the point about 'presence of the maker', and recognition of the feelings they may have felt in the process of creation, refers to the way in which we may mirror (or feel ourselves to be mirroring) the sense of concentration, or happiness, mourning, or other feeling, which we sense is contained in the clearly 'human' elements of a creative work. This is the handmade imperfection which Ruskin argued makes human craft work so special. And it is what I was referring to above, when I said that 'the viewer cannot help but smile in appreciation' at the cheap homemade details of the *Star Wars Uncut* videos.

The reference to joy, which I kept in both the short and long versions of the definition, might seem curious. It raises the question: would we say that something was 'not creative' if we somehow knew that the process of its construction involved no joy whatsoever? Well, perhaps we would. With no magical, smile-inducing spark behind it, the constructed thing is just, well, a constructed thing. And would we refuse to describe a person as 'creative' if their making process was all hard concentration and no flicker of pleasure? Again, yes, perhaps we would. I certainly like it better than the other definition, which – let us not forget – would deny the 'creative' label to people much *more* often.

Of course, the 'joy' does not need to be present throughout. Making things is often an intense, difficult, or frustrating experience. But whether the thrilling zing comes right at the start, with an exciting idea before any planning, or right at the end, when the thing is finally *done*, it's likely to be in there somewhere.

Now, the sensibly sceptical reader might at this point be wondering if I am trying to replace a well-established definition of 'creativity' with my own inauthentic version, like someone sneakily changing the rules in order to win an argument. But I would suggest that my description of creativity lines up well with regular usage. For instance, when we talk about the Web as something which gives everyday people opportunities to be creative, and to share the fruits of their creativity, we are talking about the kind of creativity that I have outlined above. We are *not* talking about the kind of creativity as defined by Csikszentmihalyi, which only counts activity as 'creative' when it has led to outcomes which have had a significant, recognized impact on the relevant field.

And similarly, when we meaningfully say 'this is all very creative', about an exhibition put on by fashion students at the local college, or about a complex marble run made by a father and daughter team, or about handmade toys at a craft fair, or an agricultural machine made by a farmer to make a regular task more efficient, we are again talking about creativity as I have outlined it, and not like the Csikszentmihalyi definition.

Although the word 'creativity' might be overused in the world today, it is rightly and reasonably used in relation to some significant everyday activities – of the kind I describe in my definition – and this is both meaningful and widely accepted. Nobody would sensibly say that you are not creative unless you have *actually* done something on a par with inventing the helicopter, or founding the radical painting movement of Cubism. And the more everyday, emotion-oriented and process-based description of creativity offered by my definition seems to work pretty well in practice.

For example, it enables us to account for the inclination to say that both the original *Star Wars* movie, and the *Star Wars Uncut* homemade remakes of scenes, score highly for creativity, whilst the process that generated the *Star Wars* Special Editions is less creative. The Special Editions are an example where the level of discernible joy, in the somewhat pointless and fussy additions, is insufficient. And this approach helps to explain why we might want to assert that a selection of amateur videos on YouTube are 'more creative' than an evening's worth of stuff on network television. The latter is likely to be polished, very professionally produced, and may be quite imaginative, but it's not quite the kind of thing that the word 'creativity' was made for. Whereas on YouTube, you have a world of people doing amazing, silly, clever, pointless, or heartfelt things, and putting them out in the world for others to experience, *because they want to*, and that seems to be much more like what 'creativity' is meant to be all about.

Creativity is something that is *felt*, not something that needs external expert verification. I rest my case, for now, although we'll come back to this later.

4

THE MEANING OF MAKING III:
DIGITAL

In the preceding two chapters we have looked at some of
the philosophy and practice of craft – the careful, thoughtful process of making something with the hands. Producing
something for the Web, or elsewhere on the internet, might
be thought of as the *opposite* of the physical, material process
of craft work. The early terms used to characterize the internet, such as 'virtual reality' and 'cyberculture', underlined
the notion that this activity is ethereal and not 'real'. The
newer notion of 'the cloud' – the virtual space where online
programs and processing as well as content are increasingly located, seemingly 'up there' and away from earthly
computing machines – gives a similar impression.

But in my experience, making things to share online is
very much a craft process. You start with nothing, except
perhaps for some basic tools and materials, which contain
no prescription and seemingly infinite possibilities. When I
started making websites, in 1997, I had to do it by typing the
HTML code into a plain text editor (which in my case was

Notepad, the very basic text editor which has been included
in every version of Microsoft Windows since 1985).[1] This is
known as 'hand coding', a term which is meaningful beyond
the simple fact that you use your hands to type, which of
course is common to many computer functions. 'Hand
coding' points to the delicate process of building up the code
bit by bit, testing it from time to time to see if there are
any bugs – tiny imperfections which typically stop the whole
thing from working. It's a process you feel your way through
– starting with a few ideas, and maybe a couple of rough
sketches, you start to put the thing together, see how it goes,
take a step back, make some changes, and see how it looks.
This may lead to some new ideas, then you change things a
bit, keep on going, until it's done. You also have to make all
the individual graphics (titles, logos, buttons, and pictures),
again starting with nothing, trying out ideas, seeing what
looks right, making all the visual bits and bobs the site will
need as you build it from the ground up.

You use keyboard and mouse, but this activity is obviously
not 'hands-on' in the normal craft sense – you can't *literally*
press your fingers into the craft material, the equivalent of
the clay or wood or paint, because it's all digital. But you can
certainly leave your metaphorical fingerprints all over the
thing you're making; indeed, it's hard not to. The personality of the maker always comes across in the finished thing.
So this process is like craft in the tinkering, weaving, 'from
the ground up' experience of making something; and it's also
like craft in that the maker imprints some of their character upon the work, and its audiences are likely to sense their
'presence' – that sense of connection which we installed in
our definition of creativity at the end of the previous chapter.

In the nearly 15 years since I started tapping bits of
HTML into Notepad, the tools have changed, but the process is pretty similar. Nowadays, helpful 'what you see is what

you get' software means that the tinkering is less often inter-
rupted by crashes or totally unexpected results, but it's still
tinkering, and it's still building from the ground up, and
you still need to make the necessary components (such as
graphics) elsewhere and then pull them into your website
workshop. And the same principles apply if you're not making
websites at all but are, say, making online video, which again
is a messy process of creating a range of material which you
then cut, select, and edit to craft a finished object. As with
physical handmade crafts, you end up with a 'polished' end
product, which may have a 'simple' appearance, but behind it
there are hours of intricate, tentative, and difficult work.

So this chapter continues our discussion of craft, and
the meaning of making things, into the digital realm –
and in particular to the Web, where today's creators have
the opportunity to easily share their work with other
internet-connected people all around the world.

The Web is, of course, vast. There's no point trying to
describe all of the creative things that happen there, because
there's just so much of it. It's not even like we're interested
in just one *kind* of creativity, such as online poetry, photography, or politics (even though you couldn't do justice to any
of them in a book chapter either). As it happens, as mentioned in the previous chapter, I edited a book called *Web
Studies* – published in 2000, followed by an all-new second
edition in 2004 – which did indeed attempt to capture all
dimensions of online creativity: 'everyday Web life, art and
culture, Web business, and global Web communities, politics and protest', as it said on the back cover. But of course,
all you could really get were some snapshots of interesting
bits of the Web, and their implications.

So here, we'll start with something both very simple and
very complex, a Web 2.0 'platform' from which we can learn
something about others: YouTube.

MAKING AND CONNECTING ON YOUTUBE

YouTube is by far the best-known and most-used online video website. You are almost certain to know this already, as YouTube has become somewhat ubiquitous on the internet, and in popular culture generally. Although it only launched in 2005, it quickly came to dominate online video, with its straightforward interface and simple tools for sharing and embedding material. Just four years later, YouTube videos accounted for 40 per cent of all videos viewed online, with closest video-hosting rivals Microsoft and Viacom way behind at 2 per cent each.[2] In 2009 it was serving more than 1 billion videos every day,[3] and hundreds of thousands of videos were being uploaded by users daily.[4]

In terms of my own dealings with online media, to be honest, I came to YouTube relatively late. Of course, like almost everybody, I had watched some videos on it. But during 2005–7, YouTube didn't strike me as a central place for participatory culture, probably because I was equating video with television. If you're interested in everyday people coming together online, making and sharing and connecting, then a site of television-ish clips doesn't sound very promising, as television is necessarily rather professional and complex, rather than handmade and simple, and not at all easy to produce. It also seems to be about watching rather than about communicating. The television model is what we were trying to get *away* from.

Of course, I was wrong. Well, mostly wrong: videos are odd entrants in the 'communal allotment' of Web 2.0 – as I described it in chapter 1 – since each item tends to be a self-contained and 'sealed' package, which means that other users cannot easily add bits to, or re-edit, a posted video. (Technically, it is perfectly possible to download a YouTube video, in lower-than-original quality, and re-edit it, but this is a much more complicated process than, say, editing a Wikipedia page, which can be done in a matter of seconds.) However, if we relate this to the 'allotment' metaphor, adding videos to YouTube is like adding plants to the garden; and then those items can be nurtured by others (through ratings and links) and responded to (through comments and further videos). Contributing diverse plants to a shared garden is a perfectly good form of collaboration: we don't actually need to be pruning, feeding, and fussing over bits of individual plants together. So it's still a Web 2.0 community, but with the level of mashability being set one notch higher.

As for the worry that videos are an unnecessarily professional and complicated type of building-block for online interaction: it turned out that I was uneasy about something which obviously wasn't bothering other people. The online community seem to be pretty forgiving about formal quality issues – and I had to remind myself that being a perfectionist isn't actually a *good* thing. I received a memorable lesson on this point when, for some reason, I found myself watching a video by Chris Anderson showing a radio-controlled blimp – a flying airship – that he had made at home. There are quite a lot of public Chris Andersons – including a jazz pianist, an athlete, and the guy who runs the TED conference, none of whom are *this* Chris Anderson. This is the one who wrote *The Long Tail* and is editor-in-chief of *Wired* magazine. In other words, he's someone who should be a master of Web 2.0, who is concerned with excellent design, who is a well-known professional.

The very striking and delightful thing about his blimp video was this: it was *messy*. Not, I should say, that it was uninteresting, or foolish, or that his radio-controlled blimp was not impressive.[5] His home-made blimp is surely very clever, and the video conveys a perfectly reasonable sense of what the thing looks like and how it operates. But the video was not at all professional in its execution: the hand-held camera was shaky, the autofocus wasn't always right, and in particular the audio was very rough, with Anderson apparently unconcerned by the crashes and shouts which his children were making in the background of his languid, unscripted commentary. Anderson clearly wanted to share his blimp-making work with the blimp-making community (yes, this is a particular hobby, with its own community of enthusiasts, and Anderson in this case seemed to be speaking to them, rather than to the broader audience – such as the readers of his best-selling books). But he was not going to spend ages cutting together the best shots, or re-recording the audio, for a more polished presentation. And the important point is that, as a viewer, I *did not mind*. It was *fine*. I liked the unshowy, rough-and-ready nature of the whole thing. It was liberating. Then I remembered that I had also recently looked at YouTube videos on sewing – to make a toy for Finn – which were educational but simply done, and I hadn't been bothered by the lo-fi recording; and I had watched a terribly ropey video of Clay Shirky doing a talk, apparently filmed by someone in the audience, and I hadn't really minded that either. I do normally like things to be presented nicely, but this focus on content rather than style conveyed the powerful, inclusive, happy message that 'anyone can do this'.

Here we find ourselves to be modern versions of John Ruskin, whom we met in chapter 2. Ruskin asserted that it is better that objects made by people should bear the marks of the effort of making them, rather than being polished but impersonal. Writing in 1849, he said that things made by people should exhibit 'the vivid expression of the intellectual life which has been concerned in their production'.[6] Such creations 'become noble or ignoble in proportion to the amount of the energy of that mind which has visibly been employed upon them'.[7]

This view appeared in *The Seven Lamps of Architecture*, where each of the 'lamps' represents a guiding principle for architects and other creative workers. This one is part of 'the lamp of *life*', where Ruskin argues that the joy of workers' creativity should be visible in the things they produce. Developing this theme three years later in his essay 'The Nature of Gothic', Ruskin suggests that a slick production is nice if you can get it, but is not the most important thing:

> If you are to have the thought of a rough and untaught man, you must have it in a rough and untaught way; but from an educated man, who can without effort express his thoughts in an educated way, take the graceful expression, and be thankful. Only *get* the thought, and do not silence the peasant because he cannot speak good grammar, or until you have taught him his grammar. Grammar and refinement are good things, both, only be sure of the better thing first.[8]

Here we must forgive Ruskin his Victorian tone, because he is at least trying to be nice, and of course is saying that we should put aside snobbish notions about the appearance of things, and instead appreciate the intellectual effort that they embody. In this scenario, I'm afraid, Chris Anderson, author of *The Long Tail* and editor-in-chief of *Wired*, is 'a rough and untaught man', and a 'peasant', but one with something to say. Ruskin continues:

> So the rule is simple: Always look for invention first, and after that, for such execution as will help the invention, and as the inventor is capable of without painful effort, and *no more*. Above all, demand no refinement of execution where there is no thought, for that is slaves' work, unredeemed.

Rather choose rough work than smooth work, so only that
the practical purpose be answered, and never imagine there
is reason to be proud of anything that may be accomplished
by patience and sand-paper.[9]

In modern terms, Ruskin is saying that spending hours on
overwrought postproduction is unnecessary, and deadens
the human connection that we would otherwise make with
the work. Thus I could see thought, life, and inspiration
in the video produced by the blimp-making peasant, Chris
Anderson, which encouraged my own creativity; whereas a
more 'professional' quality of video would only have reinforced the feeling that video-making was not something
that a 'rough and untaught' person such as myself could
participate in.

And so I started making videos for YouTube. In fact, this
story has two strands, because on the one hand I started
making 'personal' home movies, since the birth of our son
Finn had given us something really worth preserving in
moving pictures, and also, having started to get the hang
of digital video-making, I began to produce work-related
videos about some of my academic projects and research.
These appear on separate YouTube channels, giving me the
dual experience of being a domestic amateur on one channel and a public academic on the other. Chris Anderson's
noisy, shaky videos gave me the confidence to make my own;
although in practice I can't help trying to make the videos
look and sound as good as I can, so the reality is not as liber-
atingly rough-and-ready as promised. And the same amount
of effort goes into both categories of video, even though
a personal video showing highlights from Finn's first year
has only been viewed 70 times, whilst a worky one called
'Participation Culture, Creativity, and Social Change' is at
12,000.

For either type of video, I don't just think of it as a 'video' – it's a 'YouTube video'. Within a couple of years of its existence, the site's very name had become descriptive of a particular kind of audio-visual artefact: the short, fast, online video. This is the case even though being a 'YouTube video' says nothing really about the content. But YouTube is a particular kind of thing – a platform of possibilities.

YOUTUBE AS ARCHETYPE OF THE DIGITAL CREATIVE PLATFORM

Web 2.0 applications which encourage people to make and share things are often not very specific *tools*, as such, but are broad *platforms*. The word 'platform' is both the technically correct term for this kind of thing, but also the right common-sense word to describe the kind of stage which they offer for creative performance. Platforms of this kind tend not to assert a preference for particular topics or styles of material. Rather, they encourage users to express their creativity in whatever way they choose – within a particular framework, and general type of content. YouTube is now one of the most well-established of these platforms, and so makes a decent case study through which to consider the places where digital craft work happens.[10]

YouTube is perhaps unusual in that the core content, the videos themselves, cannot usually or satisfactorily be produced by direct input into an online device. Unlike a blog, for instance, which can be immediately contributed to by typing on a keyboard and hitting 'publish', production of a watchable YouTube video usually requires at least a little more work – most often recording using a digital video camera, followed by some editing – before the work can be uploaded. (This is not always the case – a growing number of laptops and phones can record video material and publish it to YouTube immediately – but such contributions are lo-fi even by YouTube standards. Another alternative is to use screen-capture software to make a video recording of, say, a PowerPoint presentation, with an audio commentary, but again this requires preparation, care, and editing.) Apart from that caveat, however, YouTube is an archetypal digital creative platform in three key ways.

1. A framework for participation

First of all, it offers a framework for participation. The key element here is the invitation to users to upload their own videos, of under fifteen minutes in duration. So, some things are set: it's primarily a place for videos, and in particular, short videos. But everything else is open. Whilst early contributions to the site seemed to be mostly youthful skateboard stunts and amateur music videos, the range soon blossomed, and YouTube is now, of course, a home for poets, engineers, medics, teachers, and a vast multitude of others, and the content is now an incredible array of material in diverse styles, on an enormous range of topics, including performance, education, video journals, sport, technology, family life, and how-to guides and discussions on everything from car maintenance to breast-feeding.

This highlights the sense in which YouTube is essentially 'just' a platform for creativity. In an unglamorous formulation, it is a database website, which invites people to add data as files, comments, tags, and links between different bits of information (notably user profiles and video content). Without the responses of users to this open invitation, YouTube would be nothing – there would literally be (almost) nothing there. YouTube could solicit material from existing media companies – as it does do, forming partnerships with numerous well-established corporations – but there is much evidence that YouTube's huge popularity, and dominance in the online video field, is due to its emphasis on establishing its framework as one which primarily supports a *community of participation and communication* amongst everyday users, rather than elite professionals.[11] (The YouTube community focus is discussed in point 3, below.)

One view of such a platform is that it is a (commercial) service offered to users who know what they are dealing with when they use it, and who are basically pleased that it gives them a stage on which to share their thoughts and their creative work, and a network through which they can connect with others, for free. A much more negative interpretation is offered by critical theorist Mark Andrejevic, who sees the user activity, freely 'given' by people as they upload videos and conduct community activity on the site, to be a new form of exploitation.[12] YouTube is a business built on the labour of unpaid video-makers around the world. In addition, as users move around YouTube, willingly indicating their interests and preferences through their searches, clicks, and ratings, they generate valuable marketing data which is gathered by the corporation and used for commercial purposes. To Andrejevic, this is 'immaterial labour', which is autonomous (you go on YouTube as a free choice) but creates an 'exploitable surplus' (valuable data). The extent to which you see this as primarily sinister and worrying is perhaps a matter of personal preference (and we'll be discussing this more in chapter 8). Andrejevic certainly seems to think that it indicates that YouTube secretly hates its users, and would be happier doing away with amateur video altogether and delivering the more profitable professional content provided by commercial 'partners'.[13] However, this seems to miss the point that without the 'amateur' content and contributions, YouTube would be much less popular, as we will see below.

A less damning perspective is offered by Virginia

Nightingale, who suggests that the companies that own online platforms such as YouTube and Flickr act as the 'patrons' of collective creative activity, retaining some power and control, but also welcoming the imaginative work of users.[14] Whichever way you look at it, the tradeoff between having a free online environment for sharing material, on the one hand, and providing a corporation with some useful data – and the opportunity to show us a few adverts – on the other, is one which millions of users seem to be more-or-less comfortable with, although that doesn't necessarily mean it's the perfect solution.

2. *Agnostic about content*

Second, within this framework, YouTube is entirely agnostic about what contributions can be made (apart from some precautions about pornographic and potentially offensive or abusive material). The platform is presented, but the opportunities for innovation in content are left open to the users. Some people have used it in ways that mimic established forms or styles, such as the music video, the interview, the comedy sketch, or the product review 'show'. A number of these individuals aspired to enter the mainstream media, and some have done so when their YouTube popularity has brought them to the attention of the traditional industry.[15] Others post examples of their professional practice (such as demonstrations of training or consultancy styles, or architectural 'walk-through' videos), in order to attract clients.

Other contributors, however, are entirely unconcerned about reaching a broad audience. Some use it to share family videos with friends and relatives. Some create what Patricia Lange has called 'videos of affinity', which are simply-produced recordings, with little or no postproduction, created

purely to connect with a community of friends and acquaintances.[16] These kinds of videos can seem trivial to those who
expect online video to aspire to 'TV standard' productions,
but any such criticism is clearly misdirected since, as Clay
Shirky has explained, when online material seems pointless
or baffling, the explanation is usually: 'It's simple. They're
not talking to you.'[17] These are just quick, reasonably tran-
sient ways to make a simple connection. The artist Martin
Creed has mentioned that one of his motivations for making
creative work is – counter to the idea of the grand artistic
statement – rather just 'to say hello',[18] and these 'videos of
affinity' sit, even more modestly, in that tradition – and also
with the 'I just called to say hello' phone call.

Not that YouTube videos are usually short on creativity:
a lot of material is made with a great deal of care and/or
ingenuity by users who hope to entertain their friends and
also, potentially, attract a wider audience. The press coverage of copyright and piracy issues can lead to the assumption
that a majority of the videos on YouTube are clips copied
from mainstream media – or put there by professional producers themselves, in a bid to assert control. But a content
analysis of 4,320 popular videos conducted by Jean Burgess
and Joshua Green in 2007,[19] found that only 42 per cent
of these came from mainstream, broadcast, or established
media, whilst just over 50 per cent were original user-created videos. (Eight per cent were from sources of 'uncertain'
status.) Video blogs (vlogs) accounted for 40 per cent of this
non-professional work, and other types of material included
user-created music videos (15 per cent), live material such
as music performance, sport, and 'slice of life' (13 per cent),
non-fiction presentations such as news and reviews (10 per
cent), and 'scripted material' – not necessarily scripted as
such – such as comedy sketches, animation, and machinima[20]
(8 per cent). A further 10 per cent were experimental or tech-

nically playful videos, where users toyed with various effects. This does not mean that they are works of little interest: for instance, the entertaining 'Original Human TETRIS Performance by Guillaume Reymond' is in this category, and has gathered 10 million views to date.

As these statistics are based on observations of the YouTube site alone, they are not able to tell us the motivations of the creators. However, on the basis of these categorizations, and the detail provided in Burgess and Green's account, it seems reasonable to suggest that their makers wish to communicate and connect with an audience, often on an emotional or intimate level, to share their knowledge or insights, to entertain and – in a perfectly valid sense – to show off, and, in doing so, to try to connect or have an impact on others. (We will consider motivations in a bit more detail in the section after next.)

3. Fostering community

Third, YouTube is more than a video archive: it is, and keenly positions itself as, a community. The tagline 'Broadcast Yourself' – which quickly replaced the original, less engaging slogan 'Your Digital Video Repository'[21] – points to the outward-facing, and possibly autobiographical, nature of the anticipated videos, but YouTube's functionality encourages much more than mere individualized 'look at me' self-exhibition. It actively encourages users to make comments, to subscribe, to give star ratings, to add friends and send messages, and to make videos responding to other videos.

These are not – or certainly not entirely – tacked-on 'social networking' features. Rather, as Jean Burgess and Joshua Green have shown, the users who have managed to become 'YouTube stars' have done so by embracing the community, and by acting as community members themselves.

Video celebrities such as Marina Orlova (who presents her own word etymology shows, *Hot for Words*, in a flirtatious style) and Michael Buckley (whose *What The Buck?!* offers camp coverage of celebrity news) have reached a point where they can appear in mainstream media, but have risen to the top of YouTube visibility not by acting as aloof stars, but by being community *participants*. They invite and respond to comments on the site, make links with others, and refer to community comments, responses and events within the videos themselves. They are actively embedded within the user community.[22] A revealing contrast is offered by the case of Oprah Winfrey's foray into YouTube. Oprah (or rather, her production company) used her TV show to promote the launch of her YouTube channel, and chose to disable certain participatory functions such as external embedding of videos, and unmoderated comments. This 'incursion of such a major corporate player into YouTube's attention economy' provoked 'an intense and immediate flurry of protest videos' and discussion.[23] Most damning of all was the perception that Oprah was neither from, nor engaging with, the YouTube community, and invited only a 'one-way conversation'. And indeed, Oprah has been relatively unsuccessful in this medium, gathering only 64,200 subscribers in two years.[24]

As Burgess and Green put it:

> However charming . . . or silly the content of their videos might be, what all the entrepreneurial YouTube stars have in common is the fit between their creative practice and the dynamics of YouTube as a platform for participatory culture.[25]

Engagement in the community is not just a route to online stardom, of course. Henry Jenkins suggests that YouTube offers 'strong social incentives' to make and share, and that users are inspired by 'the emotional support of a community eager to see their productions'.[26] He also suggests, quoting Yochai Benkler, that participation in an online culture such as YouTube's can 'make their practitioners better "readers" of their own culture and more self-reflective and critical of the culture they occupy'[27] – a claim which perhaps applies more in some cases than in others.

There is also the gift-giving dimension to YouTube's community: users give and receive homemade video 'gifts' for reasons which are to do with feelings and attachments, rather than economics. The notion of the gift economy helps us, in particular, to understand the rewards for participation – such as 'status', 'prestige', or 'esteem' – which have no (immediate) economic value.[28]

In sum, then, YouTube is a platform which offers a *framework* for participation, but which is *open* to a very wide variety of uses and contributions, and basically *agnostic* about the content, which means it has been adopted by a wide range of users for a diverse array of purposes. People use YouTube to *communicate* and *connect*, to share knowledge and skills, and to entertain. They use the *community* features of the site to *support* each other and engage in debates, and to generate the characteristics of a 'gift economy'. Whilst it is true that the majority of visitors to YouTube are viewing, not producing and participating, there are still literally millions of users who engage with this creative platform every day, and whose relationship with professional media has been fundamentally shifted because of the knowledge that they can be the creators, and not just receivers, of inventive media.

MOTIVATIONS FOR MAKING AND SHARING

This discussion of YouTube so far has been relatively 'top down' – a look at what happens when a business or organization establishes a platform and invites people to contribute to it, and make social connections upon it. Now I'd like to dig a bit deeper into *why* people make and share stuff online. For some platforms this is reasonably straightforward, because the amount of *effort* is low, and the social rewards and connections make it worthwhile. So Facebook, for instance, only requires simple and momentary inputs (adding a status update, or a link, or a photo), and in return you get to be part of an active social network, where people might make comments on your stuff, and you can comment on theirs, leading to a sense of mutual engagement and community, as well as an opportunity to try to impress like-minded people with your interests and activities.

In a similar way, Flickr provides an easy and quick way for people who take photographs – which is many people – to share them with their friends, and others: in order to show where they have been, or what they have been engaging with recently, or things they are proud of – including friends and family. They may also wish to share the aesthetic qualities of the appealing or inventive images that they have made. Or all of these things.

This regular, easy sharing of everyday personal stuff cultivates what Leisa Reichelt has called 'ambient intimacy'. In a blog post, she explains:

> Ambient intimacy is about being able to keep in touch with people with a level of regularity and intimacy that you wouldn't usually have access to, because time and space conspire to make it impossible. Flickr lets me see what friends are eating for lunch, how they've redecorated their bedroom, their latest haircut. Twitter tells me when they're hungry, what technology is currently frustrating them, who they're having drinks with tonight.[29]

Reichelt acknowledges that some people believe that they would find all this information to be just unwanted trivia and 'annoying noise'. But the success of social networking sites shows that people do get something from the regular sharing of ordinary fragments of everyday life.

> There are a lot of us . . . who find great value in this ongoing noise. It helps us get to know people who would otherwise be just acquaintances. It makes us feel closer to people we care for but in whose lives we're not able to participate as closely as we'd like.[30]

With services of this kind, there is not really a big question of 'why do users go to the *trouble* of doing this?', because it's all quite easy, and producing the content is not time-consuming. The motivation and the reward are basically the same thing: to be part of an active community, part of a conversation, and to feel somewhat more connected to people we know. Possibly also – but not necessarily – to come into contact with some new people.

Other online creative activities, though, take more *effort*, which makes the question of motivation less straightforward and more intriguing. Preparing a single video for YouTube, for example, might take several hours, or a few days. (As we have noted, you can bang out the video equivalent of a phone call in a few minutes, but videos of that kind are not the most common, and are rarely very popular.) Writing a blog is also rather time-consuming and quite hard work. So why do people do these things, putting their creative work out into the world with no financial incentive? Some people do get income from blog-writing, or video-making, it's true, but most of the content out there does not directly bring in money and is made for other reasons. So what are those reasons?

Let's start with blogs. Some blogs are everyday scrap-books, or a diary of a holiday, for instance, which are not especially difficult to produce, and which connect their authors with their friends and family in a way which is similar to the social networks mentioned above. But some blogs require rather more work.

To take one example: David Jennings, an educational consultant from London, has written one blog post every single day since 20 December 2005 – with the exception of five days when his son was born – and he's still going (www. musicarcades.com). This is a blog about everyday life – his own everyday life – which is not unusual, but it's based around his record collection. Having noticed that his collection of recorded music (vinyl, tapes, and CDs) had grown rather large, and that at some times he had acquired music at a rate which meant that he hadn't always appreciated each bit, Jennings set out to blog about each item – one per day.

Each item is listed in a database, and a random number generator tells him which one he's got to write about next. Rather than writing an encyclopaedia entry about each record – which you can usually get on Wikipedia anyway – Jennings typically writes about the personal memories and the associations that each one evokes, as well as some musical reflections and connections, notes about the sleeve, or anything else that you might like to file under 'cultural commentary'. He enjoys doing it, but this is quite hard work, taking up to an hour a day – which is a lot when you've also got a job and a young child. So why does he do it, I asked. He replied:

It's a kind of journey. It's about my love affair with listening to music, refracted through a series of snapshots. It's about trying to make sense of how music is bound up with my life. And it's also about the pathology of collecting – and means

I have to give real attention to the things I've collected, one by one, rather than just piling them up.[31]

But, I asked, why do it as a blog?

It's saying this is something I have a passion about. And it's harder to give up when it's public – there's a kind of public commitment to continue. I like the idea that people will stumble across the blog, when searching for information about some obscure record, and might feel a shared moment of enthusiasm for frankly rather a nutty project.[32]

So a project like this is partly just a personal endeavour – done because the blogger *wants* to, regardless of audience – but also connects him with other people, some of whom share ideas, feelings, and musical associations of their own, and some of whom are imagined future readers: Jennings describes his blog as 'a gift to future anthropologists', and I think he's only *half* joking.

A second example is Amanda Blake Soule, whom we met in the last chapter, as an exponent of craft-centred and creative parenting. She came to write her book *The Creative Family* (now followed by two other books) because of the popularity of her *SouleMama* blog. We know why she likes crafts and creativity, but what motivates her to record it all in a blog? In a reflective blog post, she considers:

There are so many things that get us through the days of parenting (because sometimes it's about soaring and some days it's truly about 'getting through'). . . . This blog, you see, is one of those things for me. It's a meditation of sorts. It's one of the ways in which I remind myself of the joys, the beauty and the blessings around me each and every day. . . . Writing about them helps me hold onto those moments.[33]

There is the personal need to write, then, as a way of preserving memories, and also because this drives her to create
further *opportunities* for such memorable family moments to
emerge – a cycle which she describes as a 'ridiculous joy-
addiction that feeds itself'.[34] But this is joined by a desire
to communicate, and a modest hope of inspiring others,
especially parents. As she notes in the same post:

> I write for me, but I hit 'publish' each day in the hopes that
> somehow – someway – these little ramblings of mine could
> inspire you to look for, to follow, to perhaps even create a
> moment of joy and beauty in your own day.[35]

The hundreds of comments on this one *SouleMama* blog
post alone attest that Soule's homemade writings and photographs do indeed bring comfort and support to many people
every day.[36]

To broaden our range of anecdotal evidence, and before
we turn to more systematic research, I thought I would ask
this question about motivations on Twitter.[37] I wrote: 'Not
v scientific, but can any Twitter friends tell me *why* you
make stuff to share online – YouTube, blogs, etc.?' I received
about 30 responses. Of course, this is a self-selected group,
and a very wonky small sample (people who follow me on
Twitter, *and* who happened to look at it and see my message
at the right time, *and* who could be bothered to reply), but it
was nevertheless interesting to see what people said. I have
tried to summarize and group together the different answers,
but it's still quite a long list:

- So others can learn or be entertained
- A desire to share thoughts and creative endeavours
- To chronicle my existence
- To add to the information available on the Web

- To be an active participant in the discussion of things
- To be a media maker and not just consumer
- Self-promotion/to show off
- To get feedback
- As a way to collaborate
- Contributing to and being part of a community of peers and friends
- A sense of being heard.

To simplify even further, these responses suggest that people spend time creating online content because they want to feel active and *recognized* within a community of interesting people, and because they wish to express or display aspects of themselves and their interests. So in many ways we might have predicted these kinds of reasons, and they can, if you like, be summarized as 'making is connecting'. But the theme of *recognition* comes through a little more strongly than anticipated: people want to lay down signs of their existence and their ideas, and they want this to be *noticed*. This is not surprising, but it adds a significant note to our general picture of what's going on. The 'sharing' and 'connecting' themes sound both warm and benign; seeking recognition is not necessarily very different, but it includes a harder edge, a kind of demand – 'notice me!' – which we have to understand as well.

STUDYING BLOGGERS

So now let's turn to the research literature, in the hope of finding more rigorous evidence. We'll begin with a 2007 journal article by Rosanna Guadagno and colleagues at the University of Alabama's psychology department, entitled 'Who Blogs? Personality Predictors of Blogging', which uses a personality inventory questionnaire to see what kind of person a blogger is.[38] I have to say, I don't like this kind of thing – I believe this kind of research is reductive and doesn't foster deep understanding.[39] Furthermore, rather than being based on a proper representative national sample, the researchers have only bothered to survey undergraduate students at (presumably) their own university. This is not research of the highest quality, then,[40] but it seems to have been noted in the public domain,[41] and we're short of blogger studies here, so let's take a look anyway.

The study was done in two parts with a total of 367 students, two-thirds of whom were female. Of these students, 66 reported writing a blog, and it is the difference between these students and the others which leads to the study's findings. The researchers used the 'Big Five' model of personality, which is based on the notion that individuals vary on five key dimensions: neuroticism, extraversion, openness to experience, agreeableness, and conscientiousness. Their study found that those who scored more highly for 'openness' were more likely to be bloggers, and women who were more 'neurotic' were more likely to be bloggers (although this was not the case for men). The researchers note that 'Given that the characteristics of individuals high in openness include imagination, curiosity, artistic talent, intelligence, and diversity in interests . . . it is not surprising that this is a characteristic of bloggers.'[42] The finding about 'neuroticism' sounds rather less complimentary, although this also is judged to be 'not surprising' by the authors, who say that women 'who are high in neuroticism – characterized by anxiety, worry, emotional reactivity, and nervousness – may blog to assuage loneliness or in an attempt to reach out and form social connections with others'.[43] This tick-box approach to exploring personalities and motivations leaves much to be desired, but in its simplistic way confirms what we suspected already: blogging is good for imaginative, creative people who want to make connections.

A study of Japanese bloggers, by Asako Miura and Kiyomi Yamashita, took a more direct approach by probing active bloggers themselves.[44] The researchers sent an email to all registered users of Hatena Diary, a free blog service – with the cooperation of the Hatena company – and received 1,142 usable responses to their questionnaire – a very good number, even though it's a self-selected sample. Two-thirds of the bloggers were male, and most were in their twenties and thirties (although 10 per cent were teenagers and 1 per cent was over 50). The survey questions sought to explore aspects of personality such as level of self-reflection, need for reassurance and to be understood by others, and need for information, as well as questions about the satisfaction of blogging and interest in continuing. The study found that the strongest reason for continuing to write a blog was positive response from other people, which had 'a positive effect on all kinds of satisfaction'. The authors explain:

> This suggests that positive feedback from readers, for example sympathy, support, or encouragement, worked as a strong emotional social support on the behavior of publishing a personal blog and motivated a person to continue to be an author.[45]

Negative feedback could be damaging to levels of satisfaction with self-understanding and acceptance from others, but overall was not as powerful as positive feedback – nice comments could outweigh nasty ones, in other words, especially where the latter could be explained as being due to lack of understanding. Furthermore, the researchers say:

> Satisfaction from being accepted by others had the strongest effect on the intention to continue blog writing. This

might suggest that there is additional significance in blog writing for authors beyond the merely personal act of diary writing.[46]

These findings, then, underline the importance of warm social connections, recognition, and appreciation for those who invest significant amounts of time in the creation of online content. This does not simply mean that they yearn for friendliness and praise, but rather that making things and sharing them online is a process which also creates networks of emotional support and significant social bonds.

On the more qualitative side, David Brake wrote a whole PhD based on in-depth interviews with bloggers. He interviewed 23 authors of *personal* blogs – rather than blogs about politics, technology, or any other topic (he notes that these personal blogs make up about 70 per cent of all blogs). The selected bloggers all lived in or near to London, UK, so that Brake could interview them face to face, but otherwise the bloggers were not known to the researcher, or each other, and were selected for diversity – taking in a range of different kinds of people who happened to blog. Brake's PhD thesis is full of detail,[47] but I asked him if he could summarize why it is that people go to the effort of producing a blog. He replied:

Based on my research, I would say that the people who write personal blogs have broadly speaking five motivations (though these can overlap and change through time):

- Some bloggers maintain their blogs to narrowcast their doings to friends and acquaintances, not really seeking to enter a dialogue with them.
- Some are there to maintain a dialogue with friends – what they write may be visible to others, but those others are not the target audience and the bloggers may be at

best indifferent, and at worst hostile, to their unintended readers.

- Some treat their personal blogs as PR or journalistic tools, reaching out to an imagined audience that they wish to impress to advance in their careers, but not seeking a personal connection.
- Some (which I term 'telelogic' because they are going with the 'logic' of blogging tools) genuinely want to be read primarily by people who they have not met and are not intending to meet – and some of these don't even want to be read by their friends and families.
- Lastly, and for me most intriguingly, there are those whose blogging practice appears to be 'self-directed' – people who blog because they want to master a new tool, or because they like to write, or because they want to be heard – but at a very tenuous level – or because they want to vent frustrations.[48]

To compress this further, then, we can say that Brake's bloggers primarily wanted to communicate, to connect, or just wanted to create and share. Incidentally, none of them, he tells me, experienced their blog-making as 'hard work', even when their levels of online productivity were high.

PRODUCTIVE ENTHUSIASTS

A somewhat different perspective on these questions is provided by Nancy Baym and Robert Burnett in a study of online fans of Swedish independent pop music.[49] The researchers' starting-point is the question of whether fans who produce elaborate blogs or podcasts about a particular commercial scene (in this case, Swedish pop music) are being 'exploited', because they provide 'free labour' for an enterprise which may ultimately make money for someone other than themselves. (This discussion connects with the Marxist approach to Web 2.0, which we will discuss in chapter 8.)

Unsurprisingly – since the individuals concerned are *enthusiasts*, who make their online content willingly and happily – Baym and Burnett found that these bloggers and podcast-producers did not usually consider themselves to be exploited. On the contrary, they enjoyed their creative activity and the connections which it brought to other fans, and to the musicians themselves. (Others might disagree, of course, but Baym and Burnett note that 'In scenes like this, exploitation and just reward are matters of perception.'[50]) These users spent great amounts of time maintaining their websites, but the benefits included engaging with music, working with creative people they admired, and the opportunity for self-expression, and 'to make meaningful contributions to a cultural domain that brings them such pleasure'.[51] As in the other studies, the pleasures of communication and creativity are coupled with a need to be heard which requires attention and interaction from other people to be satisfying.

Taken together, then, these studies describe some not-very-surprising reasons why people go to the trouble of making online videos, blogs, and sites, and they reflect the suggestions which were suggested by my Twitter followers. Partly people make these things and share them because *they want to* – the process of making the thing, and knowing that others may encounter it, brings its own pleasures. Partly it is to connect and communicate with others, and to be an active participant in online dialogues and communities, both giving and receiving ideas, feedback, and support. And partly it expresses a wish to be noticed, recognized, and heard.

These motivations follow on from – and are part of a continuum with – the motivations for engaging in hands-on craft activity discussed in the previous chapter. We can see that online, like the crafters offline, people like to be able to make and manage a whole thing, seeing it develop from first idea through to completion. In some cases they enjoy collaborating during the process. And they certainly like to share the process of making, as well as the finished thing, with others. They feel that they can express themselves in an 'authentic and personal' way, and connect with a like-minded community. These are all things that were cited as motivations for engagement with physical crafts and making. In the previous chapter, Rozsika Parker made a very good point about how embroidery could have 'a transformative impact on the sense of self'. Here is part of her argument again, but with references to embroidery replaced with references to blogging:

> Winnicott's theory of mirroring helps us understand how the experience of blogging and the blog affirms the self as a being with agency, acceptability and potency. . . . The blogger sees a positive reflection of herself in her work and, importantly, in the reception of her work by others.[52]

We could equally insert 'website maker', or 'YouTube video producer', of course. These motives, qualities, and desires are in many ways timeless, then, but the internet provides a platform for sharing and exchange, with unique properties of accessibility and reach.

In other words, for centuries people have liked to make things, and share them with others, in order to communicate, to be part of a conversation, and to receive support or recognition; but the internet has given us a forum where people can do this without gatekeepers, without geographical restrictions, and in an organized way that means we can find like-minded people easily – so that we can share ideas and enthusiasms with people who actually care about the things that we care about, and are likely to have meaningful, informed responses.

It is also the case that such a system might lead people to become more closed-minded and insular – only encountering and listening to the views of those 'like-minded people', and replacing a broad and varied cultural diet with lots of similar, comforting but not especially mind-expanding things. We need to be mindful of this potential. But I have seen no evidence that this is happening, and the internet seems to bring people all kinds of everything, from which they then have to actively pick and choose. This may not always be the most shockingly diverse set of resources ever collected, but it typically provides a richer experience and a wider range of messages and possibilities than they would otherwise be able or likely to access.

BEYOND THE SCREEN?

In this chapter, the online making-and-connecting hub I've mentioned most often is YouTube. But as we've noted already, YouTube is in a sense an odd illustration of the anti-television, hands-on, making-things principle, since it is about people making and sharing *video clips*, and so although it may involve all kinds of creative activity at the *production* stage, what you *consume* is essentially just more television-y stuff. Of course, making videos is often a physical, hands-on, real-world process, and the online community culture around the videos involves all kinds of sharing and communication which are much more interactive and two-way than the standard television experience (including the supposedly more interactive, but fundamentally one-way, *digital* television experience). And indeed many other Web 2.0 platforms are about making and sharing things which are not at all television-y, such as general and specialist knowledge (Wikipedia), photography (Flickr), knitting (Ravelry), or microfinance for third-world entrepreneurs (Kiva).

These are relatively conventional Web experiences compared with immersive virtual worlds, such as Second Life, where users create their own 'avatar' (representing themselves) and interact with others in a 3D environment. Do these online worlds take us a step further towards an experience which is a parallel of embodied, hands-on creative activity? The supporters of virtual worlds certainly argue that they are the opposite of television because they offer a hugely *interactive* experience, rather than one characterized by passive viewing. But for critics of television who are troubled by the notion of the population sitting glued to fantasy worlds offered on screen rather than real-life engagement, Second Life offers little comfort. The Disney movie *Wall-E* presents a chilling vision of the future where dull and overweight humans are literally unable to get out of their seats, and watch television continuously. Fans of Second Life would be horrified by the idea that their experience is much the same thing, but an external observer might disagree.

As you may detect, whilst I am usually really keen on online participatory platforms, I am not enthusiastic about Second Life. For me, it just introduces an unnecessary middle layer between myself and the ideas, information, or communication that I want to exchange. I've already got one body that I can use reasonably well, so having to use this body to control another 'virtual' one, which sits between me and the usual immediacy of the Web, is not an exciting development. Maybe this is just a matter of personal taste, and no doubt there are many educational and collaborative uses of Second Life which people find useful.[53] In the mid-2000s, when Second Life was talked of as the future of online activity, I was unconvinced, but also anxious. Was this actually what everybody wants to do online? Should I feign interest, so as not to seem like an old fuddy-duddy?

Thankfully, as it turns out, I needn't have worried. As

time has moved on, we have seen that Second Life has found its niche, but has not become the future of everything. Thank goodness. In 2009 I was relieved to see this view confirmed in a blog post entitled 'How Not to Predict the Future (or Why Second Life is Like Video Calling)'. This was by Dougald Hine, a writer and activist of great energy and vision, who observed the following:

> Video calling was expected to be huge, but it turns out hardly anyone wanted it. Text messaging, on the other hand, was an unexpected success.
>
> The technology landscape is shaped not just by what we can do, but what we choose to do – and simpler, less impressive technologies may turn out to be vastly more powerful as social tools.
>
> Again, with Second Life, people's demand for high-tech, highly immersive substitutes for face-to-face experience was massively exaggerated – while the real story turns out to be the social power of stripped down, simple bits of communication, like Twitter, that weave in and out of our First Lives.[54]

This point connects with another of Hine's favourite ideas, which is encapsulated in his notion of the '"Why Don't You?" Web'. This concept is named after the old BBC children's programme called *Why Don't You?*, which was short for *Why Don't You Just Switch Off Your Television Set And Go Out And Do Something Less Boring Instead?* The programme ran from 1973 to 1995, and – as the title clearly indicates (!) – was based on the idea that children should be encouraged to turn off their screens and do something more active. This often involved making crafty things or doing magic tricks. But the Web enables people to do much more inventive and connected off-screen activity.

Hine is one of the founders of the School of Everything, a website which connects people who are able to teach something with people who want to learn something. These can be free or paid-for arrangements, or the 'ideal type' – although the site exhibits no preference – would be a mutual exchange of knowledge or skills. In terms of the '"Why Don't You?" Web', Hine explains:

> We see School of Everything as part of a larger shift in the way people are using the web, away from spending more and more of our lives in front of screens, towards making things happen in the real world.[55]

He observes that since the early days of the Web, people have eagerly taken up online services – such as those enabling shopping, banking, reading, and chatting – which they were already doing, but could now do more conveniently, without having to go anywhere. But more recently, 'another way of using the internet has emerged', as the internet can also help people to do things they previously *didn't* do, out and about in the areas where they live. School of Everything is obviously one example of this, along with Freecycle, which enables people to give and receive unwanted stuff instead of having to buy new stuff.

Another example is Meetup.com, which enables people with shared interests to meet up locally, taking the standard idea of the virtual community – people who have something in common, who wouldn't have known about each other if it wasn't for the internet – and then throwing in the novel idea that they might actually get together for a coffee. (Of course, some virtual communities have developed into groups who might actually meet sometimes, but Meetup.com cuts straight to this level.) Hine notes: 'Interestingly, the most active early users of Meetup have been "stay at home mums", with nearly 2000 groups and 100,000 members [in 2008] – an experience which echoes that of the Open University, nearly 40 years ago.'[56]

LET'S GET TOGETHER

There are, of course, innumerable other examples of people getting together online to do things offline, and they can be found easily on the Web. Here I will list just a few examples to illustrate the range of things that people have started to do:

- Landshare (www.landshare.net) brings together people in the UK who want to grow their own vegetables, but don't have anywhere to do it, with people who 'have a spare bit of land they're prepared to share'. People also use the site to share knowledge and lend tools. Launched in 2009, it had 50,000 members within a year.
- Ecomodo (www.ecomodo.com) enables people to share tools and products that they are not currently using. The idea is succinctly illustrated on the site, where it says: 'The average drill is used for 10 minutes of its life. Most people who own a drill never actually needed to own a drill, they simply wanted to drill a few holes.' The environmental impact of a product, from its manufacture and sale through to its disposal, is huge, the site notes, 'and seldom reflected in the contribution it makes to its owner's life'. Ecomodo enables people to borrow things when they need them, without having to unnecessarily buy new ones.
- Streetbank (www.streetbank.com) similarly enables people to lend and exchange things, and skills, with their neighbours: 'Streetbank allows you to enjoy all the things within 1,000 yards that your neighbours are willing to share.' It is based on the idea that there are probably many nice

people and resources near walking distance of your home, but it often isn't easy to get an introduction in order to get to know them – hence the site.

- Brooklyn Skillshare is more of a physical happening, helped along by its website (www.brooklynskillshare. tumblr.com). It is 'a community-based, community-led, and community-building learning event' organized and taught by residents of Brooklyn, New York. Participants are encouraged to spend the day at a series of hour-long classes, such as screenprinting, bike mechanics, jewellery casting, home audio production, making your own butter and ricotta, and DIY electronics.

- Green Gyms (www2.btcv.org.uk/display/greengym), a concept developed by the British Trust for Conservation Volunteers, give people the opportunity to meet others and engage in physical activity while caring for the local environment, looking after or creating facilities for common spaces.

- Men's Sheds (www.mensheds.com.au) is a movement which has grown up in Australia, which primarily helps retired men – who may be experiencing isolation, loneliness, or depression, after a lifetime of work – to connect with each other, and the community, through activities based in a 'shed' where they can make and do things for themselves or for the community. 'Through collaboration, problem solving and decision-making, a men's shed can considerably enhance the initiation and implementation of projects . . . and improve the lifestyle of many men', says the website, which provides help and resources for finding or starting a shed.

Initiatives such as these were possible before the Web, of course, but were more difficult to organize, and in particular were liable to draw in more outgoing, gregarious kinds of people, whilst leaving others isolated. The internet gives such individuals a simple way of hearing about – and developing a sense of comfort and familiarity with – groups, activities, meetings, and projects, making it considerably easier to overcome the emotional and psychological hurdles to participation.

Making and sharing things online, engaging with people who (at first) you don't know anything about, anywhere in the world, can be very rewarding. Any kind of meaningful creative 'project' is good to have, as we will see in the next chapter. And those initiatives which bring people into *real life* contact with others can be especially helpful for happiness and well-being – as we will see.

5

THE VALUE OF CONNECTING I:
PERSONAL HAPPINESS

In the previous chapters we considered the value of making things. In this one, and the next, we will look at the importance of friendly social connections. It would be easy to think of this as a rather trivial matter: 'friendly social connections' may be nice to have, for personal indulgence and a kind of vanity, but they are hardly the stuff of important social science, economics, or social policy. But surely the very opposite is the case: without human empathy, communication, trust, and general-purpose goodwill and friendliness, society would very quickly dissolve in a horrible apocalypse of never-ending misunderstanding, crime, and conflict.

Looked at in that sense, we can see that the value of social connections has been rightly explored by social scientists for over a century in their many and diverse studies of social cohesion, the family, religion, 'deviance', economics, social policy, politics, war, terrorism, and other topics. In this chapter we will narrow this field, and look at the recent studies of happiness, which suggest that individuals are more satisfied when they are part of social networks. Then in the next chapter, we will consider the literature on 'social capital' – a sociological term for shared values and connectedness – which shows that we are all, collectively, better off as a society when we are active parts of the social fabric.

HAPPINESS STUDIES

The past decade or so has seen a sharp rise in scholarly interest regarding the topic of 'happiness'. This is partly because serious academics have finally become willing to engage with a term which previously would have been seen, outside of literary and philosophical studies, as too 'fluffy': the sensible researcher of previous generations would have discussed 'scales of social satisfaction', or 'trust', but would generally have avoided admitting that they were concerned with human happiness. This is perverse, of course, because the question of how to have happy people in a happy society addresses every politician's dilemma and has links with every social problem.

When people are asked about what would increase our happiness, we typically think that 'more money' must be at least *part* of the answer. Indeed, richer people tend to think that they need more additional income than poorer people do.[1] However, as happiness researchers have found, people are very bad at predicting what will *actually* make them happy – beyond the instant-hit burst of excitement that they can imagine when various possible treats are suggested to them.[2]

Meanwhile, the idea that money is not actually a route to happiness has been a well-known and seemingly popular one for some time. In one of his best-known parables, Jesus argued that 'It is easier for a camel to go through the eye of a needle than for a rich man to enter the kingdom of God' (Matthew 19:23–4). The Beatles echoed the sentiment in their 1964 hit *Can't Buy Me Love*, and indeed the insignificance of money in the quest for happiness underpins numerous pop songs, such as *Love Don't Cost a Thing* by Jennifer Lopez and *The Best Things in Life Are Free* by Luther Vandross, movies from *Citizen Kane* and *It's a Wonderful Life* to *Trading Places* and *Iron Man*, and in particular romantic comedies – for instance, from the many possible examples, it is the 'message' of *Notting Hill*, *Two Weeks' Notice*, and *About a Boy*, all of which happen to star Hugh Grant.

CAN'T BUY ME HAPPINESS?

As it turns out, Jesus, the Beatles and Hugh Grant all seem to be right about this one. Indeed, the starting-point for much contemporary happiness research is the observation that almost everybody thinks that they would be happier if they had more money, but that studies demonstrate that this is simply not the case – with the exception of the very poor. In general, when people get more money, they soon get used to it, and return to much the same level of (dis)satisfaction that they were at before.[3]

There is a good old Marxist argument which says that when religions, movies, or pop songs suggest that money doesn't make you any happier, this is a form of propaganda – designed to persuade the impoverished and exploited that their desire for a greater share of society's wealth is misplaced. The news that more money wouldn't make us any happier appears to contradict that. But there are two things worth noting here. First of all, as mentioned above, increased income *does* make a significant and sustained difference to those people who previously were very poor, living below subsistence level. Second, it is *relative* income which makes people more or less happy – if we are getting much less than other people, we are much less happy.[4]

Correspondingly, and rather disappointingly, these same statistics indicate that if an individual became rich, they would only be happier if their position was reasonably unique; if *everyone* became much better-off, they wouldn't all become much happier. This is not a pessimistic hypothesis, but rather can be observed as a matter of historical record: during the twentieth century in America and Europe, for example, the general standard of living rose dramatically. But recorded levels of happiness stayed remarkably constant.[5]

Because people are unrealistic as they imagine their possible futures, and fail to realize that they would simply get used to having more money, they tend to spend more and more time working – which doesn't actually make them happier – and correspondingly less time doing other things. Research in social psychology has suggested that this is part of a broader phenomenon: that human beings tend to focus on the wrong things – superficial things – when thinking about future possibilities. This is expressed in striking terms by David Schkade of the University of California, San Diego, who summarizes his research in this area with the assertion: 'Anything you can focus on isn't as important as you think.'[6]

One of Schkade's curious case studies is to do with people moving to California. Lots of people dream of making California their home. This is not some Beach Boys-inspired propaganda, but a plain fact: opinion polls have consistently shown that it is the state that most Americans would like to move to.[7] Each year, more than a million people move into California from other states. But also each year, more than a million people move out of California to make a life elsewhere. Something draws them in. But also, something pushes them away. Schkade and his colleague Daniel Kahneman argue that the people who dream of moving to California are victims of a 'focusing illusion': they have zoomed in on an appealing detail – a sunny climate – at the expense of the bigger picture, which in this case is everything else in life.[8]

The researchers supported this by conducting a survey in California, and in the Mid-Western states of Michigan and Ohio. This found that people in the Mid-West were just as satisfied with their lives as the people who lived in California. However, when asked to predict how happy *other people* would be, participants across the board thought that the Californians would be happier. And indeed, Californians were personally happier about their climate. But otherwise, their lives had not been taken onto a better, more magical plane, just because the sun was shining. And crucially, nobody really thought that the weather was that important. They rated other factors such as job prospects, personal safety, and social life as being much more significant for their own happiness, and of course this was reflected in the fact that Californians and Mid-Westerners did indeed have remarkably similar levels of self-reported happiness.

This explains the people moving out of California, as well as those moving in. Those moving in, this research would suggest, may be mistakenly fixated on the temptation of sunshine, and not really thinking about the other things that matter to them in life. Whereas those moving out are likely to be people who have tired of the famous Californian obsession with body image, or who pine for the homely charms of the state they grew up in, or who want a more secure environment for their families. Of course, people move for all kinds of reasons, but the Californian-sunshine 'focusing illusion' illustrates nicely our ability to get overly excited about 'quick hits' and forget what really matters.

HAPPINESS UNDER THE MICROSCOPE

If only we knew which things would *actually* make us happier – not just in the short term, but as a long-term quality of life kind of factor. But now we do – thanks to the new 'science of happiness', which draws upon economics and psychology. From economics, it takes the idea that you can look at data about a range of social or economic inputs and draw statistical inferences about what has positive or negative results. Unlike traditional economics, though, it does not assume that human behaviour is *necessarily* driven by money and self-interest. From psychology, it takes the idea that people's inner states are important, and that personal experience can, in broad terms, be assessed and measured. This emergent field also draws usefully upon neuroscience, sociology, and philosophy.

Rather than taking happiness as a poetic or romantic concept, the 'new science' takes the presence or absence of happiness as a hard-nosed empirical fact. Measuring levels of happiness is not difficult: you simply ask people to attach a number to it themselves, with a question such as 'Taking all things together, would you say you are very happy, quite happy, or not very happy?' In a survey, this works fine, and produces empirical data on how happy people say that they are. This is, then, a fact, rather than a feeling (although it is made up of self-reports about feelings), and when we match it up with other empirical data we find that it is a fact with consequences. For example, it has been found that happy people live longer than less happy people. This is not because the unhappy people are unhappy about some third factor which is contributing to their early demise. Rather, people with otherwise comparable circumstances seem to be sustained if they have a sunny disposition.

One especially memorable analysis, known to experts as 'the nun study', led by David Snowdon, shows this vividly. The study tracks an unusually homogeneous group – a set of American Catholic nuns. In the 1930s, when new nuns joined the School Sisters of Notre Dame, they were asked to write an autobiographical sketch. Some 60 years later, researchers looked at 180 of these handwritten accounts, written when the women were on average 22 years old, which had been kept on file. Rating their autobiographies for amount of 'positive emotional content', they found this to be a strong predictor of longevity. Of those who were alive in 1991, more than half of those who had written the least cheerful accounts – more than half a century earlier – would die before the end of the decade, whereas those who told a more contented story in their youth had significantly longer lives, with only one in five of nuns in the happiest quarter not making it through the same period.[9] In other words, it seems that happiness, regardless of other factors, means you live longer.

GREATEST HITS OF HAPPINESS

Richard Layard, well-known as an economist and now one of the leading authorities on happiness, has drawn upon numerous studies and datasets to produce what he calls the 'Big Seven factors affecting happiness'. These are:

- Family relationships
- Financial situation
- Work
- Community and friends
- Health
- Personal freedom
- Personal values.[10]

Layard explains that the first five of these are listed in order of importance, with personal freedom and personal values being additional crucial factors. He observes that except for health and income, these seven factors 'are all concerned with the quality of our relationships'.[11] Happiness therefore has a lot to do with the social bonds and connectedness that concern us in this book. So let's look at each of the relevant factors in turn.

First of all, it is perhaps no surprise that family relationships appear to have the very strongest relationship with reported levels of happiness. In spite of all the jokes that are commonly made about marriage as a kind of prison or limitation on happiness, data consistently show that married people are happier than unmarried people, and that the ending of a marriage is generally unmatched as a source of unhappiness. For instance, Layard uses data from the World Values Survey, which covers 90,000 people in 46 countries, and asks people to self-report on their own happiness as well as many other features of their life. From these statistics we can discern that becoming separated from a spouse has an impact on happiness four times greater than that of a one-third drop in family income. It is worse than becoming unemployed, having a significant decline in health, or living in an undemocratic dictatorship.[12] This strong finding in favour of 'marriage' should not be taken to be an affirmation of heterosexuality, of course. A growing number of countries are enabling same-sex marriage, or 'civil partnerships' on a similar basis, and the benefits of these public affirmations of commitment are likely to be exactly the same.[13] As Layard explains:

> The main benefits of marriage or cohabitation are obvious: you give each other love and comfort; you share resources, gaining economies of scale; you help each other. . . . Married

people are healthier and live longer. . . . We need other people, and we need to be needed. Increasingly, research confirms the dominating importance of love.[14]

This need for social bonds follows through into the third item on Layard's list, the importance of work. Becoming unemployed has a huge impact on happiness, which is only partially explained by the difficulties caused by the corresponding drop in income; it is the loss of social relationships and self-esteem associated with work which hits especially hard. Whilst any work tends to provide some sense of purpose, and social connections, the data also show that work should be *meaningful* in order to add to our happiness. As Layard reports:

> Perhaps the most important issue is the extent to which you have control over what you do. There is a creative spark in each of us, and if it finds no outlet, we feel half-dead. This can be literally true: among British civil servants of any given grade, those who do the most routine work experience the most rapid clogging of the arteries.[15]

All of these things – relationships, self-esteem, meaning – also go to explain why retired people are no happier than working people: they have gained lots of leisure time, but may have also lost a lot of social connections, and the feeling of making some kind of difference.[16]

Fourth in Layard's 'Big Seven' factors affecting happiness is community and friendship. As we will see more below, feeling a part of a helpful and trustworthy community can give a huge lift to people's general sense of contentment. This theme is perhaps magnified at the more macro level, where the ways in which governments connect with personal and community life add up to the measures of 'personal freedom', such as corruption, accountability, and effectiveness of government services. These again have a significant impact on happiness.

You might think, for instance, that local government decision-making processes could not have much to do with happiness, except perhaps that we would be very happy not to have to hear about them. But that is only because we have become used to having no control in that area – it seems boring because it is out of our hands. A study by Bruno Frey and Alois Stutzer was able to show that actually, where people had power in this sphere, it affected the mood across the whole population.[17] Their research looked at Switzerland, which is divided into 26 cantons, and where policy issues are frequently decided by referendum – but to varying degrees. In the cantons where citizens had the most rights to referendums, compared with those where these rights were least, people were 11 per cent more likely to describe themselves as 'completely satisfied' with their life. Living in a place where it was relatively easy to get the signatures necessary to trigger the mechanisms of direct democracy had this clear and sizeable impact on the happiness of the people in that canton – not just on the people launching referendums, but the whole population.[18]

Finally on Layard's list of factors affecting happiness, there is 'personal values', in other words our inner self and philosophy of life. One of the most consistent findings of happiness research, for instance, is that people who believe in God are happier than those who do not. It is possible that happy people are more likely to believe in God, rather than the belief causing happiness, at an individual level, but Layard asserts that 'since the relation also exists at the national level, we can be sure that to some extent belief causes happiness'.[19] A study by the Pew Research Center in the US (nothing, in fact, to do with church pews) seemed to find a similar connection between religion and happiness – although the finding may be more to do with the social bonds of church *attendance*. 'People who attend religious services weekly or more are happier (43% very happy) than those who attend monthly or less (31%); or seldom or never (26%)', the authors report.[20] They also note that this correlation 'has been a consistent finding in the General Social Surveys taken over the years'.[21] Even amongst those of the same religious faith, actually *going* to church makes a very significant difference to reported levels of happiness. Church attendance may reinforce faith, which, as noted above, makes people happier, but it additionally involves regular participation in a local network of goodwill and community, which – as we have also seen – is a strong propagator of happiness.

GET A PROJECT

Looking at Layard's 'Big Seven', we might think that all we need to do to attain a super level of happiness would be to align a reasonable number of these factors around ourselves and simply wait for the happiness to flow in. If we move to an especially democratic canton in Switzerland, get married, turn up regularly at work and church, invite some friends round, and get some decent medical and financial advice, we should be able to score 100 per cent happiness.

However, although all of these things might help to *support* our efforts, happiness does not follow from passive participation. Similarly, the idea that you can be happier if you merely lower your expectations, doesn't really work. People need something to strive towards. Richard Layard puts it very nicely: 'Prod any happy person and you will find a project.'[22] As Tibor Scitovsky argued in his 1976 book, *The Joyless Economy*, individuals in modern societies tend to have reasonable amounts of money and free time, but this is no good if they are simply bored. Traditional economics has tended to be blind to such issues, since it would assume that gains in money and leisure are inherently positive.[23]

However, happiness researchers such as Sonja Lyubomirsky and her colleagues Kennon M. Sheldon and David Schkade are able to point to a number of studies which demonstrate that goal-oriented activities are a major contributor to happiness.[24] Indeed, comparative studies have shown that the intentionality of *choosing* to do a particular activity adds considerably to the pleasure, when compared to pleasant changes in circumstance which have merely happened.[25] And, unlike most things that give a boost to happiness – even marriage – the pleasure of working on projects does not fade over time.[26] You could say that this statistic is a little unfair, as people can readily create new and stimulating projects for themselves, whereas exciting new marriages, or delightful new homes, say, cannot be generated easily, and come with costs. But such is the nature of projects: relatively easy to create, and a source of pleasure, even when you haven't really done much about them.

Happiness, then, is about family, community, and well-being. It cannot be determined by a certain level of material comfort. Instead, it stems from having meaningful connections with others, and meaningful things to do. These projects are especially valuable if they are not contained at the individual level but involve some form of sharing, cooperation, or contribution to other people's well-being. As Richard Layard says at the beginning of the conclusion to his *Happiness* book:

A society cannot flourish without some sense of shared purpose. The current pursuit of self-realisation will not work. If your sole duty is to achieve the best for yourself, life becomes just too stressful, too lonely – you are set up to fail. Instead, you need to feel you exist for something larger, and that very thought takes off some of the pressure.[27]

This means we need to broaden our focus from individual happiness to activities within the social fabric more generally. This brings us to the discussion of 'social capital', which is the focus of the next chapter.

6

THE VALUE OF CONNECTING II:
SOCIAL CAPITAL AND COMMUNITIES

The happiness research, discussed in the previous chapter, has indicated factors which typically make *individuals* happier, and which can often be encouraged or stimulated at government level, thereby helping society as a *whole* to be happier. For instance, support can be given to couples and families – in the form of centres and activities for parents and children, and relationship support – and the benefits of marriage can be extended to same-sex couples.[1] Governments also obviously play a crucial role in the stability and legislation of work; support for and prevention of ill-health; and in levels of freedom and active democracy. So, although the government can't 'make you happy' per se, it can give support to some of the structures that might help to foster individual happiness.

A slightly different way of looking at similar issues is found in the literature on 'social capital', which is the focus of this chapter. This discussion also begins with individuals, in the sense that social well-being is a responsibility of us all, and then it tends to reach towards a more inclusive, participatory, community-based view of the solutions. 'Social capital' has become a buzzword amongst policy-makers and think-tanks since the 1990s, so there is again a question of what the state can do to support social capital – but also an idea that social capital might help the state. The 'happiness' and 'social capital' studies are not mutually exclusive fields: the research mentioned in the previous chapter which suggests that collaboration and social projects are good for happiness, for instance, could also be absolutely central to social capital scholars making their case.

Compared to 'happiness', 'social capital' is a less self-explanatory term, and – as is often the way with academic jargon – is understood differently by different writers. Before we look at the different approaches, I will try to outline the meaning of the term in a general way. It started life as a metaphorical mirror of financial capital: just as a supply of money can enable you to do things that you otherwise could not do, a stock of social relationships will also make it easier to do things that otherwise you could not. These relationships are central to the smooth running of a society. L. J. Hanifan, who seems to have been the first person to use the term, wrote in 1916:

> The individual is helpless socially, if left to himself. . . . If he comes into contact with his neighbour, and they with other neighbours, there will be an accumulation of social capital, which may . . . bear a social potentiality sufficient to the substantial improvement of living conditions in the whole community. The community as a whole will benefit by the cooperation of all its parts, while the individual will find in his associations the advantages of the help, the sympathy, and the fellowship of his neighbours.[2]

Hanifan's notion of 'social capital' failed to capture the general imagination at that time, and remained generally invisible for several more decades. Indeed, those who started talking about social capital from the 1980s onwards may well have been ignorant of this earlier usage. However, Hanifan's outline of social capital is remarkably close to its accepted use today. It is worth clarifying that social capital (being about social networks and relationships) is distinct from other forms of non-financial capital that people might talk about these days, such as human capital (individual expertise), physical capital (equipment), and cultural capital (individual cultural knowledge). The thing that these different forms of capital all have in common – the thing that makes them 'capital' rather than just 'know-how' – is that they are all used to create further capital.

Generally, the social capital writers are concerned with social relationships based on cooperation, reciprocity, goodwill, and trust, oriented towards a society that's nice for everybody to live in. Inevitably, they generally have to admit that there is a 'dark side' to social capital as well: even the most brutal, selfish, antisocial person tends to have social networks, and indeed they can achieve their goals much more efficiently if they have a good stock of social relationships. The advocates of 'social capital' would be in favour of mutually supportive community groups of enthusiasts with shared interests, but the Ku Klux Klan is a mutually supportive community group of enthusiasts with shared interests. So although social capital can seem like a wonderful 'happy glue' for society, solving all its problems, its functions are not *necessarily* always wholesome, kind, and ethical. Nevertheless, the social capital literature does seem to suggest a path towards a better society, which we should not dismiss just because there are – as always – possible antisocial applications of the idea.

WHY WE'RE LOOKING AT SOCIAL CAPITAL

To be clear: the reason why you're reading a chapter on social capital in this book, is because the social capital research is all about the value of people doing things (making and connecting) in communities, versus what happens when they don't.

By the end of this chapter, it will hopefully be clear that people doing stuff together in communities is really valuable for a number of reasons, whereas when they don't – when they remain isolated, strangers to their neighbours, not communicating – then society enters a downward spiral. That doesn't just mean 'a bit less friendly', but really *falling apart*, with higher levels of crime, distrust, depression, and illness.

The social capital literature doesn't directly and completely prove that 'making is connecting', but it does show the value of connecting through doing things together. The additional job of showing that creative activity is better for this than anything else is hopefully done in the other chapters.

THREE APPROACHES TO SOCIAL CAPITAL

In the past two or three decades, scholars have taken an interest in three different perspectives on social capital in particular. These are based on the ideas of Pierre Bourdieu, James Coleman, and Robert Putnam. The first two are part of the background story, and I wrote a few pages on them for this book – but then needed to make the book a bit shorter, and so now I've cut those out and put them on the book's website instead (www.makingisconnecting.org). So here we'll cover Bourdieu and Coleman rather briefly, and then discuss Putnam – the king of social capital writers, and the key source for most discussions of the topic today – in more depth.

French sociologist Pierre Bourdieu (1930–2002) was interested in the ways in which society is reproduced, and how the dominant classes retain their position. He wisely observed that this could not be explained by economics alone, and developed a model based on cultural capital, and social capital, as well as economic capital. Cultural capital refers to the ways in which people would use cultural knowledge to undergird their place in the hierarchy (most easily pictured as pretentious displays of middle-class taste).[3] Social capital, meanwhile, refers to the advantage gained 'by virtue of possessing a durable network of more or less institutionalized relationships of mutual acquaintance and recognition'.[4] This definition, in itself, is similar to other definitions, such as those that we will see below, and Hanifan's approach above. But where other writers see social capital as a fundamentally heartwarming network of social connections, Bourdieu uses it to explain the cold realities of social inequality. Here, social capital is a way of showing how the middle and upper classes make sure that their spheres remain exclusive. Although distinct from economic capital, and operating in a different way, it is inseparable from it. Clearly, this relates to a real phenomenon in social life: studies continue to show that social mobility remains something of a myth, and that tomorrow's wealthy professionals are most likely to be the children of today's wealthy professionals.[5] But social networks are not *always* just the exclusionary tool of elites, and so Bourdieu's approach to the concept of social capital is rather limited and deterministic.

Around the same time, in the late 1980s and early 1990s, the American sociologist James Coleman (1926–95) was also writing about social capital. Coleman also linked social capital with economics, but in a different way. He wanted to combine the insights of sociology and economic theory, seeing social capital as a way of adding a human and more collective social face to the overly rational and individualistic models of traditional economics. Coleman's approach leads to a broader view of social capital, where it is not seen only as stock held by powerful elites, but notes its value for all kinds of communities, including the powerless and marginalized.

He proposes a model in which social capital is one of the potential resources which an actor can use, alongside other resources such as their own skills and expertise (human capital), tools (physical capital), or money (economic capital). Unusually, though, social capital is not necessarily 'owned' by the individual but instead arises as a resource which is *available* to them.[6] So, for example, if you live on a street where you can rely on your neighbours to look out for your children, then you have access to a form of social capital which other people, in less trusting or well-bonded streets, do not. Furthermore, this is not a resource which you could give or sell to your friend on the other side of town. To get access to it, she would have to move into your street (or one like it) and establish some relationships with her neighbours – all of which would take time and effort – because social capital is a resource based on trust and shared values, and develops from the weaving-together of people in communities.

Coleman also highlights the role of social capital as a source of useful everyday information, and of norms and sanctions, which can facilitate certain kinds of actions, but may also be restrictive.[7] In particular he singles out 'one effect of social capital that is especially important: its effect on the creation of human capital in the next generation'.[8] This 'human capital', such as a secure sense of self-identity, confidence in expressing one's own opinions, and emotional intelligence, enables young people to become better learners, and so helps them to be more successful in the education system and in society. This human capital emerges out of social capital, because this kind of development depends upon *relationships*, most obviously within the family (or other support network).

In this model, then, social capital – in any context – relies on people looking beyond themselves and engaging in supportive or helpful actions, *not* because they expect a reward or immediate reciprocal help, but because they believe it's a good thing to do. Coleman himself seems to struggle against the gravitational pull of traditional economic theory, and is barely able to accept this conclusion. Nevertheless, he usefully highlights the significance of social capital as part of a potential solution for marginalized learners, and its importance in parenting, for people of any social class.

ROBERT PUTNAM AND ALEXIS DE TOCQUEVILLE

Bourdieu and Coleman are well-known within academic circles, but Robert Putnam is perceived as the popular, public face of 'social capital' theory. A professor at Harvard University's John F. Kennedy School of Government, Putnam's article 'Bowling Alone: America's Declining Social Capital' was published in the *Journal of Democracy* in 1995, and, surprisingly for an academic article, shot its author to fame – or, at least, fame amongst journalists and policy wonks – as he was invited to meet President Clinton and other influential officials. Putnam then turned his short article into a substantial and thoroughly researched book, packed with data, also entitled *Bowling Alone*, and discussed it on a tour of numerous venues and radio stations across North America and Europe.

Putnam's work is often described as 'neo-Tocquevillian', suggesting that he is reviving the spirit of Alexis de Tocqueville, the nineteenth-century French author of *On Democracy in America* (published in two volumes, 1835 and

1840). This book is well-known in the USA, and in a sense forms part of American mythology. For this reason it is worth delving into this bit of backstory, for a short while, in order to help us understand the impact of Putnam's argument.

Alexis de Tocqueville was a civil servant and social thinker, from an aristocratic background, who travelled across the USA in 1831. In his book, which draws upon the experiences of this journey, he seems to assume that a large democracy with such levels of freedom and equality in the eyes of the law should produce an anarchic level of individualism, and general chaos. (This seemingly high level of freedom and equality was relative, of course, being limited to white males.) However, de Tocqueville seems compelled to report that, contrary to his expectations, he found an impressive level of community spirit and mutual support at all levels of American society.

He notes that American citizens 'enjoy unlimited freedom of association for political purposes', and observes that this seems to *also* encourage civil associations, a term which covers all the non-governmental, and not explicitly political, clubs and organizations, including charities, religious groups, bee-keepers' associations, volunteer fire brigades, sports clubs, parenting groups, and so on. De Tocqueville marvels at how 'Americans of all ages, all conditions, and all dispositions constantly form associations' for a huge range of purposes,[9] and he emphatically 'admires' this capacity.

It is easy to see how American readers will have swelled with pride, through the nineteenth and twentieth centuries, at this famous European assessment of their civic connectedness and community spirit. De Tocqueville was especially impressed that Americans, as he saw it, did not pin their hopes on individuals, and did not ask or wait for the government to act on their behalf – as he asserts the English or the French would do – but instead have 'carried to the highest perfection the art of pursuing in common the object of their common desires and have applied this new science to the greatest number of purposes'.[10] He asserts:

> Nothing, in my opinion, is more deserving of our attention than the intellectual and moral associations of America. . . . As soon as several of the inhabitants of the United States have taken up an opinion or a feeling which they wish to promote in the world, they look out for mutual assistance; and as soon as they have found one another out, they combine. From that moment they are no longer isolated men, but a power seen from afar, whose actions serve for an example and whose language is listened to.[11]

Despite its grand tone, this observation is not to do with American political associations, which the author is also aware of and impressed by, but with all other shared social or cultural needs or interests. He writes that 'the art of associating together' is essential if civil society is to be maintained. Modest connections create the conditions which enable more substantial ones to grow:

> The greater the multiplicity of small affairs, the more do men, even without knowing it, acquire facility in prosecuting great undertakings in common.[12]

This apparent American capacity to form mutually supportive groups and associations seems quite wonderful and has become part of America's proud story. This helps to explain why, 160 years later, a Harvard professor's book about civic engagement became so widely discussed – as it suggested that de Tocqueville's dream society was rapidly collapsing.

PUTNAM'S *BOWLING ALONE*

Robert Putnam's argument is that this healthy tendency of Americans to make connections and form associations, between people who otherwise would not have known each other, has been collapsing in the latter half of the twentieth century. Like de Tocqueville, Putnam does not have a special interest in people organizing for political purposes: any kind of association is considered to be valuable, whether social, sporting, religious, musical, hobbyist, or whatever. The bowling league is one example of just such an association.

Putnam's memorable title, however, can create some confusion. The phrase 'Bowling Alone' suggests a remarkable degree of isolation, as we are apparently invited to picture individuals going out on their own, to roll a lonely ball down their local ten-pin alley. Have people – or specifically, Americans – really become so disconnected and friendless? Well, no. The *Bowling Alone* website seeks to clarify, right at the top, by saying: 'We are bowling alone. More Americans are bowling than ever before, but they are not bowling in leagues.'[13] In other words, they are actually *not* bowling alone. Not at all. They are going out as groups of family and/or friends – and, as it says here, they are actually doing so more than ever. The thing that has declined is the bowling league, a more competitive structure where teams compete against each other. You could certainly wonder whether this is a real loss. Although the team relationships, and even inter-team rivalries, were likely to be friendly, the bowling league obviously required a level of sporting prowess, since teams would almost inevitably want to win. By contrast, the purely 'social' bowling that has more-or-less replaced the league competitions is less to do with bowling aptitude, and more to do with having fun and spending time together. So it's not 'bowling alone' at all.

We cannot conclude from this, of course, that Putnam is all wrong and that American associational life is healthier than ever. Putnam's headline example is easily misunderstood, and weirdly equates being with family or friends with being 'alone'. This perhaps points to the way in which Putnam mourns older forms of association while not entirely recognizing newer ones. Nevertheless, Putnam has data on his side, as we shall see. And the bowling league example is not entirely arbitrary. As John Field explains, league bowling serves in Putnam's discussion as:

> a metaphor for a type of associational activity that brings relative strangers together on a routine and frequent basis, helping to build and sustain a wider set of networks and values that foster general reciprocity and trust, and in turn facilitate mutual collaboration.[14]

Thus, bowling, or singing, or railway modelling, are all activities which may not have a direct impact upon society in themselves, but when people meet up to engage in their shared enthusiasm, this provides really valuable social glue, bringing people together and fostering relationships of trust and reciprocity. This is what 'social capital' is, for Putnam.

He writes that the essence of social capital theory is that 'social networks have value', because social contacts are a resource which boosts the 'productivity of individuals and groups'.[15] He defines social capital as:

> connections among individuals – social networks and the norms of reciprocity and trustworthiness that arise from them.[16]

Therefore social capital is not merely about the *willingness* to be socially helpful or community-minded, but relies on the actual existence of functioning networks accompanied by actually existing expectations.

Putnam then makes a distinction, which he attributes to Ross Gittell and Avis Vidal, between *bridging* social capital and *bonding* social capital. Bridging social capital draws people in, and embraces diversity, making links between different people and groups. Bonding social capital, on the other hand, is more exclusive, tying together people who are already similar, or have interests in common. Both forms have their uses, and it is not necessarily that one is 'better' than the other. Bonding social capital is that which binds together a bunch of rich white men in their golf club, for instance – the kind of exclusive elite connection that Bourdieu was concerned about – but it is also bonding social capital which connects an ethnic minority group in a particular area of a city, providing vital social and psychological support, and help with finding shelter, advice, and employment. Bonding social capital can be pictured as a tight-knit circle of comrades; whereas bridging social capital has its arms outstretched, to welcome people in. We should note, incidentally, that it's not a matter of one or the other; different groups or communities might have some degree of *both* kinds of social capital.

In *Bowling Alone*, Putnam marshals his data not only to demonstrate that associational life in the USA has declined, but – crucially – also to address the questions 'Why?' (in other words, what has caused this decline?) and 'So what?' (does this matter, and what are the consequences?). First let's briefly list some of the declining activities which Putnam analyses – these have typically all fallen dramatically since the middle of the twentieth century. In political participation, he finds that citizens may be reasonably interested and well informed, but their behaviour shows a sharp decline in electoral voting, attending public meetings, and engagement with political or civic organizations, especially in terms of face-to-face meetings. In terms of the non-political civic associations which so fascinated de Tocqueville, such as hobby clubs and voluntary groups, Putnam finds a sharp decline, with people increasingly joining organizations such as Greenpeace, to which they donate money but never meet up with other supporters – 'mail-order membership', as Putnam ruefully calls it.[17] In terms of religious participation, American religious belief remains strong – as is well known – but church attendance is down, and churches are less well connected with the wider community.

All of these examples are likely to be somewhat familiar to the modern reader, and could potentially be explained by suggesting that the American public have shifted towards a less formal culture, where people like to 'hang out' in a loose but friendly way – which should still be high in social capital – even though the rather stiff-sounding gardening associations or choral societies have waned in popularity. Surprisingly, though, Putnam's data show that even informal socializing has dropped – for instance, the number of times American adults had some friends round to visit them at home fell by 45 per cent between the late 1970s and the late 1990s. This is not because they have chosen to go out for meals together instead – no significant rise there, Putnam reports, and meanwhile going out to bars and nightclubs had also dropped by 40–50 per cent in the same period. It's possible that within these numbers, Putnam has refused to recognize fast food outlets as social spaces (because he dislikes them so much), and may have missed off some of the more recent rise of Starbucks-type coffee houses, but overall it's a clear picture of much less open and outward social connection, and much more family-based staying-in.

An illuminating example of how Putnam links apparently banal social practices with serious social concerns comes in his discussion of people playing card games, such as Rummy, Poker, Spades, or Blackjack. You might think that such games may be fun, but trivial, and have little to do with holding together the fabric of society. But Putnam thinks differently, and has even done some sums to illustrate his point:

> As recently as the mid-1970s nearly 40 per cent of all American adults played cards at least once a month, and the ratio of monthly card players to monthly moviegoers was four to one. Between 1981 and 1999, however, the average frequency of card playing among American adults plunged from sixteen times per year to eight times per year. . . . American adults still play five hundred million card games a year, but that figure is falling by twenty-five million games a year. Even if we assume, conservatively, that community issues come up in conversation only once every ten card games, the decline of card playing implies fifty million fewer 'microdeliberations' about community affairs each year now than two decades ago.[18]

Card games are just one example from several social activities covered by Putnam. Clearly, not all card games are opportunities for heavy discussions of civic affairs, but Putnam is not saying that they are: instead, he offers a rough calculation which shows – even if it's not quite right, even if such conversations only occur in every 20 or every 40 card games – that the *opportunities* for such possible 'microdeliberations' appear to be on the wane.

Putnam's book was written at a time when the internet had *started* to connect people in new ways – potentially making up for the lost card games and public meetings, I mean – but had not really begun to blossom as it has today. We will consider Putnam's discussion of the internet in a few pages. Meanwhile, some of his preferred examples are a little old-fashioned, or just odd: for instance, singing songs around a piano is good for social capital, in Putnam's book, but visiting art galleries or exhibitions is not[19] – even though one might expect the latter to prompt more stimulating conversations. His view of video games as socially isolating may have been credible at the time of writing, but today the social aspect of online gaming is the key to their popularity (although – one supposes – not often leading to discussion of civic affairs). And, of course, Putnam's data only represent the USA, but are likely to mirror *roughly* similar shifts in everyday life across the developed world – although Scandinavia remains a notable exception, having seen some similar social changes but retaining very healthy levels of social capital. Overall, in any case, you can see where Putnam is coming from, and it is easy to sympathize with his concerns, in spirit even if not in detail.

So, if social capital is in decline, if people are connecting less with others, we have to ask: why? How did this happen?

THE CAUSES OF COLLAPSING SOCIAL CAPITAL

Putnam's discussion of these questions is again considered at length, and with lots of data. Here he is able to show that, despite his apparent fondness for the 'good old days', he is not a social conservative. He finds no reason to blame changes in family structure, or women's much greater employment outside the home, or the growth of the welfare state. He does not feel able to blame capitalism in general, since America has 'epitomised market capitalism for several centuries', whilst his observed collapse of social capital is a more recent phenomenon. However, he does note that the increasing nationalization and globalization of shops, banks, and businesses is having an impact. Part of this problem is that big brand-name shops, rather than independent stores, would be less likely to act as local hubs of information and social connection, and would be less likely to take their stock from local makers and producers. Putnam's focus, though, is largely with the decline in civic commitment on the part of business leaders. Philanthropy and community engagement used to be of importance to American business people, whereas today – as one contact complained to Putnam – 'They're all off at corporate headquarters in some other state.'[20] This is likely to be a significant factor 'as regards larger philanthropic and civic activities', Putnam muses, but it 'is less clear why corporate delocalization should affect, for example, our readiness to attend a church social, or to have friends over for poker, or even to vote for president'.[21]

Having considered a range of possible explanations, Putnam arrives at four main factors that he says have caused the decline in civic engagement and social capital:

- *Generational change:* This is Putnam's biggest factor, accounting for 'perhaps half of the overall decline', as 'an unusually civic generation' born earlier in the twentieth century are slowly replaced by their 'less involved' children and grandchildren.[22] 'Generational change' is not really an explanation in itself, of course: the *actual* explanation seems to be that the experience of World War II cemented the centrality of community, solidarity, and self-sacrifice, in a way which subsequent conflicts and causes have not.
- *Television:* Hard on the heels of generational change and the experience of a world war comes the seemingly mundane arrival, and vast popularity, of television, accounting for 'perhaps 25 per cent' of the decline in civic engagement.[23] This is largely for the straightforward reason (which we discussed briefly in chapter 1) that it 'privatizes' leisure time, keeping people at home, on their sofas, for

literally several hours every day on average. 'Nothing else in the twentieth century so rapidly and profoundly affected our leisure', Putnam notes: 'In 1950 barely 10 percent of American homes had television sets, but by 1959, 90 per- cent did, probably the fastest diffusion of a technological innovation ever recorded.'[24] Since then, Putnam's data show, people became less likely to switch on to watch a particular selected programme – as they typically did in the earlier days of television – and more likely to have the TV on anyway. Household life would be directed towards a television set, and their connection with the outside world would become filtered through the television. Drawing on various sources of data, Putnam finds that 'Nothing – not low education, not full-time work, not long commutes in urban agglomerations, not poverty or financial distress – is more broadly associated with civic disengagement and social disconnection than is dependence on television for entertainment.'[25] And, in a surprising and disturbing killer blow, he finds that people don't even really enjoy it: 'Like other addictive or compulsive behaviours, television seems to be a surprisingly unsatisfying experience. Both time diaries and the "beeper" studies [when a beeper prompts participants to record how they are feeling at particular more-or-less random moments during the day] find that for the average viewer television is about as enjoyable as housework and cooking, ranking well below all other leisure activities and indeed below work itself.'[26]

• *Suburbanization, commuting, and sprawl:* Rather than living and working in their local communities, people increas- ingly travel some distance from home to work, which reduces their engagement with the community that they live in, and also takes up time in the day, leaving less time for friends and neighbours, and community engagements. This urban 'sprawl' also contributes to social segregation, and damages bridging social capital, as people choose to locate their home lives amongst other people 'like them'. Putnam finds that 'the residents of large metropolitan areas incur a "sprawl civic penalty" of roughly 20 percent on most measures of community involvement'[27] and that, as increasing numbers of people come to live like that, this accounts for around 10 per cent of the overall decline of social capital.[28]

- *Everyday pressures:* Finally, Putnam finds that 'pressures of time and money' have also contributed to the problem by around 10 per cent. These factors might seem rather timeless and not necessarily a recent phenomenon, but surveys show that the pressures of work, time spent at work, and a general feeling of busyness and having no spare time have all risen dramatically since the 1960s. Economic worries and 'the pressures associated with two-career families' also do not help with civic engagement.

Overall, we can see that the latter two factors make only a small contribution, and that generational change seems to be very significant, but is also a rather vague factor that we probably couldn't do much about (unless the idea of a massive and very punishing world war sounds like an appealing plan – which it surely doesn't). This leaves us with one clear suspect making a significant contribution to the decline in civic engagement and social capital: television.

Putnam does not seem to be one of those TV bashers who find ways to attack popular culture because of a general disdain for young people's interests, or modern life in general.[29] On the contrary, he has gathered data from a broad range of sources and considered a very great number of possible causes for the particular phenomena that concern him. Television does not seem to have been targeted, but rather it *emerges* as a significant cause from Putnam's investigations.

And so, surprisingly perhaps, electronic entertainment seems to be a key culprit behind a very considerable shift in society.

THE CONSEQUENCES OF COLLAPSING SOCIAL CAPITAL

Next we have to consider whether this decline in social capital actually matters. Turning to this 'So what?' question, Putnam says:

> An impressive and growing body of research suggests that civic connections help make us healthy, wealthy, and wise. Living *without* social capital is not easy, whether one is a villager in southern Italy or a poor person in the American inner city or a well-heeled entrepreneur in a high-tech industrial district.[30]

His evidence demonstrates that social capital has a considerable impact in a wide range of areas. For example, local environments are both cleaner and safer where there is a higher level of civic engagement. Putnam has even mapped which US states are more or less 'pugnacious' – measured by the proportion of people who agree with the statement 'I'd do better than average in a fist fight' in the DDB Needham Life Style surveys – and found that states high in social capital are less pugnacious. To put it another way, wandering into an area with lower social capital means that people are somewhat more likely to fancy the idea of beating you up.[31] Similarly, the problems of crime and violence in inner cities, his data suggest, cannot be read off from economic factors alone but are most serious where there is a lack of 'community monitoring, socialising, mentoring, and organizing'.[32] When we look at child development, we find that it is heavily influenced by the levels of trust and goodwill, and supportive networks, within the child's family, school, and community. Indeed, as we have seen already, health and happiness for people of all ages are linked with social connectedness.

Social capital is not a supernatural force, of course, and Putnam identifies particular ways in which social capital leads to these positive results.[33] For instance:

- It enables citizens to resolve problems more easily;
- It helps communities to advance because members know that they can rely on each other;
- It fosters awareness of the ways in which our fates are interlinked, and encourages us to be more tolerant, less cynical, and more empathetic.

Since Putnam assembled his landmark book in the late 1990s, we have come to think of the internet as a major, mainstream way of connecting people, as discussed in chapter 4. Here it is still worth looking at Putnam's findings in this area, based on his observation of the first few years of the World Wide Web.

THE INTERNET AND SOCIAL CAPITAL

A little historical context might be useful here. When Robert Putnam was writing the book *Bowling Alone*, in the late 1990s, the internet and the World Wide Web were not entirely new, and everybody seemed to be talking about them. But at the same time, they were clearly *not* as embedded in a majority of people's everyday lives as they are today. In 2000, when Putnam's book came out, only 44 per cent of the US population were internet users. By 2010, this had grown to 77 per cent. Of these, almost all (90 per cent) had broadband access, giving swift access to online video, audio, other substantial downloads, and live online gaming experiences and virtual worlds.[34] Their counterparts ten years earlier were receiving content on dial-up modems which were literally several hundred times slower.[35]

In the UK, the story was similar, but from a slower start. In 2000, only a quarter of households had access to the internet, a number which itself had doubled since the start of 1999, when only 13 per cent of households had access.[36] By 2010, 77 per cent of the population were regular internet users, with 73 per cent of households being online. Of those, as in the USA, almost all (90 per cent) had a broadband connection. A UK Office for National Statistics report shows that in 2010, the great majority of the population were regular internet users, with almost all young people using it regularly (97 per cent of those aged 16–24), and strong usage continuing into the middle-aged bracket (84 per cent of those aged 45–54, and 72 per cent of those aged 55–64, had used the internet in the previous three months).[37] The drop-off for older people, which pulls down the overall average, only really affects the over-65s, 32 per cent of whom had accessed the internet in the previous three months.

If we return to *Bowling Alone*, then, we can see that Putnam did well to include a reasonably substantial section on the new-ish phenomenon of the internet.[38] In general, he tries to be fair-minded on this topic, and is certainly open to the idea that the internet might help to restore some of the broken bonds in society. This is made more difficult, though, by the 1990s view of the internet as a kind of potential *replacement* for, rather than enabler of, real-life social connections. 'Within a few years of the Internet's launch', he notes, 'simulacra of most classic forms of social connectedness and civic engagement could be found on-line.'[39] This isn't necessarily good: 'simulacra' is the key word here, and Putnam notes the appearance of 'cyberweddings' and 'virtual funerals', the largely unwelcome late-1990s online versions of social occasions where families and friends traditionally get together for solace or celebration, and which are so important in bringing the 'tribe' together (crucial 'bonding capital', in other words). The defence offered by the 'virtual funeral' creators – that it's better than missing it, if you're too busy to actually go – is hardly the kind of argument that is going to persuade Robert Putnam.

Putnam therefore begins by wondering whether 'virtual social capital' is simply a contradiction in terms. This is a crucial question. The classic, heartwarming vision of social capital brought to mind by de Tocqueville and Putnam – an association of volunteer firefighters handing out Christmas gifts to poor children on the village green, that kind of thing – doesn't immediately seem to translate into the apparently soulless activity of people sitting at computers. And at a more general level, we might think, don't warm social bonds depend on seeing a person's face, hearing their voice, being in their physical presence?

On the other hand, by the late 1990s there was a growing awareness that online communities were not necessarily just about hobbies and information – engineers sharing hardware tips, as it were – but could also be strong sources of genuine support for new parents, or people with similar illnesses, the divorced or bereaved, or teenagers wondering if anyone else feels like they do. Howard Rheingold's famous 1993 book, *The Virtual Community*, painted a picture of the author's engagement with an early online community, The WELL (The Whole Earth 'Lectronic Link), which was full of heart, kindness, and mutual sympathy. Right near the start of the first chapter, for instance, Rheingold describes the following case:

> Jay Allison and his family live in Massachusetts. He and his wife are public-radio producers. I've never met any of them face-to-face, although I feel I know something powerful

and intimate about the Allisons and have strong emotional ties to them. What follows are some of Jay's postings on the WELL:

'Woods Hole. Midnight. I am sitting in the dark of my daughter's room. Her monitor lights blink at me. The lights used to blink too brightly so I covered them with bits of bandage adhesive and now they flash faintly underneath, a persistent red and green, Lillie's heart and lungs.

Above the monitor is her portable suction unit. In the glow of the flashlight I'm writing by, it looks like the plastic guts of a science-class human model, the tubes coiled around the power supply, the reservoir, the pump.

Tina is upstairs trying to get some sleep. A baby monitor links our bedroom to Lillie's. It links our sleep to Lillie's too, and because our souls are linked to hers, we do not sleep well.

I am naked. My stomach is full of beer. The flashlight rests on it, and the beam rises and falls with my breath. My daughter breathes through a white plastic tube inserted into a hole in her throat. She's fourteen months old.'

Sitting in front of our computers with our hearts racing and tears in our eyes, in Tokyo and Sacramento and Austin, we read about Lillie's croup, her tracheostomy, the days and nights at Massachusetts General Hospital, and now the vigil over Lillie's breathing and the watchful attention to the mechanical apparatus that kept her alive. It went on for days. Weeks. Lillie recovered, and relieved our anxieties about her vocal capabilities after all that time with a hole in her throat by saying the most extraordinary things, duly reported online by Jay.

Later, writing in Whole Earth Review, Jay described the experience:

'Before this time, my computer screen had never been a place to go for solace. Far from it. But there it was. Those nights sitting up late with my daughter, I'd go to my computer, dial up

the WELL, and ramble. I wrote about what was happening that night or that year. I didn't know anyone I was "talking" to. I had never laid eyes on them. At 3:00 a.m. my "real" friends were asleep, so I turned to this foreign, invisible community for support. The WELL was always awake.

Any difficulty is harder to bear in isolation. There is nothing to measure against, to lean against. Typing out my journal entries into the computer and over the phone lines, I found fellowship and comfort in this unlikely medium'.[40]

This section alone seems to singlehandedly answer the question of whether you can build social capital online. Clearly you can. And online networks of this kind would potentially be powerful both in terms of bridging capital – bringing diverse people together, with no geographical limitations – and bonding capital – creating a strong 'in-group' spirit as they share both knowledge and emotions. Putnam seems to accept this, but isn't sure if it's quite enough.

For one thing, his survey datasets contain no sign that internet users are more civically engaged than the average, once the higher educational qualifications of these early(ish) adopters is controlled for. However, he readily admits that it would be 'much too early to assess the long-run social effects of the Internet empirically', and moves swiftly on to consideration of its *'potential'*.[41]

This potential is certainly not lost on Putnam, who writes:

Communication is a fundamental prerequisite for social and emotional connections. Telecommunications in general and the Internet in particular substantially enhance our ability to communicate; thus it seems reasonable to assume that their net effect will be to enhance community, perhaps even dramatically. Social capital is about networks, and the Net is the network to end all networks.[42]

He notes that the internet is a 'powerful tool' for sharing information between people across geographical distances; 'The tougher question is whether that flow of information itself fosters social capital and genuine community.'[43] On the one hand, online communities may be more egalitarian, since views can be discussed through written text without the contributor's physical attributes such as sex, race, age, or beauty having any effect on how the words are perceived. On the other hand, when the 'threshold for voicing opinions' is lowered in this way, it can mean that, 'like talk radio, it may lead not to deliberation, but to din'.[44]

Today it can seem easy to 'participate' in campaigns with the click of a mouse: in some cases, campaign groups have created online tools which enable users to instantly send a readymade message to a politician or business leader – messages which inevitably will be seen by their recipients as mass-produced 'spam', regardless of the virtue of their arguments. Putnam wisely observes that this kind of thing can 'simply exacerbate the imbalance between talking and listening that is a prominent feature of contemporary civic disengagement'.[45]

In particular, Putnam lists four 'serious challenges' to the notion that the internet can fix the *Bowling Alone* problem of civic disengagement:[46]

- First is the digital divide – lack of access to the internet – a problem which has diminished since the 1990s, as noted above, and which Putnam considers 'serious but not insurmountable', if libraries and community centres can also provide access and support. Nevertheless, it remains the case that lack of money, knowledge, awareness, confidence, and/or skills can mean that millions of people do not benefit from the internet.
- Second is the lack of non-verbal (or non-textual) cues in

online communication, which strips a rich layer of meaning from interactions. This means that less solidarity is fostered within groups, and can lead to misunderstandings, higher levels of abusive behaviour, and dishonesty. This point can be true, when people interact exclusively online with no chance of real-life encounters, but seems to me to be relatively insignificant compared to the benefits.

- Third is the threat of 'cyberbalkanization', the concern that specialist online interest groups are so narrowly focused – with everyday chitchat being roughly dismissed as 'off-topic' – that a new form of exclusive homogeneity is created online. Interactions in the real world, Putnam notes, 'force us to deal with diversity', whilst online shared-interest groups may not. This, I would say, is sometimes true, but on the other hand, the online community who come together because of a shared love of rabbits, green energy, Lego, or *The Simpsons*, may be incredibly diverse – much more so than one's own neighbourhood. Also, as Putnam notes, people are very likely to be part of several groups – 'an interwoven community of communities' – which reduces the level of specialist isolation.

- The fourth and final challenge concerns whether the Web would develop and flourish as a medium of active social communication, or merely turn into a new variety of passive television viewing. At the start of the century, Putnam had to admit that it could go either way, and that his data could provide no firm clues. However, he warned that 'The commercial incentives that currently govern Internet development seem destined to emphasize individualized entertainment and commerce rather than community engagement.'[47] From our vantage point a decade later, we can see that this one perhaps didn't go as badly as feared: the success of online social networks such as Facebook and Flickr reflects the recognition amongst internet entrepreneurs that social interaction and community are what drive people to a site. In other words, it's precisely the non-television dimension of online services that makes them attractive. Even in the more 'TV-like' corners of the internet, such as the massively popular video site YouTube, the platform includes a social network. For sure, the majority of YouTube visitors arrive there just to watch a video – perhaps following a suggestion from friends or contacts on another network – and may not engage with YouTube's networks and communities. As we saw in chapter 4, however, for many of those who *produce* and share YouTube content, these communities are a vital part of the experience – they are what creates motivation and meaning for their creative endeavours. As the research by Jean Burgess and Joshua Green, and others, has shown, without the interaction and dialogue with other YouTube users and fellow creators, community members would be much less motivated to produce, share, and publicize their creative activities.[48]

In summary, then, these four 'serious challenges' do not seem to be especially devastating. Not that Putnam necessarily intended to shoot down the claims which enthusiasts have made about the internet's potential: on the contrary, he seems to be cautiously optimistic, admitting at the end of his discussion that, 'In fact, it is hard to imagine solving our contemporary civic dilemmas *without* computer-mediated communication.'[49]

Of the four challenges, the first and last seem to be the most potent, ten years on. It remains the case that differential access to the internet – not just in terms of having the equipment and being connected, but more crucially about the skills, confidence, and awareness necessary to use available resources and tools in a fruitful manner – creates a barrier for a significant minority. And it is also still the case that commercial drivers might incline the powerful online media companies to try to make our Web experiences more television-y than participatory. This is a challenge we will discuss in the next two chapters, but for now we can simply note that people clearly *like* online participation, and they seek out and recommend to each other the sites where they can communicate and share with others.

We can also take some comfort from the fact that internet users are a responsive and fussy crowd, who will swiftly turn their backs on online services which become annoyingly commercialized. They will simply go elsewhere. To take the most obvious example, Google's rise to ubiquity was achieved by a combination of a search system which seemed to give users the relevant results that they wanted (rather than paid-for listings), plus a very clear layout with clearly labelled text adverts set aside from the main section of non-sponsored results. Literally millions of users soon fled from the banner-advert festooned search engines like Yahoo and AltaVista, in favour of this simple and seemingly less commercialized (although ultimately hugely profitable) approach. The fact that users can so easily abandon one service in favour of another (unlike the more fixed array of TV stations), and tend to resist garish commercialism, suggests that it would be difficult for anyone to foist an unwanted 'couch potato' version of the Web upon us.

That's the optimistic view, anyway. Some critics, notably Jonathan Zittrain, seriously fear it could go the other way if mainstream users decide that they would prefer – or passively wander into accepting – a neat and tidy prepackaged version of the Web, rather than the more experimental, anything-goes version that we have (mostly) been familiar with so far.[50] Zittrain lists several reasons to be concerned, but it is difficult to imagine that most people would like to shift over to a locked-down, restricted, limited version of the Web. History supports this view, since an alternative, family-friendly, restricted version of the Web was offered to consumers before: they called it AOL, an internet service provider which in the 1990s sought to keep you on its AOL pages and was reluctant to release you onto the treacherous seas of the proper World Wide Web. But this model collapsed once users realized that the supposed horror and anarchy of the Web was mostly invisible unless you went looking for it, and that online diversity was not scary but just meant that there were all kinds of wonderful resources created by all kinds of wonderful people. Being in a protected bubble, presented with AOL news, AOL reviews, and AOL advice, did not seem to be good value once customers realized that the collective wisdom of people from all around the world was available just on the other side of AOL's picket fence.

On the other hand, we shouldn't be too complacent. The rise of different kinds of online devices, such as mobile phones and the iPad, can mean that ways of accessing things via the internet gets gently reinvented into a more 'consumer' rather than participatory model. This is presented to users as pleasant and convenient, but represents a threat to the ideals of the World Wide Web. (We will discuss this in the next chapter.)

In sum, Putnam was rightly cautious about the hype surrounding the internet, but was also generous in recognizing that online communication at least has considerable *potential* as part of the solution to declining civic engagement.

CRITICS OF PUTNAM

In this chapter I have discussed Robert Putnam's work at some length. I have questioned some of his assumptions, but generally have embraced his approach as interesting, well-meaning, and potentially fruitful. Putnam is not universally popular, however. To balance things out, we should briefly note some of the key criticisms offered by others.

One common complaint is that Putnam is so enthusiastic about social capital as a positive force that he neglects the role of government, politics, and social policy. He could be seen to be suggesting that if only we could get everyone to help each other out on a local community level, we could do away with formal social and health services altogether. For this reason, Putnam has occasionally been accused of having a 'neorepublican' interest in eroding the welfare state.[51]

This seems deeply unfair. Putnam is, presumably, aware that the state does not have the magical power to guarantee that society will be cohesive, kind, safe, and trusting, and – based on evidence that these things, or perception of these things, are in decline – engages in an evidence-based discussion of solutions which are largely based on communities, groups, or individuals, and are potentially self-starting. He does not suggest that more 'top down' approaches or interventions are not required, or that government support for social and health services is not necessary.

Uneasiness about Putnam's solutions may be amplified in today's economic climate. In the UK, for instance, the newly elected coalition government in 2010 loudly declared enthusiasm for the idea of a 'big society' – representing the opposite of 'big government' solutions – where volunteers would step in to provide educational, environmental, and social services which previously were delivered, at a cost, by the state. As we have seen, community engagement is a good thing, and is rewarding for participants and their neighbour-hoods, but it should be built *above* the baseline of necessary services – not as a money-saving replacement for them. The point of Putnam, as far as we are concerned in this book, is to highlight the value of social connections, and connected social projects – not to offer a right-wing excuse for slashing public services.

Putnam is also accused of seeing social capital in an overly rosy light. Although he includes a short chapter on the 'dark side' of social capital in *Bowling Alone*, he mostly ignores the in-group favouritism, aggressive competition, and bully-ing that can be fostered within like-minded groups, instead seeing social connections as typically warm, benevolent, and fruitful. This gloomy criticism doesn't stand up to the evi-dence, however. Although there certainly are unpleasant and offensive groups strong on bonding capital (they appre-ciate people who are like themselves), but low on bridging capital (they hate everyone else), this is not the ideal type. More crucially, Putnam mines his data to show that this is not the common form: looking at the trends of economic and civic equality, and comparing them with his social capi-tal data – across different US states, and across time – he finds that 'the evidence powerfully contradicts the view that community engagement must necessarily amplify inequal-ity'.[52] The evidence that lack of social connections is bad for society is emphatic; whereas the fact that *some* social connec-tions prompt cruel or exclusionary behaviour is true but not such a widespread phenomenon. Clearly, if we are talking about whether social connectedness and people's willingness to help those around them are a good thing for society, the answer is bound to be yes.

A similar criticism concerns Putnam's indifference to the *content* of people's connections. This is reflected in a story told by Michael Edwards, in his book *Civil Society*, where Putnam had been invited to address a seminar at the Harvard Divinity School, and was explaining the virtues of choirs, choral societies, and other voluntary groups, only to be stopped by an audience member who said: 'But Bob, what is the choir *singing*?'[53]

This point reminds us that just because people have come together to do something collectively, this does not mean that their activity will meet expectations about a good or progressive society. Even if their content is not obviously antisocial – if they have avoided songs in celebration of Satan or suicide bombers – their hymns might reinforce traditional values at odds with the 'liberal' agenda. So should we worry about content at all – is it *only* important that people come together to sing, or should we worry about the messages being sung?

Putnam implies, overall, that any kind of communal activity is better than slumping, isolated, in front of the TV. There is perhaps also an assumption that greater levels of social interaction will, generally speaking, lead us to appreciate differences, and to get along better with a diversity of people. Edwards ends up concluding that a mix of activities and memberships, combining groups with informal and formal qualities, is bound to be healthy: 'it is the ecosystem that matters, not the characteristics of its individual components'.[54] A good mesh of people and groups engaged in action around different kinds of interests is also likely to challenge narrow perceptions and prejudices: a group of bigots who stay in their little club, moaning about the world, aren't very high in social capital anyway. Get them out in the world, communicating and working with people on things, and their assumptions will be challenged.

SOCIAL CAPITAL – IN CONCLUSION

There is now a significant body of literature on social capital, and we've only scratched the surface here. In particular, I have based this discussion around the arguments made by the most notable modern driver of social capital theory, Robert Putnam, and don't really have space to discuss the additional avenues developed by his followers and others – although of course you can follow those up for yourself, if interested.[55] Although some of these publications suggest that they have made significant advances since the publication of *Bowling Alone*, it's probably more accurate to say that Putnam did the main job, laying out a huge canvas, and then the others have added some extra detail and colour, and the occasional extension.

At the end of his overview of a wide range of social capital theory and research, John Field makes a good, clear argument for the value of the general concept:

> What social capital brings to social theory is an emphasis on relationships and values as significant factors in explaining structures and behaviour. To be more precise, it contributes new insights by focusing on 'meso-level social structures' such as family, neighbourhood, voluntary associations and public institutions as integrating elements between individuals and wider social structures. Moreover, it allows social scientists to examine the role of these meso-level structures in a systematic way since it has a structural dimension (networks), a behavioural dimension (participation) and a cognitive dimension (norms).[56]

In particular he emphasizes that social capital is not only a theoretical tool for thinking about the importance of social connections and civic engagement: rather, there is 'abundant evidence that social capital actually affects the outcomes of social behaviour' and is therefore 'a variable in its own right'.[57]

The social capital research, like the happiness research, has provided clear evidence that having friendly social connections and communication, and working together with people on shared projects, is not merely pleasant-but-optional 'icing on the cake' of individual lives, but is absolutely essential both for personal well-being and for a healthy, secure, trustworthy society. Both spheres of research tend to concern geographically based lives rooted in physical communities, but they have obvious implications for online social activity as well.

In the next chapter we'll move on to discuss the ideas of Ivan Illich, who was also concerned with the qualities of a good life – and who also didn't talk about the Web, since it hadn't been invented yet – and then steer back towards Web 2.0 for the second half of that chapter, and the one after that.

7

TOOLS FOR CHANGE

So far in this book we have considered the qualities of 'making things' and have found, amongst other things, that individually crafted items are expressive of a personality, and of a presence in the world; that everyday creativity is central to the health of a society; and that making and sharing your own things, rather than accepting mainstream manufactured or broadcast things, is positive in both political and emotional terms. We have seen evidence that personal creative projects are good for individual happiness, and that when people organize to make things together, it can transform the quality of life in communities. Hopefully that means I have laid some pretty solid groundwork for this chapter, which is possibly (even) broader in scope, and primarily concerns the work of Ivan Illich.

Here we encounter a level of argument which might tie things nicely together, because it's *big*. For Illich, making is not just an act which might brighten your day, or which might help to develop a social connection. What I take from Illich is that *making changes everything*.

So let's explore that.

Ivan Illich (1926–2002) was born in Vienna, studied in Italy, and worked as a parish priest in New York City. Following a position in Puerto Rico, and travels across South America, he set up a cultural and political institute in Mexico. This was followed by further travel and some university positions in the USA, Mexico, and Germany. In other words, he had a complex biography, and somewhat nomadic existence, with few possessions. More importantly for us, Illich became known in the 1970s for his radical notion that overdeveloped institutions were crushing the life out of society.[1]

Whilst big, uniform systems may have been developed with the intention of helping people on a broad and democratic scale, Illich argued that they always reach a point beyond which they cause more harm than good. Schools, for instance, are originally intended to provide an *education* – of course – but once they are established into a institutional system they become machines to deliver *schooling* – conformity to rules, and memorization of a set body of knowledge without necessarily learning or understanding – which is then measured as an end in itself. Therefore, Illich suggests, the institution of school makes people stupid, institutionalized medicine makes people sick, and the institution of business ruins the planet. This sounds gloomy, then, but his solutions, based on more individual and community-based engagement, helpfulness, and creativity, may be of interest.

DESCHOOLING

Illich first became well-known for a book called *Deschooling Society*, published in 1970. As the title suggests, it is primarily a critique of the compulsory education system, and as such formed part of a challenge to established models of education, alongside the work of other thinkers, such as John

Dewey, John Holt, and Rudolph Steiner. But *Deschooling Society* also brought to the public's attention the key seeds of Illich's more general argument about large institutions – and the ways in which people could reclaim a more local, healthy, and useful way of doing things based on convivial, supportive, and relevant interactions between people.

The problem with schools, according to Illich, is that they train students to be dependent on the 'treatment' offered by big institutions. Schools aim to create people who can do well in school tests, but not people who can think for themselves. Perhaps their cruellest manipulation is that they lead people to believe they are *unable* to do things for themselves and that the big institutional solution – the one offered by schools, hospitals, and government departments – is the only legitimate one. He says:

> Rich and poor alike . . . view doctoring oneself as irresponsible, learning on one's own as unreliable, and community organisation, when not paid for by those in authority, as a form of aggression or subversion.[2]

This creates a double problem for the poor, who already experience a lack of power over their circumstances, but then, in addition, are schooled into a way of thinking which represents 'a loss of personal potency'.[3]

The solution, Illich says, is not to change the detail of what happens in schools, as replacing one compulsory education machine with another one would not address the problem. On the contrary, we need to create 'a new style of educational relationship' between people and their environment,[4] based on helping people to learn about things that they want to learn about, when they want to do so – rather than bribing or compelling people to acquire a particular stack of information at a particular predetermined time. He writes:

A good educational system should have three purposes: it should provide all who want to learn with access to available resources at any time in their lives; empower all who want to share what they know to find those who want to learn it from them; and finally, furnish all who want to present an issue to the public with the opportunity to make their challenge known.[5]

Illich outlines a number of ways to achieve this, including skill exchanges (where people can seek others to learn skills from, and can offer to share their own expertise), peer matching (where people can find others with similar interests, so that they can learn together), and new forms of libraries (containing all kinds of 'educational objects'). Rather than education being something that has to be forced upon young people by government, education is here a lively, *chosen* activity which occurs naturally across 'learning webs' of enthusiastic individuals and groups. Illich easily solves any funding issues by assuming that the finance from the existing school system can be redirected towards supporting these schemes, which means that there would be a huge pile of money available to support facilitators, computers, equipment, and learning spaces.

The idea that we should simply drop the whole carefully planned institution of education – to be replaced by the apparent anarchy of people just learning about whatever they want to learn about, whenever they want to – seems shocking, and perhaps even ridiculous, precisely because we have learned to accept the natural superiority of a uniform and imposed system. As Illich says:

School has become the planned process which tools man for a planned world, the principal tool to trap man in man's trap.[6]

Rather than trusting each other to be supportive and help-ful, and instead of relying on friendliness and goodwill, we create systems and laws which aim to remove uncertainty and chance, but at the cost of both meaningful human rela-tionships and ordinary usefulness. The helpless, bored child asks her teacher, 'Why do I have to learn this thing now?', and the answer might be, 'Because it will be good for you', or 'Because you've got a test on it next week', or simply 'Because I told you to'. This prepares her for a lifetime under other institutions which also provide 'Because I said so' as an explanation for required compliance.

This might seem to be a simple-minded critique of the necessary instruments of social organization. We might object that society needs some systems to preserve basic law and order, to offer support services to the needy, and to ensure that children receive an education – because left to their own devices, we fear that they might not get one. But we do not (necessarily) have to take from Illich that all social organizations and institutions must be disbanded. His point is more that these institutions become too big, and take on a life of their own, where the means become the ends. Therefore we should seek to develop small, local approaches, focused on people's needs, rather than the big bureaucratic operations which inevitably become focused on the needs of their own bureaucracy. Most crucially, I would say, Illich highlights the *loss of joyfulness in everyday experience* that comes with an overplanned system.

TOOLS FOR CONVIVIALITY

In his next book, *Tools for Conviviality*, Illich developed these ideas further. The planned systems, such as the one for education discussed in *Deschooling Society*, are here cast as 'tools' – because a tool is anything used to produce some thing or effect: a means to an end. Therefore, for Illich, the term 'tool' describes hammers and brooms, as well as cars and power stations, and schools and hospitals.[7] This broad use of the term enables him to pull together everything that is designed to do something, whether that is to dig a ditch or to create an 'educated' or 'healthy' person.

Tools for Conviviality was intended to be a pamphlet, for people to discuss, where Illich could set out his 'general theory of tools'.[8] The word 'conviviality' is carefully chosen. It does not refer to drunkenness, of course. 'Conviviality' for Illich is a meaningful kind of communication and engagement between people – people who are friendly, meaningfully connected, and alive in the world:

> I choose the term 'conviviality' to designate the opposite of industrial productivity. I intend it to mean autonomous and creative intercourse among persons, and the intercourse of persons with their environment; and this in contrast with the conditioned response of persons to the demands made upon them by others, and by a man-made environment.[9]

So conviviality is about being vigorously engaged in relationships, conscious of values and meanings; and it is about having the capacity to communicate yourself directly, and to create the things of your world yourself. Illich is interesting on the material world – things and objects – because he does not simply argue that we should do away with all 'stuff' (which can seem to be the implication of some critiques of modern consumer societies). For Illich, the things and objects we have in our lives are significant, but there are important questions about where they came from, the role that they play, and what meanings they embody:

People need not only to obtain things, they need above all the freedom to make things among which they can live, to give shape to them according to their own tastes, and to put them to use in caring for and about others. Prisoners in rich countries often have access to more things and services than members of their families, but they have no say in how things are to be made and cannot decide what to do with them. Their punishment consists in being deprived of what I shall call 'conviviality.' They are degraded to the status of mere consumers.[10]

Conviviality is therefore about having the power to shape one's own world. Illich makes it clear that individuals *must* retain this power – society must not seek to drain it from them. This is, then, a moral position, akin to that of Morris and especially Ruskin, whom we discussed in chapter 2. As before, I do not mean it is associated with moralism – the wish to impose particular traditional values – but rather that Illich's argument is powered by a moral belief that this kind of zesty freedom is crucial to the well-being of society, an irreducible core of what is necessary. As he explains,

I consider conviviality to be individual freedom realized in personal interdependence and, as such, an intrinsic ethical value. I believe that, in any society, as conviviality is reduced below a certain level, no amount of industrial productivity can effectively satisfy the needs it creates among society's members.[11]

Conviviality therefore also represents the joyfulness which is so easily lost when we try to organize human interests into systems and institutions. Illich makes it clear that human beings, and their societies, are quite adept at producing bad tools – or rather, we create tools with good intentions, but when scaled up, the bureaucratic process becomes an end in itself, and the tool goes bad. A society needs tools – tools that can be controlled and used to good purposes – but they cannot be allowed to become too big and powerful, or we become enslaved by them.

Nevertheless, we can create good tools if we are careful, and try to be aware of the positive and negative potentials of any instrument. As the title suggests, *Tools for Conviviality* sets out Illich's vision of how society needs tools which encourage individual creativity, enabling people to give shape and character to their own lives, rather than those tools which tend to impose a mass sameness. Therefore this is about individuals being able to make their mark on the world, rather than only have the world stamping its mark upon them.

ILLICH AND TECHNOLOGY

Illich does not want to dispose of all industry and technology, although he admits that it is now 'difficult to imagine' a modern society where scientific progress and industrial development are balanced in harmony with human needs.

Our vision of the possible and the feasible is so restricted by industrial expectations that any alternative to more mass production sounds like a return to past oppression or like a Utopian design for noble savages. In fact, however, the vision of new possibilities requires only the recognition that scientific discoveries can be useful in at least two opposite ways. The first leads to specialization of functions, institutionalization of values and centralization of power and turns people into the accessories of bureaucracies or machines. The second enlarges the range of each person's competence, control, and initiative, limited only by other individuals' claims to an equal range of power and freedom.[12]

This is a model which, for instance, connects directly with debates about the World Wide Web which have been pressing ever since the Web became publicly visible (about 20 years after the publication of *Tools for Conviviality*). On the one hand, the Web could be used to centralize a lot of power in one place – we might think of Google here – and to draw people, via attractive toys, to reduce their individuality to the level of a database – we might think of Facebook. These are concerns which will be discussed in the following chapter. More optimistically, the Web could be used – as its creator, Tim Berners-Lee, intended – to increase people's knowledge, and their connections with other people; to extend their ability to have an influence upon the things and environments in their lives; and to enable them to do more things for themselves.

Illich does not talk about computers or electronic networks in any amount of detail[13] – but *Deschooling Society* includes an interesting technological fantasy in the chapter presciently entitled 'Learning Webs'. Illich notes the amount of money which had been poured into providing television services in Latin America in the 1960s, and speculates on the possibilities afforded if this had been spent on tape recorders instead. One in five adults could have been issued with a tape recorder, and 'the money would have sufficed to provide an almost unlimited library of prerecorded tapes, with outlets even in remote villages, as well as an ample supply of empty tapes'.[14] It is these 'empty tapes' which are key. Rather than the wall-to-wall content of television, produced for mass consumption, the emptiness of the tapes waits to be filled by the diverse voices of the people:

> This network of tape recorders, of course, would be radically different from the present network of TV. It would provide opportunity for free expression: literate and

illiterate alike could record, preserve, disseminate and repeat their opinions.[15]

Where television would only spread 'institutionally produced programs' giving a voice to the establishment, and their sponsors, the tape recorders would enable people to express themselves, learn, and share knowledge.

Followers of Illich were surprisingly quick to translate these ideas into the world of information technology and networks. For instance, Illich's arguments struck a chord with the Homebrew Computer Club in San Francisco, who in the mid-1970s were starting to play with computer technology as a tool for freedom. The Club fuelled the passions of several future technology stars, including Steve Jobs and Steve Wozniak, the co-founders of Apple, and Lee Felsenstein, who designed the first mass-produced portable computer, the Osborne 1.

As early as 1973, Felsenstein and a group of friends worked on a project, 'Community Memory', directly inspired by Illich. The project initially linked just two terminals, one in a record shop and one in a library, to a central computer. It was the first public computerized 'bulletin board' system, and the terminal at the record shop end was literally positioned next to their *actual* bulletin board, where people would post messages about meetings, accommodation, and gigs. The electronic version was originally intended to be a means of sharing countercultural information and resources, but soon developed into a place for all kinds of culture and chat.[16] Its creators described it as:

An actively open information system, enabling direct communication among its users with no centralised editing or control over the information exchanged. Such a system represents a precise antithesis to the dominant uses of electronic media which broadcast centrally-determined messages to mass passive audiences.[17]

This was probably the first attempt to create a 'tool for conviviality' in direct response to *Tools for Conviviality*, and also of course now looks like a very early model for Web 2.0 – in particular the open communication, social networking, and tagging of content so that others can find it.

Clearly, for Illich, the tools we have available to us are crucial to the character of our existence. The best tools are not merely 'useful' or 'convenient' additions to everyday life, but can unlock possibilities and enable creative expression, which are essential components of a satisfactory life:

> A convivial society should be designed to allow all its members the most autonomous action by means of tools least controlled by others. People feel joy, as opposed to mere pleasure, to the extent that their activities are creative; while the growth of tools beyond a certain point increases regimentation, dependence, exploitation, and impotence.[18]

Convivial tools are those which can be freely used, by those who wish to employ them; which do not require particular qualifications; and which 'allow the user to express his meaning in action'.[19] In Illich's terms, an online service would be a convivial tool – and therefore part of the solution to the problems faced by modern societies – insofar as it offers the opportunity for free and unconstrained expression and sharing of ideas and culture. If such a service is moderated by an institution, or is unnecessarily complex, or requires specialist knowledge, proprietary codes or licences, or cannot be freely shared, it becomes an 'industrial tool', and part of the problem.

Such tools – whether good ones or bad ones – are not just accessories, but are a fundamental part of everyday social interactions. As Illich argues:

> Tools are intrinsic to social relationships. An individual relates himself in action to his society through the use of tools that he actively masters, or by which he is passively acted upon. To the degree that he masters his tools, he can invest the world with his meaning; to the degree that he is mastered by his tools, the shape of the tool determines his own self-image. Convivial tools are those which give each person who uses them the greatest opportunity to enrich the environment with the fruits of his or her vision. Industrial tools deny this possibility to those who use them and they allow their designers to determine the meaning and expectations of others.[20]

THE POWER OF ILLICH

I have quoted Illich quite extensively in this chapter, in the hope of conveying some of the passion of his argument. His writing feels earthy, and engaged with real things – actual social relations, real communities, hands-on creativity. Much 'revolutionary' or would-be society-changing writing considers social forces with academic or economic detachment, and implies that a new bureaucratic machine, preceded by a big battle, could be the solution. Illich, to his credit, clearly has no appetite for either fighting or bureaucracy, and is much more interested in unlocking the potential of individuals and communities, and trusting them to be loving, sharing, and imaginative. Being opposed to big systems, he thankfully does not wish to provide a planned or centralized solution. Indeed, Illich does not assume that he could predict what a future happier society would look like, exactly, because he knows that it should rightly emerge through diverse, non-centralized creative acts:

> Industrial innovations are planned, trivial, and conservative. The renewal of convivial tools would be as unpredictable, creative, and lively as the people who use them.[21]

The idea that a person should be enabled to 'express their meaning in action' has the feeling of rough reality, and movement; and the line which makes a particular link between joy and creativity ('People feel joy, as opposed to mere pleasure, to the extent that their activities are creative') is warm, memorable, and powerful. Furthermore, Illich's clear opposition between convivial and industrial tools gives us a straightforward means to assess the quality of new innovations (although there would always be debate about their qualities, and some haziness where new tools offered some characteristics of both kinds).

Certainly, when we think about new (or old) forms of media, the extent to which they enable free and creative self-expression is, I think, absolutely crucial. On the one hand, this seems obvious – and therefore barely worth writing about. But, on the other hand, a concern for individual everyday creative autonomy is frequently *not* raised as a critical dimension when new technologies, applications, or toys are being evaluated. Often, video games and online applications are launched with hype about their 'interactive' or networked 'collaborative' features, but are actually more-or-less closed worlds which do not enable the users to make their mark on the system, and consequently deny them the opportunity to 'express their meaning in action'.

The launch of Apple's iPad device in 2010, for example, prompted vast amounts of discussion in the press. (As *Private Eye* magazine in the UK put it, 'You may not yet be reading *The Guardian* on an iPad, but you can hardly avoid reading about the iPad in *The Guardian*' – and the other newspapers were not far behind.) This was partly, of course, because newspaper and magazine publishers were filled with anxious hope that the iPad would provide them with a clean, locked-down way to sell their content electronically to consumers, without those consumers being easily able to share and exchange this material without paying. And this explanation itself points to a characteristic of the iPad which was not explicitly highlighted in many of the published features, reviews, and discussion: the iPad was a step backwards in the evolution of personal computing devices, towards media *consumption* rather than media production. Without a camera, or even a proper keyboard, it lacked the basic tools of bloggers and YouTubers, and encouraged a 'sit back and enjoy' orientation, as demonstrated by Steve Jobs, the Apple chief executive, using it on a couch at its launch.

This could be an unfair 'criticism', you might say, since the iPad was a *new kind* of device, and was *not meant* to be the same as a full-blown computer – which Apple would also happily sell to you. Therefore, it would be unfair to criticize the iPad for lacking certain features which appear on bulkier and less beautiful devices – although, on the other hand, Steve Jobs and his chief designer, Jonathan Ive, do also seem to believe that the iPad indicates the future of computing.[22] In any case – and even if, by the time you read this, new versions of the iPad have emerged with more built-in production tools – the point here is that many newspapers and commentators discussed the new machine so warmly, as a thrilling computer/internet device which could easily replace the laptop or netbook, without seeming at all concerned by its positioning of the user as a viewer, reader, and player, but not as publisher or producer. In other words, Illich's argument for convivial rather than industrial tools is not as obvious to everyone as we might hope.

TINKERING AND GENERATIVITY

A similar point is made by Jonathan Zittrain, of Harvard Law School, in his 2008 book *The Future of the Internet And How to Stop It*.[23] Despite the implication in the title, Zittrain doesn't want to stop the internet, but he does want to avoid a future internet where everything has become proprietary and fixed and non-tinkerable. Zittrain coined the notion of 'generativity' – which is basically the right and the opportunity to be creative – and 'generative technology' – which is technology that enables you to do whatever you want to do with it, to create stories and ideas and uses for yourself. 'Generativity' is therefore a version of Illich's 'conviviality', as applied to technology, and means basically 'Does it want you to do your own thing, or does it want you to do *its* thing?'

One example which Zittrain uses to illustrate this is, again, from Apple. Zittrain begins the story by recalling the Apple II, which was really the first mainstream personal computer produced by the company, in 1977. The Apple I, created in 1976, was a computer purely for hobbyists; each one was soldered together by hand, by Apple co-founder Steve Wozniak, in the garage of his new business partner, Steve Jobs. To be precise, it was his parents' garage – Jobs was 21 at the time.

The Apple II was meant to have broader appeal, and a magazine advert from 1977 explains how the whole family can learn to take the system 'as far as your imagination can take it', by programming the machine in Apple BASIC.[24] (That's not silly – that's what we did back then: personally, I spent many hours of my early teenage years writing games in BASIC on my Commodore Vic-20, a home computer of the early 1980s.)[25] Charmingly, the Apple ad includes a picture of a microchip-packed circuit board in the corner, mentioning:

> Apple II is also available in board-only form for the do-it-yourself hobbyist. Has all the features of the Apple II system, but does not include case, keyboard, power supply or game paddles. $798.

The Apple II, as the immediate product of guys who loved to hack and tinker with technology, was a machine which, like many early home computers, didn't 'do' anything when you switched it on, but waited for you to do something with it. Modern users might find this weird and unhelpful, but the positive view is that the creators of the system didn't *mind* what you did with it. You could do *whatever you wanted* (with the necessary skills – and within the limits of possibility). This consequently meant that sales of Apple II took off for reasons which Jobs and Wozniak had no control over and were not necessarily even aware of. For instance, it was only when Apple sought to investigate why sales of the Apple II had taken a sudden upward swing that they discovered that business people were buying the machine just so that they could use Visicalc, which was the first ever spreadsheet program. Like most Apple II software, Visicalc was created by an external developer, and when Apple executives happened to have seen an early version, they had not recognized it as anything very special.[26] But of course, they were later very happy when it helped to boost sales of their machine. Although they had not planned Visicalc itself, they *had* planned the unpredictable possibility of its existence.

As Zittrain puts it:

> The Apple II was quintessentially *generative* technology. It was a platform. It invited people to tinker with it. Hobbyists

wrote programs. Businesses began to plan on selling software. Jobs (and Apple) had no clue how the machine would
be used. They had their hunches, but, fortunately for them,
nothing constrained the PC to the hunches of the founders.[27]

So the Apple II, and other early home computers, offered a
huge open door to creativity and innovation. Programming
the computer for yourself was not a 'back stage' activity, per-
formed by qualified professionals, but was what the machine
assumed you were going to do when you took it out of the
box.

Over time, this level of openness and generativity led to a
problem – unhelpful users were able to bring about viruses,
spam, and identity theft. These unwelcome innovations led
to a desire amongst the weary public for a 'clean', quality-
controlled, and therefore censored version of the internet
– and it is this desire for a locked-down replacement for one
of humankind's greatest inventions which is the 'future' that
Zittrain wants to 'stop'.

In 2007, some 30 years after the Apple II, Steve Jobs
launched the iPhone. Zittrain observed how things had
changed since the invention of that computer:

> The iPhone is the opposite. It is sterile. Rather than a
> platform that invites innovation, the iPhone comes pre-
> programmed. You are not allowed to add programs to the
> all-in-one device that Steve Jobs sells you. Its functional-
> ity is locked in, although Apple can change it through
> remote updates. . . . The machine was not to be *generative*
> beyond the innovations that Apple (and its exclusive carrier,
> AT&T) wanted.[28]

Zittrain notes that Jobs even described these restrictions
at the iPhone launch, boasting: 'We define everything that

is on the phone.' Appealing to a fear of amateur creativity, he went on: 'You don't want your phone to be like a PC. The last thing you want is to have loaded three apps on your phone and then you go to make a call and it doesn't work anymore.'[29]

Since then, famously, things have changed, since one of the main selling-points of today's iPhone is the huge number of 'apps' available to users, produced by third-party developers. In the two years since the launch of the 'App Store' in July 2008, at least 225,000 third-party applications have been offered there, with over 5 billion total downloads.[30] So the iPhone today is not quite as wholly Apple-directed as Zittrain suggested. Becoming an iPhone developer is not prohibitively difficult or expensive – you sign up for membership of the developer community, and for access to the necessary software, on the Apple website for US $99.00 per year (in UK terms that's about £5.50 per month) – although you also need an Apple Mac computer to create and test the software on (as well as the limitation, common to all programming, that you need the skills to be able to program).

Nevertheless, this is a long way from the machine that anticipated individual, creative programming when you switched it on. This is a device which you *can't* program just by switching it on. Furthermore, crucially, every app has to be distributed via the App Store, and every App Store app has to be reviewed and approved by Apple itself, before it can go anywhere. Apple typically approves most apps, but this is a process of approval for publication – the very opposite of the now well-established open-publishing ethos of the internet and the World Wide Web. The approval process takes an unpredictable length of time, and apps can be rejected for reasons which are disputed. (The Wikipedia article on 'App Store' contains examples.) This, again, is a long way from the approach celebrated in the famous Apple TV ad, shown during the 1984 Super Bowl, where a colourful runner, representing creative individualism, is seen hurling a hammer through a giant screen showing a 'Big Brother' style dictator intoning judgements to rows of grey-faced drones.

It can be objected that Apple does not seek to stifle creativity – instead it has *supported* the distribution of thousands of diverse apps by creative amateurs as well as professionals, and enabled them to share their work for free, or for payment (in which case, Apple takes a cut of 30 per cent, and the creator gets 70 per cent). When apps are rejected, this is usually for reasons which are reasonably predictable as they are in breach of Apple bylaws about pornography and taste – although satirical political content has also been rejected.[31] Regardless of one's feelings about these decisions, the crucial point is that the company which produced the device *is making decisions* about which programs the machine can run and which ones it can't. And it's the same for the iPad, even though we might expect things to be different on the larger, more 'tablet computer'-like machine. This model of a multinational corporation as gatekeeper and protector, to whom content creators are subservient, is a control-freak reversal of the generative ideal of computers, the internet and the Web.

This argument reflects concern about a possible future direction of the internet, and computer technology, where people will not be free to do whatever they like any more. So it is not just about Apple – which perhaps just gets picked on as the more surprising case, since its old rival Microsoft is normally thought of as the more locked-down, less open corporation. But, for good measure, Zittrain also cites Microsoft's video game platform, the XBox, as another chilling example of locked technology which does not foster generativity.[32]

PRESERVING THE OPEN CREATIVE WEB

In terms of the World Wide Web, we should be worried about technologies or websites which promise to bring users 'the best of the Web' or 'specially selected websites'. This happens especially when businesses are developing ways of presenting the internet on television, phones, or other devices. Various companies are developing or producing things like this – even the non-commercial BBC is leading development of a service called YouView, which would enable viewers to watch video on demand from a range of sources, and also helpfully lead you to 'your favourite' websites such as Facebook and YouTube. None of those intentions are evil, but the subtle re-positioning of the internet as a thing which basically brings you some professionally produced channels, that you can enjoy watching, and which you can trust because they are produced by a handful of big companies, is the opposite of what online culture has generally been about.

When Tim Berners-Lee invented the World Wide Web, the idea was that any piece of online information could link to any other piece, simply and easily, anywhere in the world, enabling the maximum sharing of ideas and experiences. As he explained in his testimony to the US House of Representatives Subcommittee on Telecommunications and the Internet, in 2007:

> The success of the World Wide Web, itself built on the open Internet, has depended on three critical factors: (1) unlimited links from any part of the Web to any other; (2) open technical standards as the basis for continued growth of innovation applications; and (3) separation of network layers, enabling independent innovation for network transport, routing and information applications.[33]

The Web grew at a fantastic rate because this arrangement meant that there were no gatekeepers, and nobody had to ask anybody for permission to share what they had to say. Berners-Lee notes that today we are so familiar with these characteristics of the Web that we can easily overlook them as 'obvious' or 'just unimportant'. But of course they are not. They have enabled the Web to become the outstanding resource that it is – something which does indeed seem to be forgotten by those who seek to present a 'simpler', top-down, 'consumer'-oriented version.

Explaining the role of the World Wide Web Consortium (W3C), which he directs, and the general importance of open standards, Berners-Lee said:

> The special care we extend to the World Wide Web comes from a long tradition that democracies have of protecting their vital communications channels. We nurture and protect our information networks because they stand at the core of our economies, our democracies, and our cultural and personal lives. Of course, the imperative to assure the free flow of information has only grown given the global nature of the Internet and Web. As a Federal judge said in defense of freedom of expression on the Internet: 'The Internet is a far more speech-enhancing medium than print, the village green, or the mails. . . . The Internet may fairly be regarded as a never-ending worldwide conversation'.[34]

That is why the Web is – and must remain – a universal platform: 'independent of any specific hardware device, software platform, language, culture, or disability', as Berners-Lee says.[35]

The importance of this approach – where the internet works in a way which carries all content equally, and in the same way, regardless of what it is or who has made it – is

highlighted in the frequent spikes of concern about 'net neutrality' amongst the followers of technology news. As Mehan
Jayasuriya explained, in 2010:

> The internet was designed to respect the so-called 'end-
> to-end' principle, which places control at the ends of the
> network with users and ensures that all traffic is treated
> equally. The upholding of this principle has come to be
> known as 'net neutrality', which has been the status quo for
> as long as the internet has existed. But as the internet has
> grown to become the 21st century's most powerful engine
> for economic growth, internet service providers (ISPs), the
> middlemen of the internet, have begun greedily eyeing the
> web, hoping to wring additional fees out of users and con-
> tent providers alike by instituting a tiered system similar to
> that of pay TV.[36]

The lack of clear rules about whether ISPs have to uphold
the 'end-to-end' principle, in many countries, including
the US and UK, means that ISPs have started to make up
their own plans. The threatened 'tiered system' could mean
that content from the biggest companies, such as Google or
Disney, would load quickly, whilst material on the everyday
'public internet' would be put on a slower track. This kind
of proposal causes immense consternation amongst the nice
people who want to preserve a fair and equal internet, but
that doesn't mean it won't happen.

The attractiveness of the Web for many people is very
much to do with the fact that you can join the conversation
– whether at a light level (such as commenting on blogs, or
posting pictures on Flickr) or a deeper level (by creating
your own site, network, or service). It only remains a convi-
ial tool while these possibilities are obvious and centre-stage.
If the Web becomes a place where people are not typically

creative, where the anticipated mode of engagement is consumption rather than creativity, then it will have become an industrial tool, and its positive potential will be destroyed.

CONVIVIAL TOOLS EVERYWHERE

Of course, the World Wide Web is not 'the solution' to the problems and social needs outlined by Ivan Illich. Indeed, the idea that a combination of electronic hardware and software, applied on a global scale, could be the answer to our problems might seem laughable. But, of course, the Web is not just technology – most importantly, the Web is *people*. Diverse, interesting, creative people, sharing their ideas and pictures and information and stories.

Illich felt that human beings flourish through warm, supportive, personal friendship connections. The Web helps to create these, although when conducted *only* through a screen we might be concerned that this is not the warmest and most natural form of connection. But as we saw in chapter 4, the '"Why Don't You?" Web' is increasingly helping people to use online tools to make connections in real life. And of course, the Web isn't everything. As we saw in chapter 3, people create their own networks and experiences around the process of making things, because they like to see and to share the whole fruits of their own creativity, and to feel connected to other inventive people, and to feel part of meaningful, productive social processes which have a past and a future. This urge appears to be timeless and enduring, but we do need to encourage the conditions and tools that will help it to grow.

8

WEB 2.0 NOT ALL ROSY?

So far in this book we have generally seen Web 2.0 as a good thing. In this chapter we'll consider some of the more critical views. Some of them are relatively predictable, and seem to come from those who have not sought to engage with the culture, and have rather inflexible views about its obvious badness; but others, such as the knowledgeable critical argument made by Jaron Lanier, are more worrying.

First of all, let's recall the positive arguments for Web 2.0. This is not a definition or a list of the primary features of Web 2.0 – the kind of thing which appears briefly in chapter 1 – but rather the reasons why Web 2.0 services are especially helpful for people making and connecting:

- Services such as YouTube, WordPress, and Flickr provide users with easy-to-use platforms which enable them to place their creative work (such as videos, songs, writing, or photography) online.
- These services are typically free (or inexpensive) to use.

- Being part of a big, popular platform makes it easier for your work to be found by others.
- The commenting and community facilities enable others to engage with and respond to the content, and help to build relationships, and possibly collaborations, between creators.

Before Web 2.0, you could do most of these things online yourself, but it was often expensive or difficult. For instance, my own Theory.org.uk website aims to offer nicely presented text and images, which I've been able to do using simple tools since the mid-1990s, but most of the 'interaction' has been via email. I have never hosted video on my own site, because of the *Catch-22* problem that I'd want to drive people to watch it but then would be worried about the potential 'excess bandwidth' charges. (Instead, I put my videos on YouTube and link to them.) I've hosted other people's work on my site – but only when they've sent it to me and then I've manually added it. The database skills needed for a system where people can add their own content, or even just comments, are probably beyond me. (I've never tried to learn, but I assume it's rather difficult and/or time-consuming.)

Compared to all of that, the easy, accessible, sociable, and free Web 2.0 services seem like a wonderful phenomenon. How could anyone have a problem with them?

FREE PLATFORMS AS EXPLOITED LABOUR

Web 2.0 platforms give us a place to share our stuff, and discuss it with others, for free. But this situation can also be stated in rather less cheerful terms: Web 2.0 sites provide no content themselves, but instead become highly valued and (in some cases) profitable businesses off the back of the creativity of their users. In this view, the site owners are the lazy, greedy factory owners, whose wealth is built upon the hard labour of thousands of creative workers. These workers generate value, which the owners exploit by selling advertising opportunities, alongside their work, to other businesses.[1]

This does indeed sound like exploitation, and is true from a macro point of view. But from the point of view of individual users, it's quite different. On the whole they never hoped or expected to be able to make any financial gain from sharing their work – for them, that's not the point, and in most cases it would be unrealistic to expect any. Furthermore, it's a financial *advantage* that they don't have to pay to have their work hosted online.

Users are likely to recognize that sites such as YouTube, Flickr, and Facebook are able to exist because they are funded by advertising, and generally accept this as part of the deal. (In fact, up to now, at the time of writing, YouTube has not placed adverts next to much of the non-professional content – advertisers are wary of the unpredictable messages that their products might be promoted alongside – and Flickr doesn't seem to bother with adverts either. But *even if* there were adverts, of a not-too-intrusive variety, I think we can anticipate that users would understand that this is how it works: no adverts would generally mean no free sites.) I don't mean to support or celebrate advertising: it's not part of my vision of an ideal society. And I certainly don't agree with Chris Anderson's unlikely thesis, in his book *Free* – discussed further below – that a seemingly endless supply of advertising money means that more or less everything can become free.[2] But as the means by which, in a capitalist culture, companies are able to offer 'free' services to users, it's a system which people seem to think is OK.

The critical argument here can be put in different ways. The writer and consultant Nicholas Carr has said:

By putting the means of production into the hands of the masses but withholding from those same masses any ownership over the product of their work, Web 2.0 provides an incredibly efficient mechanism to harvest the economic value of the free labor provided by the very, very many and concentrate it into the hands of the very, very few.[3]

This formulation poses the problem rather well – although on a precise level it is somewhat flawed, as none of the well-known Web 2.0 services try to take ownership of work away from their creators; typically, the user keeps copyright and all other rights over their work, but provides the site with a licence to reproduce it.[4] And, as I've said, the 'free labour' which is 'harvested' is happily and voluntarily given by users who *want* to share their creative work. They have no thought for 'economic value' except, perhaps, for being glad that sharing their creative work online is not costing them money. So making them sound like slaves in a workhouse is a rhetorical device which doesn't, I think, line up with most people's own experience. After all, if they felt that they were being punished or exploited, they would simply do something else.

Toby Miller, a professor of Media and Cultural Studies at University of California Riverside, puts a similar case much more grandly:

The pride with which gullible 'MIT-like/lite' subscribers to digital capitalism and the technological sublime welcome the do-it-yourself elements to YouTube is part of the managerialist, neoliberal discourse that requires consumers to undertake more and more tasks for free or at their own cost.[5]

This argument seems to rest on the assumption that making media to share with others is a job of work – a 'task', as he calls it – which is onerous and tiresome. Miller's apparent anger that people would be 'required' to do this 'for free' only makes sense if your view of creative work is incredibly two-dimensional, so that you think that the 'work' of making a video to share with your friends is no different from the 'work' of coal mining or street cleaning. It makes sense in the old media model: for instance, if a commercial television station got me to work as a camera operator on a drama series, but refused to pay me, that would indeed seem unfair. But when applying these expectations to YouTube, I think Miller has made a category error. The creative social acts which we see the results of on YouTube are not the equivalent of work, which you would reasonably expect to get paid for. They are more like the act of putting together a photo album, to show to friends, or the act of recording some music that you have composed, so that you can replay it to a fellow enthusiast. If you asked your friend, or some third party, to pay you money for this experience, you would seem rather wacky. And if your friend informed you that your creative endeavours made you a 'gullible subscriber to the managerialist, neoliberal discourse' then you might be understandably puzzled.

Of course, it is indeed the case, as noted above, that sites such as YouTube do aim to make money by hosting content which the content creators do not get paid for; in that sense, insofar as those videos having an audience creates value, then YouTube does indeed 'pocket the lot'. (To be fair, we should note that creators of much-viewed videos can become YouTube Partners and participate in a revenue-sharing scheme; but this does not apply to most users.[6]) This 'exploitation' argument appears to make sense on the macro level, where we note that YouTube has copies of millions of videos and is (generally) keeping all the money it makes from showing them to eager viewers.

But if we switch back to the micro level again, each *individual* video has a very small value indeed. If YouTube has about 200 million videos in its library, and takes advertising revenue of US $240 million – as it did in 2009 – then the average video is worth $1.20, or about 80p in UK sterling, each year.[7] This is a rough calculation based on estimated figures, since Google does not publish separate accounts for YouTube. But in any case, it's going to be a very small amount. As a video-maker, I don't mind YouTube keeping my 80p. Indeed, video-hosting is an expensive business, and I'd happily *pay* YouTube at least 80p per video, each year, so it could be shared with my friends and whoever else wanted to watch it.

Furthermore, in real life – and I don't know if the economic reality is of relevance when debating Miller or not, but anyway – the actual cost to YouTube of hosting each video, and delivering it to users on demand, is almost $3 a year.[8] So the idea of YouTube stealing all that surplus value is just imaginary anyway, at the moment, since there simply isn't any.

In any case, I have here joined Miller in mistakenly treating everyday users' YouTube videos as economic objects. As I've already said, that's surely not the point. Sharing videos with friends, and interested others, on YouTube *really is* parallel to singing songs around the campfire in the evening, when the day's labour is done. Maybe my singing voice is beautiful and I could, if I wanted to, print tickets and ask the people around the fire to pay me a fee, but that would completely change the atmosphere and our sense of mutual understanding. Not every aspect of life has to be 'monetized' – even though there is usually someone, somewhere, trying to extract economic value from any activity.

(In the same article, Miller appears to say that the opportunity to share homemade videos with the millions of YouTube users is only the same as the claim that 'You are the star!' made by the host of the old TV show *Candid Camera*.[9] But, for very obvious reasons, these are really not the same thing at all. Are we really going to say that all the people who offer their handcrafted videos of information and entertainment on YouTube are just the same as the chumps trapped like zoo animals in an old prank show on television? Isn't that in any way insulting?)

GOOGLE KNOWS YOU INSIDE OUT

Critics argue that Web 2.0 services are actually built on a *double* exploitation. First of all, as discussed above, they thrive on the unpaid labour of content creators. Second, they 'exploit' the 'labour' of all site visitors, who generate valuable data about their interests and activities as they click around a site. Clearly, again, this is not the common sense understanding of 'labour', as almost no-one would think that watching a few YouTube videos and checking out some Facebook fan pages was the same thing as a hard day at work. Nevertheless, these activities produce data which, in aggregate, are of value to marketers, who want to know what people are interested in, and what interests are linked to other interests, so that they can ever-more precisely target consumers with relevant messages designed to increase sales.

Mark Andrejevic, for instance – whom we met briefly in chapter 4 – notes that this fits Marx's understanding of exploitation: 'forced, surplus and unpaid labour, the product of which is not under the producers' control'.[10] Technically he's right, of course: marketers can generate financial value from the trail of data that is produced as we wander around websites. But this only really makes sense when you've got data about millions of users; on the individual level, my web-browsing activity is worth almost nothing.

The argument about Web 2.0 services storing vast amounts of data about our online activities works much better as an objection based on ethics, rather than economics. And to be fair, Andrejevic's outrage seems to be based in a general sense of injustice which goes beyond the economic analysis:

> The offer of control over productive activity is redoubled online as a form of exploitation – except in this case, the captured product is rendered in commodity form: that of the data captured by marketers. . . . Palpable evidence of exploitation in this instance takes the form . . . of alienation: the ability to create, view and share user-created [material] is accompanied by the extraction of user-generated data. This data is captured in order to be returned to its producers in the form of an external influence: the congealed result of their own activity used to channel their behaviour and induce their desires.[11]

By turning data about you – data which you have produced, by wandering around the Web – into a changed online experience, which aims to lead you via ads and links to other things that you might like, the interactive economy aims for 'increasingly accelerated consumption', Andrejevic says.[12] It gives you the freedom to communicate, and the opportunity to wallow in a mirrored pit of your own preferences, all in one go.

More generally, too, the rise of online surveillance can obviously be considered a worrying trend: as we do more and more everyday activities online, including all kinds of personal messaging on services such as Facebook and Google Mail, as well as commenting, searching, navigating, and shopping, the trail of information we leave about our 'private' lives and our interests is immense. And, even though they come in enormous quantities, these data *are actually being stored*, because companies find them valuable now or are working out ways to make them valuable in the future. Governments are also eager for records to be kept of all emails sent and all websites visited, for 'security' purposes.[13]

THE CRITICAL CONDITION

There are real issues to be concerned about with Web 2.0, then. But these important debates can be undermined by the black-and-white worldview of the academics who write about these matters, who wear their single-mindedly 'critical' stance as a badge of honour. People who say descriptive or positive things about aspects of Web 2.0 are dismissed as naïve optimists, and – as I have found myself – if you try to encourage some curiosity about the *possibilities* of shareable digital media you are summarily accused of being a 'technological determinist' – the worst of all things to be.[14] But of course, thinking about how certain kinds of technology might be used is not 'determinism' of any sort.

These critics are rightly concerned about the desire of big business to own and control everything – I worry about that too – but that shouldn't stop us from thinking about the more positive potential of these technologies as well. The approach of these critics is not just pessimistic about the intentions of corporations, but takes an especially dim view of ordinary people, who are assumed to have little creative capacity of their own and are liable to fall for whatever trick the media barons might push at them. There is a kindly concern for what people might have *done to* them, but no interest in what people might be able to *do for* themselves. So this narrow 'critical' literature could get rather frustrating.

Then along came Jaron Lanier.

JARON LANIER: CREATIVITY UNBOUND

Jaron Lanier was one of the original digital pioneers, and led the field in virtual reality – a term which he is said to have coined – in the 1980s. He is a musician and philosopher, as well as being a computer scientist, and has created all kinds of things from early computer games to cutting-edge medical simulations, and advanced internet applications. In other words, he *really knows what he's talking about*. And you would expect him to be a kind of leading-edge techno-enthusiast. The fact that he isn't, and that he's worried about a particular way in which the Web has developed, means he's instantly intriguing.

In 2010, Lanier set out his concerns about the Web – in particular the idea of Web 2.0 – and what this means for online creativity and self-expression, in a book entitled *You Are Not a Gadget*, which we will consider here.[15]

TEMPLATE IDENTITIES

The standard positive view of Web 2.0 social network sites such as Facebook is that they have made it much easier for people to express themselves online, and to communicate aspects of their identities. That was certainly my view, before I read *You Are Not a Gadget*. Explaining the benefits of such easy-to-use sites to my students, I would recall the early days of the Web, in the 1990s, when individuals would use basic tools such as Microsoft Notepad to make their 'personal homepages'. These handcrafted websites were often messy, informal, and self-indulgent. As I mentioned in chapter 4, that's certainly how I started: as a rather late early-adopter, in 1997, I learnt how to make an HTML page with Notepad, and lay it out using tables, mostly by looking at the source code of other people's pages. (Eventually I got a book, of the *HTML for Dummies* variety.) This was quite laborious, although at the time it was a geeky challenge, and contributing to the internet – contributing to the *actual internet*, with your stuff visible to people *around the world* – seemed wildly unusual and rewarding.

Since those days – well, actually, *during* those days – personal homepages became derided as places where friendless nutters would write poems about their cats, or post pictures of their favourite biscuits. They came to be seen as rather pointless, narcissistic sites, which in any case were hard to find and didn't help people to link with friends except when they explicitly added links to each other's homepages. And because making graphics yourself was not the easiest thing in the world, homepages were often decorated with random images swept up from around the Web, a mix of garish colours, corny animations, and – horror of horrors! – blinking 'under construction' messages.

So, fast-forward a decade and compare this with Facebook, where almost any moderately literate internet user can create a profile. This is so easy to do, and results in a nice neat set of boxes of pictures and information – it's clearly an improvement. But, Lanier argues, it's not. He puts individual creativity, and self-expression, above all else – and therefore concludes, with a surprising but clear logic, that the diverse, handcrafted personal homepages of the 1990s were *much* more preferable than the formulaic, template-driven expression of identity pushed by Facebook. It doesn't matter if they were messy, or had an unexpected tone of voice, or lacked a uniform mode of navigation – on the contrary, those are the things that made them *unique* and *special*.

Now, you might object that templates are simply *help-ful*. Design templates help users to present what they want to express clearly, avoiding mess or usability problems, and helping them to make their material look presentable without having to study the nuances of graphic design. Blogging tools used by writers, such as Wordpress, and sites where musicians can share their work, such as Bandcamp, help their users to present the fruits of their creativity in a clear, straightforward, and shareable way, by offering a choice of templates (which can be customized to some extent). Whereas those 1990s personal homepages often looked awful, and could be difficult to use, and even the flexibility of MySpace was frequently abused by people who just seemed to want to make a mess. But remember that Lanier is concerned about how individual *identity* is expressed online. We should always be willing to spend a bit of time making a characterful and personal representation of our identity, he implies – we can't allow our very *selves* to be reduced to a template.

This is one of Lanier's key concerns: that digital systems reduce everything to the level of simple bits of information, so that they can be processed. Sometimes, this is fine and necessary: for instance, when we file a tax return, we reduce our working activity to a set of numbers in a database; but everybody knows the difference between real life and the numbers in a tax return. However, he says,

> the order is reversed when you perform the same kind of self-reduction in order to create a profile on a social networking site. You fill in the data: profession, marital status, and residence. But in this case digital reduction becomes a causal element, mediating contact between new friends. That is new. It used to be that government was famous for being impersonal, but in a postpersonal world, that will no longer be a distinction.[16]

When we reduce our humanity to fit in with the requirements of a machine (or a database, or a piece of software), Lanier warns, we lose something of ourselves.

To illustrate the point, he tells the story of how European missionaries preserved some aspects of indigenous musical cultures, but 'de-alienated' them – keeping the more familiar sounds, which they would have been most comfortable with, but removing the strange and alien elements that would be necessary for the most rich and meaningful experience to be preserved. He goes on to say:

> Something like missionary reductionism has happened to the internet with the rise of Web 2.0. The strangeness is being leached away by the mush-making process. Individual web pages as they first appeared in the early 1990s had the flavor of personhood. MySpace preserved some of that flavor, though a process of regularized formatting had begun. Facebook went further, organizing people into multiple-choice identities, while Wikipedia seeks to erase point of view entirely.[17]

The uniform nature of Facebook profiles keeps things simple and predictable; but, Lanier reminds us, human beings are worth cherishing because of their rich, distinctive, individual natures, not because they are simple and predictable. 'We shouldn't seek to make the pack mentality as efficient as possible', he writes. 'We should instead seek to inspire the phenomenon of individual intelligence.'[18] These quotes lead us to another Lanier theme, that Web 2.0 reduces individual creativity to a general 'mush'.

INDIVIDUAL CREATIVITY VERSUS THE 'HIVE MIND'

The spirit of Web 2.0, as we have seen earlier in this book, is associated with the exciting promise of collaboration: people coming together, online, to do creative things that otherwise would have been difficult or impossible to organize. But Jaron Lanier argues that interesting works of creativity aren't normally produced by lots of people throwing stuff into a big pot and giving it a stir. That's the 'mush-making process' mentioned in the quote above, where the individual voice is diluted or silenced in the name of collaboration.

He's got a point, hasn't he? There's a reason why the phrase 'designed by committee' is never meant as a compliment. Wikipedia is the best example of a successful online collaboration that we've got, and it works because everyone basically understands that an encyclopaedia is meant to be reasonably bland and descriptive. In the collaborative process of making Wikipedia, all the rough edges are shorn off, and that's a good thing because an encyclopaedia isn't meant to be a creative form of individual expression anyway. Wikipedia 'seeks to erase point of view entirely', as Lanier put it above – but that's OK when you're making an encyclopaedia.

For anything more artistic, creative, or expressive, though, if you're inviting the whole world in to contribute, the 'mush-making process' is obviously a problem. YouTube and Flickr work because they enable users around the world to come together to make a site full of interesting videos, or photos, but each unit of collaboration is quite substantial – by which I mean, you don't generally collaborate on the *content* of each YouTube video, or Flickr image, which are individually prepared as self-contained things before they are uploaded to the site; the collaboration is more to do with adding these building-blocks together to make an interesting collection, and then enhancing the experience of fellow users through comments, ratings, and responses. On Wikipedia, of course, the unit of collaboration is much more fine-grained: people aren't just adding the building-blocks (such as whole articles about a topic), they are fiddling with, debating, and sometimes fighting over every little detail of each block (for instance, adding punctuation, or a reference, or removing a word to change the tone of a sentence, *within* individual articles).

Lanier doesn't seem to mind Wikipedia too much: he admits that it's a convenient starting-point, but is concerned that it may begin to acquire a status as 'the overarching, primary text of the human experience'.[19] He also argues that to get a good understanding of a topic, we should look beyond the high-ranking Wikipedia search result to find information 'in more contextualised forms, with more visibility for the authors and with a greater sense of style and presence'.[20] This is a fair point, but since Wikipedia only aspires to be a neutral encyclopaedia, and does not insist that we forsake all other sources – indeed, on the contrary, it only seems convinced that statements are valid when they are accompanied by references to other sources – then Wikipedia's status as an amazing and generally useful massive collaborative project remains intact.

If we leave encyclopaedias aside, though, Lanier's point is powerful. Great works of art, or great scientific ideas, are not *usually* produced through an entirely open and free-for-all method of collaboration. That's not to say that collaboration doesn't work: collaboration between smallish groups of people focused on a task can produce wonderful things – scientific innovations, music recordings, political strategies, or whatever – which are substantially greater than what the individuals involved might have produced if working separately. But here we're not talking about that, we're talking about the notion of online 'collaboration' which consists of a drizzle of thousands of fragmentary contributions coming in from all over the place.

As we saw in chapter 1, writers such as Clay Shirky and Charles Leadbeater assume that this model, the Wikipedia model, might be a prototype for other diverse kinds of online collaboration. And so it might turn out to be, in some cases. One instance might be the astronomy research site Galaxy Zoo (www.galaxyzoo.org), which makes use of the intelligent perceptions of human amateur star-gazers around the world, asking them to place galaxies into different classifications. This is a job which humans can do much better than computers, and has been highly successful. As one of the research papers based on the resulting data says: 'The public response to the launch of Galaxy Zoo in July 2007 was overwhelming, achieving over 36 million classifications within a few months and results that agree exceptionally well with those of professional astronomers.'[21] Since then, the project has developed into new phases with more complex goals, again using the distributed brainpower of everyday volunteers (or 'citizen scientists') to achieve results which would take professional scientists far longer to produce. So this example shows people collaborating online to do something that is scientifically valuable. But, without wanting to say anything negative about the project, these people are clearly doing the 'grunt work' of astronomy – nobody would claim they were producing original art or scientific ideas. And we should note that this is not *exactly* collaboration – it's the aggregation of millions of individual contributions.

Wikipedia still seems to stand alone as a great example of massive online collaboration which has really worked. It has been effective for an encyclopaedia, because an encyclopaedia is the classic kind of project to be worked on in this way, with millions of people all contributing their bit of knowledge to make up a great whole. Their work is all in little bits, but that's fine because an encyclopaedia is something you only look at in discrete chunks, and it's not intended to be a work of imagination, or to take you on an emotional journey.

If the product being worked on was a movie script, or a symphony, you can imagine that the 'mush' problem – the 'designed by committee' problem – would kick in very quickly. As mentioned above, we must acknowledge that when you have a smallish number of people who share a creative vision, they can collaborate to produce brilliant things: the best American TV dramas and comedies are produced in this way, and numerous musicians will testify that great, unanticipated musical works arise when their band works together to make something new. But conversely, every movie-goer knows the sinking feeling you get when the credited writers number more than the fingers on your hand. It's usually the sign of a patchy, inconsistent movie which is more like a set of sketches than a coherent narrative. If you doubt this claim, I could sit you down to watch *Dance Flick* (six writers) or *Scary Movie 2* (seven), although the United Nations may have classed this as a form of torture. So what hope for a script authored by 1,000 eager volunteers?

This is not an elitist point. If each of the 1,000 volunteers wrote their own, personal script, telling a story that was especially meaningful for them, we could cherish every one. Or they might like to work with one or two other people whose ideas complement their own, with fruitful results. We are strongly in favour of everyday creativity, and meaningful, focused collaborations. But it may not be sensible to support the exaggerated idea of online collaboration which fails to recognize that in art and design, distinctive individual voices may be more engaging than a combined swamp of ideas. Jaron Lanier thinks that the technologists have simply got carried away:

> A fashionable idea in technical circles is that quantity not only turns into quality at some extreme of scale, but also does so according to principles we already understand.[22]

But he says this is nonsense. Computer scientists, Lanier suggests, have failed to be sufficiently modest, both about their knowledge and their ambitions, and have got carried away with the dream of the 'hive mind' or 'noosphere', which is a kind of global superintelligence which they believe will emerge, distinct from any individual: the sum of all the human brains connected through the internet.[23] The ultimate version of this idea sees humans leaving their earthly bodies and having their consciousness uploaded to a networked computer-based superconsciousness – known by believers as 'the Singularity' – which then, possibly, takes over the planet.[24] This seems like pretty far-out stuff, although Ray Kurzweil's breathless, bonkers book on the subject, *The Singularity Is Near*, was a bestseller in 2005 and is heartily recommended by Bill Gates on the cover.[25] I don't know if all computer scientists really dream of merging into an unworldly superconsciousness, or if this is just about some Californian millionaires wanting to live forever, but we don't need to worry about that here.

At a more pragmatic and earthly level, relevant today, we have the question of whether linking everybody together produces things that are more valuable than the fruits of individual creativity, or the creativity that can arise in small groups or familiar communities. Lanier says:

> At any rate, there is no evidence that quantity becomes quality in matters of human expression or achievement. What matters instead, I believe, is a sense of focus, a mind in effective concentration, and an adventurous individual imagination that is distinct from the crowd.[26]

You may recognize that this argument echoes John Ruskin's 'The Nature of Gothic', and Richard Sennett's *The Craftsman*. And if we accept this point, it helps us to refine what is most important about Web 2.0. What we seem to have learnt here is that: (a) the view that Web 2.0 tools enable people to easily make and share creative things is strong, but (b) the view that *mass* collaboration will bring about untold artistic and creative riches may be weak. But actually – to refine our findings further – this view is only weak if you expect collaboration to be at the most fine-grained level, where participants are meant to craft a cultural product by sticking their spoon into a cooking-pot which has another million spoons in it (the Wikipedia model). If you are happy with a kind of mass collaboration where people are working together to create an interesting landscape by placing their creative items upon it (the YouTube model), then you're fine.

And this perhaps shows that Jaron Lanier can afford to be less anxious about the Web 2.0 hype about collaboration, because here is a version of collaboration which is about creative individuals assembling a kind of library of brilliant things – which he would probably like – and is not about creative individuals having to mush together all their ideas, individuality, and self-expression, which he definitely wouldn't like.

To be fair to the 'hive mind enthusiasts', such as Clay Shirky and Charles Leadbeater, it is also worth noting that the types of collaboration that they are excited about are not necessarily ones intended to produce instances of human creativity and self-expression such as poetry, movie scripts, or symphonies. Their intentions are usually much more pragmatic. For instance, Shirky's book *Here Comes Everybody* is not subtitled *Blending Our Brains to Make Great Art*. Rather, the subtitle is *The Power of Organizing Without Organizations*.[27] The focus is on people organizing themselves to do things without any centralized leadership or hierarchies. The first chapter is entitled 'It Takes a Village to Find a Phone', and opens with an example which shows how the use of social networking tools enabled someone in New York City to get their stolen phone back. The intended goal is thoroughly practical, not artistic.

Other examples are about the sifting and sorting of information. Shirky notes that rather than media content having to be selected by gatekeepers, such as magazine editors, in anticipation of readers' interests, the Web's 'publish, then filter' model – as mentioned in chapter 2 – means that people can publish whatever they like online, and then networks of enthusiasts identify and share material that is of interest within like-minded communities. The 'hive mind' here has not taken over individual self-expression and creativity, it is just helping people to find stuff that they might like, more efficiently.

And the case of Wikipedia – perhaps the ultimate example of the 'hive mind' at work, for now – is presented as a solution to the *organizational* problem of putting together an encyclopaedia. This is perfectly reasonable, as putting together an encyclopaedia is a huge organizational and administrative challenge, as any editor of reference books will tell you. If Shirky discussed the writing of *War and Peace* as an organizational problem best solved by a collective, you might think it was strange, because the job of writing a haunting epic novel is much more than just a matter of making sure there are 400 factually reliable words on every page. But he doesn't. Similarly, Charles Leadbeater's discussion of *We Think* works well when focused on the ways in which the Web enables people to put elements together, without any need for 'top down' organization, to make valuable new interactive collections of information and resources.[28] Leadbeater does seem to have a dream of high-quality mush – full collaborations at a fine-grained level – but his limited number of examples suggest that this would be for scientific and information applications, not for artistic communication or self-expression. So, again, the claims and aspirations for Web 2.0 are more modest than Lanier seems to fear.

PAYING THE CREATIVES

A further strand of Jaron Lanier's critique sees 'Web 2.0' as the name given to an ideology which, for businesspeople, means that online services can be funded by advertising, or other ways to shield the consumer from the direct cost, and for consumers means that everything should be 'free'. The consumer point of view is a combination of the old hacker belief that 'information wants to be free', and the spirit of the file-sharing music downloaders in the early 2000s, who argued that the music industry was a vast, greedy profit-machine which deserved a bit of Robin Hood-style redistribution.

The business point of view is represented by Chris Anderson's 2009 book, *Free: The Future of a Radical Price*, which I've mentioned in passing above, and which I'll say a little more about here. Let's start with a bit of background. In 2006, Chris Anderson published *The Long Tail*, an intelligent and readable 'big idea' book, which pointed out that the internet made available a 'long tail' of items – such as music, films, and books – which are not currently popular, and therefore not considered to be worth stocking in a shop or library with limited shelf space.[29] Although these things are not in great demand, he pointed out, there will always be someone *somewhere* who wants one, and the number of such items that can be sold on any one day is roughly the same as the number of current 'hit' products likely to be sold on the same day. So a service like iTunes or Amazon can shift just as many almost forgotten, unloved, back-catalogue items as it sells 'Top 10' hits, as it is not limited by high-street shelf space. Whilst this latter point made *The Long Tail* a successful business book, it was also good generally on how minority or niche interests could find a home on the Web, and full of interesting examples. Chris Anderson is also a keen 'maker' – I happened to mention his YouTube video about a radio-controlled blimp in chapter 4. So his follow-up book, *Free*, was quite keenly anticipated. Naïve readers, such as myself, without really thinking about it too much, imagined that it might show us ways in which all kinds of things which we had previously, very tiresomely, had to pay for, could suddenly become free.

But any commercial item worth having has to be paid for somewhere along the way – and, as it turned out, Chris Anderson didn't have an alternative to that. The book is littered with eye-catching boxes with headings such as 'How can a car be free?', 'How can a textbook be free?', and 'How can air travel be free?' But the answers are either things you've come across before, or – and perhaps this is worse – are things that are more *annoying* than anything you've ever come across before. So, for instance, a 'car can be free' on a familiar system modelled on mobile phone subscriptions, where you get the hardware 'free' at the start but pay a monthly subscription for many months, which at some point covers the cost of the device.[30] It's not exactly free, then, for the old-fashioned reason that you're actually paying for it.

Air travel could be 'free', Anderson suggests, with a slightly more radical version of the Ryanair model, where the price of the ticket is very low, but there are numerous additional costs for such high-living luxuries as taking luggage, drinking water, or going to the toilet; supplemented by income from intrusive and constant advertising and gambling opportunities.[31] So, in a curious double-whammy, you can spoil the environment by travelling within a contained environment which is already maximally horrible itself.

The 'free textbook' example is rather better, since it suggests a model where the textbook *really is* given away free online, but the company makes money by selling handy chunks of it – in the form of easily printable PDF chapters, MP3 audio chapters, and even flash cards – to students who want a quick fix of the material rather than dealing with a relatively unwieldy online book.

None of these examples is terribly noble, then. The 'free car' offer simply hides the hardware cost within a monthly subscription, and the flight example replaces a straightforward ticket cost with a range of half-hidden 'additional' fees, plus obnoxious ads and gambling promotions. And the textbook example seems to suggest that the genuinely free knowledge offered online should be presented in an inconvenient manner, so that people who want a better experience can be enticed to pay for a more user-friendly version.

Meanwhile, the consumer idea of online Robin Hoodery – why should we poor peasants have to give money to your bloated, prosperous music industry? – collapsed on the hurdle of regular logic, when it turned out that those greedy record companies ceased to be able to support anybody, if nobody was putting money into the system. Today there is a sort-of 'free' model around musicians, which suggests they can still make money from gigs and merchandise, whilst giving music away for nothing (or, at least, not expecting it to be their main source of income). This has indeed, apparently, proved to be a solution for certain artists.[32] But this seems to be only a very small number of them, who were already famous from the old order, or who had a rare lucky break.[33] Furthermore, like the other 'free' examples, it seems a rather tawdry solution – why can't a talented musician make a reasonable living from recorded music? Who decided that music recordings had the status of air, which only a greedy and selfish monster would seek to charge money for, whilst an honourable musician's income should more properly be raised via an unhealthy and environmentally damaging journey around the world's stadiums, selling £50 tickets and £25 T-shirts, with an income top-up via corporate sponsorship?

Let's recap at this point, as things can be a little confusing in this new world. There are the people who are saying that stuff online should be freely given away to the citizens – so they must be the anti-capitalists, the people's heroes, right? And there are those who say that it's only reasonable to charge people money for the fruits of creative labour – and so, being money-chargers, they must be the capitalists, yes? But actually, it's not like that, and it's *almost* the other way round.

Jaron Lanier, a musician himself, is understandably distressed that many musicians cannot make a living by selling music any more. But he doesn't weep for the music *industry*. He's not sad that music-biz executives cannot throw wild parties on private jets any longer. Instead, he has a characteristically gentle, humanistic view, that creative people have a right to be paid for their work – living as we do in this kind of society, where people can usually derive an income from the things that they produce. It's not about sticking up for capitalism, however. On the contrary, he is angry that all the money in the system has gone to content aggregators and advertising distributors: faceless companies which are the opposite of individual creative people.

The solution, he suggests, would be an easy-to-use, widely accepted micropayments system, in which Web users would pay a little bit of money when they wanted to access a video, song, article, knitting pattern, or whatever, and the money would go directly to the creator of the item. This is not a new idea, and it's just the kind of thing that the internet should make possible. (There *are* sites that can offer this kind of facility, but a common, simple micropayment system isn't built into the everyday Web.) We might wonder, then, why early internet pioneers did not embed and popularize a system to do this. The answer, in a sense, is heartwarming, in that the universe of internet users has turned out to be much more creative than anticipated. According to Lanier, in the 1980s, the dominant view was that a system rewarding individual contributions would be elitist, since the makers of creative or expressive material would only ever be a small minority. Today, we know that the interest and capacity for creative expression is widespread, but now it's too late, and the income derived from the dissemination of this material is going to the aggregators and advertising brokers (primarily Google).

To be fair, we should note that this part of Lanier's complaint is similar to that made by Mark Andrejevic and Toby Miller, whom I found, earlier in this chapter, to be less convincing and somewhat exasperating. So why am I happy to agree with Lanier, making much the same point? The difference may lie in their tone and spirit (which is a bit embarrassing to admit to, since it's not a wholly rational way to respond to arguments). Toby Miller, in particular, seemed to have no sympathy for everyday people making and sharing creative material on Web 2.0 services – they were like the 'gullible' suckers queuing up to be on *Candid Camera*, he said. Jaron Lanier, however, understands them, is one of them, and is on their side. Rather than 'critical' posturing, he's genuinely worried about our current situation and wants to work towards fixing it.

On the micropayments solution, Lanier says:

> Someday I hope there will be a genuinely universal system along [these lines]. I believe most people would embrace a social contract in which bits have value instead of being free. Everyone would have easy access to everyone else's creative bits at reasonable prices – and everyone would get paid for

their bits. This arrangement would celebrate personhood in full, because personal expression would be valued.[34]

Such a system, he explains, might bring a substantial short-term reward to the maker of an amusing YouTube video, but also, over time, might bring a decent amount of income to a writer or programmer whose work was available online. This would be a marketplace, not so much in the modern abstract economic sense, but more like the direct (and possibly social) exchange found in a traditional village market. The idea may sound nostalgic, but the internet could make it work on a global scale.

WEB 2.0 FUTURE:
HUMAN, CREATIVE, SUSTAINABLE?

To sum up, then: Jaron Lanier reminds us of the *human* dimension, and the risks, of dealing with computer-based systems. The idea that data, 'information', can take on a life of its own, and perhaps become a 'hive mind' greater than the sum of its parts, might seem appealing, and can make sense for the sifting of information or the organization of tasks. If taken into the sphere of more creative thought or expression, however, it is more likely a new and terrible form of alienation. 'Information' is nothing until processed by human minds, where *meaning* is created. And an over-enthusiasm for combining and aggregating things in digital systems is more likely to create a 'mush' than it is to create something distinctive and amazing – because you need *people* to work on and develop the ideas of others, in the delicate art of creating and making meaningful things.

Lanier can seem to be opposed to everything Web 2.0, but actually he's perfectly happy with Web 2.0 tools which allow expression of the individual voice. The systems or services he doesn't like are those which try to reduce the person to the level of the machine, or self-identity to the fields in a database; or which force us to simplify our self-expression, or want to 'mush' it together with the work of others at the cost of distinctiveness and individuality.

I would agree with that. One of the things this discussion has revealed is that 'Web 2.0' is quite a broad term which takes in a number of things, from a list of particular online services to a number of ideologies – some of which are rather vague. This doesn't mean that 'Web 2.0' is meaningless – just that we have to be clear what we're talking about.

Lanier is right that the special, valuable, distinctive thing about the Web is that it enables the sharing of diverse, individual voices and their creative offshoots. ('Individual' doesn't have to mean one person, of course – it can also mean the distinctive work of a group of people who operate as a unit.) Before Web 2.0, there was perhaps more individuality and worthwhile 'strangeness' online, but the difficulties of setting up an online presence meant that many people did not avail themselves of this self-expressive opportunity, and the world of separated sites was rather individualistic. Web 2.0 has brought us easy-to-use tools which mean that people can place their creative work on collective sites, and can group, rate, and comment on other people's items, helping other like-minded users to find other things that they might be interested in.

To some extent, this may be accompanied by an ideology which seeks to mush everything together, at the cost of distinctive individual voices, or may try to reduce individuality through the use of templates and other simplified ways of representing the self. But these are things which we can guard against, and insofar as they don't add value, they are unlikely to be widely welcomed anyway. Nobody prefers bland and boring 'mush' content to more interesting content: on this point, at least, faceless corporations agree with zingy individuals – if only because they're more likely to make money from it.

Nevertheless, the rise of the money-makers is the most worrying aspect of Web 2.0. The 'collective allotment' of Web 2.0 space – as I described it rather optimistically in chapter 1 – is not collectively *owned*. Instead – to repeat the observation made earlier in this chapter – you license your material to a giant media company such as Google or Yahoo, who present it in a manner over which you have little control, and who can slap unpredictable adverts alongside or even on top of your carefully made content. This is far from being a perfect solution. (There is also a parallel problem on a technical level, as certain applications which are widely used on the Web, such as Adobe Flash, are proprietary, so their free use cannot be guaranteed, and users cannot modify or develop these tools.[35])

In this case, funnily enough, we can again turn to Wikipedia for an alternative model – not in terms of how the content is produced, but in terms of how the service is funded. Wikipedia carries no advertising and exists as a 'public service' kind of offering run by the Wikimedia Foundation, a non-profit charitable organization, which survives on donations and grants. Answerable to its board of trustees, but not to any shareholders, it is able to pursue wholesome goals:

> The mission of the Wikimedia Foundation is to empower and engage people around the world to collect and develop educational content under a free license or in the public domain, and to disseminate it effectively and globally.[36]

On its website, the Foundation explains that it pursues its mission in four key ways:

- The Wikimedia Foundation owns the more than 300 servers used to run our projects, along with all the associated domain names and trademarks. It keeps the projects free of charge and free of advertising.
- We support strategic software development work on the MediaWiki software and associated tools which allow more people to participate, or allow the existing volunteer community to work more effectively. This includes tools specifically related to quality assurance.
- We develop learning resources, support workshops and strive to think intelligently about other ways to bring in new contributors, and to grow Wikimedia as an international movement for free knowledge.
- We try to bring the educational content from Wikimedia's projects to people in as many forms as possible. In particular, we want to help disadvantaged communities with limited connectivity to access free educational content, and to contribute to it.[37]

Some of these attractive goals are also claimed by profit-making companies, of course – Google, for instance, presents a corporate philosophy online which also emphasizes the broad and international sharing of information ('our mission is to facilitate access to information for the entire world and in every language'), the 'democracy' of their search algorithm, and the power of knowledge, aiming 'to bring all the world's information to people seeking answers'.[38] But the Wikimedia Foundation is able to make much more convincing claims regarding its mission to do these good works without charging for access and without including intrusive advertising – or any other kind of ads or sponsorship.

So could we have something like YouTube (not *actually* YouTube, but something offering the same kind of services) offered in the same 'public service' kind of way?

It's certainly possible – in the sense that anything is possible, and helped by the fact that Wikipedia itself would seem to be a pipe dream, if not for the fact that it actually happened and really exists. But I think there are two main reasons why a public service user-generated encyclopaedia is more likely to exist than a public service user-generated video site, unfortunately. (I mean unfortunate that the very good public service encyclopaedia is unlikely to be joined, any time soon, by a very good public service video platform.)

The first is cost. In the second half of 2009, the Wikimedia Foundation incurred costs of US $3.9 million, so over a year at that rate, running Wikipedia (and a number of other Wikimedia services) cost less than US $8 million – and that includes all salaries, office and operating costs, as well as servers and bandwidth.[39] This figure is relatively low, as Wikipedia is mostly serving millions of pages of text, which are small files. As we saw above, all of YouTube's bandwidth-hungry videos mean that it is far more expensive to run, with operating costs estimated at being somewhere between US $400 and 700 million a year (in 2009).[40] Whilst YouTube currently operates at a loss, Wikipedia is financially healthy. In the second half of 2009, the Wikimedia Foundation had income of US $10.6 million, more than two and a half times its costs.[41] But if it had to serve 2 billion videos a day, as YouTube does, it would probably be bankrupt within a week.

The second reason why I would guess that a public service encyclopaedia is in a stronger position than a public service video site is 'worthiness'. The Wikimedia Foundation has benefited from hundreds of thousands of smallish donations from everyday users,[42] as well as from major grant-making bodies such as the Ford Foundation, because Wikipedia seems so rare, valuable, and worthwhile. A video-sharing site which was basically YouTube without ads (and probably, for some time, with less recognition and popularity), might not seem such a distinctive and admirable proposition.

It is appealing to think that a government, or set of governments, might see the civic advantage in establishing a publicly funded video-sharing site, where creative audio-visual work could be developed and shared in an online space free of advertising and commercial concerns. Running a public service version of YouTube for, say, US $500 million (£330 million) isn't even *that* much – it's less than 8 per cent of the operating costs of the BBC, for instance.[43] But a publicly funded version of something that already exists commercially is, to say the least, unlikely – especially in the present economic climate.

A different solution to these problems would be if a site like YouTube ran without advertising, but charged the content creators small, fixed amounts of money for each item uploaded. Personally, I would be happy to pay, say, £3 (that's around US $4.50) for each video I uploaded to a YouTube-like site. Isolated examples of this kind of model may exist at the moment, but it would be nice if they were more popular, central community hubs, like YouTube is.[44] On the one hand, users who have come to expect that all online services should be free may be reluctant to embrace this model. On the other hand, as Jaron Lanier would suggest, quality content, priced fairly, might be something of value and therefore worth paying for.

To conclude this discussion, then: at the moment, as I've said, the ads on a site like YouTube seem to be a reasonable 'price to pay' for such a broad and effective platform. But this may change, and as time goes on, it may become evident that such a service cannot survive financially, or cannot do so without making the advertising more intrusive – which may, in turn, affect not only the site's attractiveness, but also its popularity. So the future of pleasant free sites for the sharing of creative content is not assured, and we may need alternatives, supported by public funding, charities and foundations, individual payments, or some combination of these.

9

CONCLUSION

In this concluding chapter I will begin by summarizing and pulling together key arguments from the book. This starts with a section about our philosophical heroes, John Ruskin and William Morris, as I want to reiterate their core points and connect them with today's issues. Then everything else is boiled down into a set of five key principles, namely:

1. A new understanding of creativity as process, emotion, and presence
2. The drive to make and share
3. Happiness through creativity and community
4. A middle layer of creativity as social glue
5. Making your mark, and making the world your own.

I will outline each of these, and then discuss the political connotations of the 'making is connecting' thesis. Finally, I will describe some 'imagined futures', where we will look at the potential implications of this book's arguments in the areas of media, education, work, and politics and the environment.

THE LESSONS OF RUSKIN AND MORRIS

We started the book with a discussion of the ideas about everyday creativity suggested by the Victorian social critics John Ruskin and William Morris. These arguments, after 150 years, remain extremely powerful and relevant. We saw that making things is part of the process of thinking about things. Making leads to pleasures and understandings, gained *within* the process of making itself, which otherwise would not be achieved.

We also saw how amateur craft, and what I call everyday creativity, has been consistently derided over two centuries. The manufacture of everyday objects, and the media of entertainment and information, has become professionalized, and it is in the interests of those companies and professionals to run down the work of amateurs (although they do not *always* do so).[1] Meanwhile, 'art' itself has also become a professional field of experts and elites, who carefully police the borders of their practice. A significant part of the joy of craft, and online creativity, is of course that it does *not* rely on hierarchies of experts and elites to be validated, and does not depend on editors and gatekeepers for its circulation.

Ruskin made the excellent point that roughly made and non-professional things embody a kind of celebration of humanity's imperfections – the very fact that we are *not* machines. The collaborative mish-mash that characterizes many Web 2.0 services is a heightened version of this. Ruskin argued that human creativity must be unleashed, and should risk failure and shame, so that the richness of humanity could be properly expressed. You may remember that he was thrilled by the sometimes silly and ugly sculptures to be found ornamenting Gothic cathedrals, as they were signs of the uninhibited life and freedom of quirky individual artisans. This is rather like the point made by internet commentator Clay Shirky, in his 2010 book *Cognitive Surplus*, that even daft websites – such as those collecting silly photos of cats with comic captions – reflect a zesty, everyday, creative liveliness which we should embrace and value, especially because they suggest to other everyday amateurs that 'You can play this game too.'[2]

Ruskin also helped us to make the connection from *individual* creativity to the 'big picture' of social stability. He showed that societies may establish apparently rational systems, which are intended to 'cure' inefficiencies, but which as a side effect silence individual voice and strangle independent creativity, and so ultimately create a much greater sickness. This Ruskin point also has a modern-day counterpart, in the recent work of Nick Couldry, which we will discuss in a few pages.

Ruskin's enthusiastic supporter, William Morris, was a creative *producer* throughout his life, as well as critic of industry and politics. He drew our attention to the fact that we need *models* of good practice. Criticizing present realities is important but insufficient. It can be hard to picture what the future would look like, and so to be making things, as examples of future creative diversity, in the here and now, offers a powerful and tangible form of inspiration to others – and challenges the apparent inevitability of the present. This idea is shared by the makers of punk zines, and the knitters, stitchers, and guerrilla gardeners, as well as the makers of YouTube videos and Audioboo recordings, who show by vivid example that you do not have to accept all of mainstream culture, and can start to create your own alternatives instead.

Morris contended that people need to be able to make their mark on the world, give shape to their environments, and share knowledge, ideas, and self-expression. Ivan Illich made the same points, in a different way, 100 years later. Both thinkers observed that these opportunities provide a feeling of joy – or, when they are lacking, a dull misery. These arguments are today more vital than ever, and since we live in a world with so much media – and, now, so much *potential* for everyday personally made and distributed media – they offer a kind of prescription for how we should proceed.

Since – as critics of this book may like to point out – the majority of people remain, most of the time, viewers and consumers of mainstream professional stuff rather than makers and sharers of amateur material, this is a prescription that may seem ambitious and radical. But there are clearly many signs of this potential – not least of all in the staggering growth of people using social networks where personal creative material is shared. Facebook went from zero to 500 million active users in six years; and in five years, the number of videos viewed on YouTube went from zero to 2 billion every day.[3] These particular platforms may not, in the future, be the ultimate sites of everyday creativity, but they certainly show that people are willing to give it a go.

FIVE KEY PRINCIPLES

This book has highlighted a number of key principles, which I offer as tools for thinking about everyday life, creativity, and media. Here, I have tried to draw together the main points, and numbered them from one to five.

1. A new understanding of creativity as process, emotion, and presence

The standard definition says that creativity should be judged on its outcomes, which are required to be original and paradigm-shifting. I argued that this way of understanding creativity is unsatisfactory because it rejects everyday activity that we would normally describe, in a 'common sense' way, as creative; and especially because it is about the final product, rather than the process. There also seemed to be a philosophical flaw in a definition of creativity which would not enable anyone to identify 'creativity' unless they happened to be in possession of a God-like overview of the history of previous innovations in that sphere. A new definition was therefore proposed, in longer and shorter forms (see the discussion on pages 75–9). The shorter one was this:

Everyday creativity refers to a process which brings together at least one active human mind, and the material or digital world, in the activity of making something which is novel in that context, and is a process which evokes a feeling of joy.

This approach to creativity is valuable, I would say, because it correctly recognizes the imaginative process of, say, knitters and bakers, amateur engineers, gardeners, Lego enthusiasts, bloggers, and YouTube video-makers, as the creative activity that it is – engaged in because the makers *want* to, and because it gives them *pleasure*. In the longer version of the revised definition of creativity, we also recognized that others may be able to sense the *presence* of the maker, in the thing they have made – the unavoidably distinctive fingerprint that the thinking-and-making individual leaves on their work, which can foster a sense of shared feeling and common cause, even when maker and audience never meet.

2. The drive to make and share

It is clearly the case, as we have seen from a range of offline and online cases mentioned in this book, that people like to make and share things. This may not be *all* people, partly because modern life has sought to render personal creativity unnecessary, but it is *some* people, with the potential to be many. They enjoy making and sharing things without the need for external rewards such as money or celebrity; although low-level recognition and reputation – being able to impress the people around you – may be a motivating force. But they just do it anyway.

In the discussion of motivations in chapters 3 and 4, we saw that people often spend time creating things because they want to feel alive in the world, as *participants* rather than viewers, and to be active and recognized within a community of interesting people. It is common that they wish to make their existence, their interests, and their personality more visible in the contexts that are significant to them, and they want this to be *noticed*. The process of making is enjoyed for its own sake, of course: there is pleasure in seeing a project from start to finish, and the process provides space for thought and reflection, and helps to cultivate a sense of the self as an active, creative agent. But there is also a desire to connect and communicate with others, and – especially online – to be an active participant in dialogues and communities. These are impulses which should be supported and developed by the websites and technologies of the future – as well as the toys and games, education and government programmes, and everything else of the future, as we will discuss in the 'implications' section below.

3. Happiness through creativity and community

We have seen that humans are very bad at predicting what will make us more happy. Indeed, it is a matter of historical and current fact that we typically allocate time to activities which are the wrong ones, working harder in an attempt to increase wealth, at the expense of the social engagement which can actually improve our enjoyment of life.

Happiness research shows that happiness is strongly associated with the quality of our relationships and our connections with others. Nothing else comes close. Richard Layard, a leading economist and happiness researcher, even ends up saying: 'Increasingly, research confirms the dominating importance of love.'[4] In chapter 5 we saw that happiness is also heavily associated with self-esteem, and having projects to work on; and that work needs to be *meaningful* if we are to be satisfied and healthy. Crucially, we saw that although the happiness research identifies a number of variables and circumstances which should be able to assure humans of greater happiness, we cannot simply line up the 'correct' lifestyle elements and expect happiness to flood in. Happiness has to be worked towards, and it flows from action, not passivity.

All of this suggests that creative projects, especially when either online, or offline but linked via online platforms, are invaluable for human happiness. We should also remember Layard's stark warning that shared purpose is essential for human stability, otherwise we can find ourselves unexpectedly crushed by loneliness and stress. 'The current pursuit of self-realisation *will not work*', he says, least of all from the consumption of readymade products.[5] Communication, exchange, and collaboration in the production of everyday life, ideas, and community, is much more rewarding.

4. A middle layer of creativity as social glue

Social scientists have traditionally analysed social life at the level of individuals, groups, and families – the down to earth 'micro' level – or in terms of organizations, institutions, and governments – the more abstract 'macro' level. More imaginative analysts, such as sociologist Anthony Giddens, have sought to connect the two levels by showing how the perception of macro-level expectations influences individual micro behaviour, and how everyday practices can in turn reinforce, or change, the macro established order.[6]

The discussion in this book, however, has often concerned activity in what we might call a middle layer. Social capital theory, as we saw in chapter 6, suggested that 'meso-level social structures' could act as 'integrating elements' between individuals and society.[7] Making and sharing activities, online and offline, can be seen as a disorganized (or, rather, lightly self-organized) cloud of creative links which can bind people together. These ties may not necessarily forge links between individuals and formal institutions, but they certainly connect people with others in unexpected, unplanned, and perhaps rather anarchic ways. This creative cloud carries no single coherent message, but its existence, representing people doing what they want to do, *because they want to do it*, raises a challenge to the lifestyles of individual consumers, and to the ambitions of organized businesses and governments. These are people who want to make their own stuff, rather than only having stuff that is made commercially or on an industrial scale; and who are interested in that kind of thing made by others. This brings us to the last of the five principles.

5. *Making your mark, and making the world your own*

Human beings need to be able to make their mark on the world, and to give shape and character to the environments that they live in. They need tools to do this, as Ivan Illich showed (see chapter 7). Ideally, these are tools which can be used in any way that a person likes, to do whatever they want. Tools which only offer a predetermined set of opportunities, or which are scaled up to provide uniform 'solutions', Illich warned, deny creativity and impose the fixed meanings of others. But mastery of a creative tool means that an individual can invest the world with meaning, and thereby 'enrich the environment' with the fruits of their vision.[8] This is not a specific roadmap towards a better society: the vision is only that there must be the ever-present possibility and potential of unpredictable and unplanned creativity – and that the *tools* for this must be readily available and easy to use.

This mention of such tools may lead modern readers to immediately think of Web 2.0: but it also has implications for what Web 2.0 should really mean. It means that Web 2.0 tools should be as open and as inviting of creativity as possible; and offer platforms where people can truly make their mark, express themselves, and shape the environment. As Jaron Lanier has argued (see chapter 8), it cannot involve simplistic templates where identities are reduced to a tickbox level. Expressive messiness, rather than Facebook-style neatness, is therefore to be encouraged – even by those of us who, for whatever psychological reason, prefer things to be tidy. Furthermore, distinctive creative contributions, and individual expressive voices, should be distinguishable – and therefore the idea of pooling all human knowledge and creativity into one mushed-together repository (or unified electronic consciousness) is not necessarily a wonderful idea.

In addition to the websites and software, new internet *devices* should also be naturally enabling of making and sharing – something which, for instance, as discussed in chapter 8, the first version of the celebrated Apple iPad was emphatically not. The idea that Apple can turn the internet into a neat and tidy experience, which is easy to use and rather beautiful, and where Apple has generously checked every possible program for suitability before allowing it to be available to you, may have a straightforward appeal to many users, but is also an underhand threat to the free Web that we have become used to.

Furthermore, our creative activity should be able to live on platforms that are *sustainable*. To date, commercial companies have created the most successful platforms, such as YouTube, Blogger, and Flickr; and they have generally managed *not* to ruin their sites, or the user-created content, with too much intrusive advertising. But things change, and licensing your carefully crafted material to an unpredictable and possibly unprofitable website may not be the best way to ensure that it is still visible, and nicely presented, in five years' time. The solution? Ideally, a consortium of enterprising governments would support a global online repository and community for digital creative work of all kinds, run by an independent non-profit foundation. Like YouTube and other such platforms, it should have no gatekeepers and a minimum amount of restrictions. This idea is not, at the moment, on the cards; but the fostering of everyday creativity is one of the most crucial things any government should do, as we will discuss below.

THE POLITICAL CONNOTATIONS OF 'MAKING IS CONNECTING'

This book is built on a broad general understanding that people are happier, more engaged with the world, and more likely to develop or learn, when they are doing and making things for themselves, rather than having things done and made for them. This lines up with liberal and countercultural notions of self-reliance and independence, and with the generally left-wing anti-consumer movements. This view suggests that big businesses cannot sell us the route to happiness and self-fulfilment – despite the implied or explicit claims of their marketing and advertising – and that the level of bland sameness which they bring to local, national, and international cultures is unwelcome and makes everyday life less interesting. In an education context, this perspective reflects approaches to learning and child development which are typically thought of as left-wing or 'alternative' – being child-centred, seeking a relationship with nature, and focused on imagination, self-expression, and creativity – rather than the conservative approach based on teaching 'facts' and conducting a lot of tests.

However, this approach could also appear to steer close to core right-wing or reactionary ideas: that the poor and disadvantaged do not deserve our support, as they are simply people who have failed to do the necessary things to ensure their own well-being; who expect to have 'things done for them' rather than solving their own problems. Of course, this is not my intention. 'Making is connecting' suggests that society is stronger, and kinder, when we take time to listen to the voices around us, when we pay attention to the diverse stories presented through the everyday creativity of our fellow human beings, and when we engage helpfully in the world. To suggest that it is rewarding and inspiring to make and fix things for oneself, rather than relying on external forces, is not at all to say that there should not be external services which provide security and support for individuals, families, and communities.

In particular, when we are talking about media, art, and culture, a kind of do it yourself individualism, or do it with others collaboration – with wide participation across the population – is highly defensible, since otherwise we only have a choice of large-scale *monolithic* solutions (such as broadcast television stations) or more distinctive but *elite* ones (such as the artworld system of 'star' artists and international galleries, where having the right kind of education, sponsors, and jargon, are necessary markers of worthiness).

Compared with mass-market populism on the one hand, and pretentious elitism on the other, the multitudinous and diverse fruits of the 'make it yourself' ethic, or the 'make it with others' ethic – as seen across YouTube and the rest of the Web, and in craft fairs, guerrilla gardening interventions, and elsewhere – are easily the winners.

The DIY ethic in everyday culture is wholly different from, say, the Thatcherite do it yourself notion which is encapsulated in Norman Tebbit's famous 1981 statement that his unemployed father had 'got on his bike and looked for work', a phrase often slightly misremembered as a direct command to the unemployed to 'get on your bike' (which, although a misquote, represents the implied meaning). This right-wing version of self-reliance, which implies that poverty or unemployment are a consequence of personal laziness, stems from the view that all of life is fundamentally a marketplace, within which some products (or people) will succeed, whilst others fail. This is the mindset which today is known as neoliberalism – the idea that markets and market forces are the primary way to understand and organize not only economics, but also politics and society.

I would say that the ideals associated with 'making is connecting' – individual and collective creativity, self-expression, and sharing – offer a *challenge* to the neoliberal vision of society, consumerism, and education. I am helped in this by the recent work of Nick Couldry, the Goldsmiths, University of London professor who has emerged as one of the sharpest analysts of the intersection between politics, culture, and communications on multiple levels. In his 2010 book, *Why Voice Matters: Culture and Politics after Neoliberalism*, Couldry charts the ways in which neoliberalism has become naturalized in social and political life over the past couple of decades, and argues that human 'voice' may be the most powerful tool to erode its power. As he explains:

Voice as a process – giving an account of oneself and what affects one's life – is an irreducible part of what it means to be human; effective voice (the effective opportunity to have one's voice heard and taken into account) is a human good. 'Voice' might therefore appear unquestionable as a value. But across various domains – economic, political, cultural – we are governed in ways that deny the value of voice and insist instead on the primacy of market functioning.[9]

Being opposed to neoliberalism does not mean that one is opposed to markets per se. Markets may be a good way to organize a number of things, such as trade and employment – with some regulation to ensure decent practices, such as minimum wage laws. Neoliberalism, however, is the belief that markets are the *only* lens through which to run anything, or to assess the value of anything. It is manifested in many ways, and becomes apparent when individuals are seen as simply customers and consumers, and workers become faceless 'service providers'. It means that the 'voice' of people is denied, because they can only express themselves through choices within the existing market, which is not genuine self-expression at all.

The perspective of neoliberalism, Couldry argues, seeps into all aspects of society and culture, shaping our assumptions and expectations, and ultimately making some approaches common sense and other views alien. For example, in education, the influence of neoliberalism means that students become 'customers' who assume that their purpose is to purchase and extract a qualification as simply as possible, rather than engage in a process of discovery, learning, and growth. For their teachers, the work becomes a matter of handing over the relevant packages of 'knowledge' in a uniform manner – the practice which can be most simply unified and audited, at the cost of individuality and creativity.

In businesses and organizations, the influence of neoliberalism means that individuals become 'brand representatives',
whose work takes over more and more of their lives and
demands a particular performance of passion and enthusiasm, the better to sell the brand, but not as an invitation to
genuine self-expression.

In media and communications, we see the growth of false
platforms, such as reality TV shows, which use individual
identities – such as the personalities of *Big Brother* contest-
ants – as tools to sell a product to a mass audience. Despite
their apparent promise, the programmes do not really give a
voice to the individuals who participate; the ideas most clearly
expressed are only those of the marketing plan and the 'story
development' decided in advance by the producers. Similarly,
in popular music we get the *X Factor* effect: interchangeable
performers who are not creative artists themselves, but the
puppets of Simon Cowell's hit factories and marketing staff.
More worrying is that this role becomes the aspiration of
young people – for one's identity to be processed by PR professionals into an effectively selling hit product, rather than a
self-expressive artist in their own right.[10]

CREATIVITY AND BEING HEARD

My own argument here would be that, although mass-market
broadcasting, consumerism, and 'neoliberal rationality' are
currently well embedded in our society and culture, we have
seen in this book the seeds of a possible new direction. Part
of the way people may now be finding a voice is by using
the internet in particular ways. Couldry's *Why Voice Matters*
acknowledges online communication at various points but is
not primarily concerned with it; and his brief discussion of
online political practices generally involves a conventional
understanding of political activity (such as online circulation

of photographic evidence by activists; anti-war and environmental campaigning websites and networks; and other online means to communicate and organize protest and opinion to governments). However he does also point towards a rethinking of what politics means – a 'politics of politics' which would aim to re-imagine and re-enable collective participation in public affairs[11] – which, in the 'everyday' contexts we are concerned with here could, I think, involve finding new meaning within our own participation in society through creative making and sharing.

If we are willing to consider an optimistic possibility, I would argue that the 'making is connecting' power of the internet, which in turn may be seeding and inspiring other offline (or both on- and offline) activities, offers us a potential way to disrupt the inevitability and dominance of the one-size-fits-all broadcasting and consumerism model, and to enhance the power of voice. For voice to be meaningful, people need opportunities and tools for self-expression, but – as Couldry asserts – they also need to be effectively *heard*. As we saw in chapter 8, the existence of Web 2.0 technologies, or companies, does not guarantee this in any way, and indeed the commercial nature of the tools can be the basis of some concern. Furthermore, the resources of skills, techniques, networks, and contacts which can help some people to get heard are not equally distributed – some people can speak with much louder voices than others. This can be seen on Twitter, where there seems to be a class of 'ordinary' users, who typically have fewer than 100 followers, and a class of high-status Tweeters, who are likely to have well over 1,000, and are much more active.[12] And of course, a majority of people are not on Twitter at all. Similarly, the very point of the 'long tail' of videos on YouTube is that most videos, whilst available, are very rarely watched by anybody.[13]

However, what we do know about online communication is that, although the capacity to be 'heard' is not evenly distributed, it does not only follow traditional or straightforward patterns either. In terms of being able to make attractive online content, an individual needs to acquire and develop certain skills. Anyone with the basic equipment can do this, although some amount of literacy and computer literacy are necessary, and a certain flair for design, and self-promotion, can also be helpful. In terms of becoming *heard* – a distinct further step, once the content has been created – the sensible individual makes use of existing online networks in a bid to push their material in front of others who may then pass on the links to yet more others. The same kind of 'anyone' can do this too. Previously existing fame or status can definitely help – that's a fact – but it is not at all necessary. Many people have become popular bloggers and YouTube video-makers even though they had no previous platform, celebrity, or relevant contacts. In the online discussion of social and political matters, it is true that college-educated professionals, and in particular already-established journalists, commentators, politicians, organizations, and think-tanks get a huge boost in visibility (which is largely the point of Matthew Hindman's book *The Myth of Digital Democracy*[14]). But it is still true that unconventional, minority, and non-professional voices also can get heard.

It is worth noting that in order to feel supported and encouraged in their creative efforts, people do not necessarily need a huge audience or network. The pleasure in connecting with other people through creativity, and therefore feeling more connected with the world – becoming heard and recognized, and starting to feel that there may be some point in trying to make a difference – can occur through interactions with small numbers of like-minded people, and so this kind of activity doesn't need to meet a large number of 'eyeballs' to be meaningful. This means that expectations can be very different from those applied to broadcast media, or even the kinds of websites and blogs which predominantly want to broadcast their message to readers.

We should remember that for those who wish to have a voice, and be heard, all of this is much, much different to the previous situation, just 20 years ago, where you had to be one of the absolute elite, employed by a media organization, and selected to produce content, to even get to speak. Today, a lot of non-elite, non-professional people are creating and sharing media, making their mark on the world, and sharing what they have to say about an incredibly diverse range of spheres and subjects, from parenting to painting, ecology to economics, diabetes to discrimination, lifestyles, poetry, science, and everything else. They also make things which are simply meant to be beautiful, inspiring, or entertaining.

It is partly for these reasons that this book has not primarily concerned itself with explicitly 'political' activity online, or with the work of 'craftivists' who combine craft activity with political activism. I have not focused on these more obvious centres of political activity because this book is about the idea that making and sharing is *already* a political act. Taken bit by bit, it's small stuff. Each little pebble of creative activity is easily lost in the general landscape, which is dominated by various big beasts such as social institutions, popular broadcasters, and giant supermarkets.[15] But those pebbles all add up, and *cumulatively* could reach as high as any of the big beasts. We have already seen that the huge numbers of people engaging with a vast array of homemade things on YouTube present a severe challenge to the professional mass-market TV stations, which until recently had assumed that they were the natural providers of what people wanted. If we were willing to be optimistic, this could just be the start of a substantial shift from the one-size-fits-all industrial fast food culture of the twentieth century, towards a homemade, slow-cooked, highly diverse feast of meaningful engagement, sharing, and playfulness in the twenty-first. This would be based on an ethics of understanding, self-expression, recognition, and respect, rather than a general assumption that people shouldn't mind parking their own personalities under a readymade platter of mass-market identities.

SOME IMAGINED FUTURES

In this section we will consider the implications of 'making is connecting' in different contexts. The argument of this book, and the five 'key principles' listed above in particular, have pretty straightforward implications for the kinds of services and experiences that it would be valuable to see developed in the future. Compressed and summarized even further, the generic points are:

- People should be given opportunities to express their creativity through tools which do not seek to shape or determine the outcomes; and which enable people to express their unique presence in the work; and which mean that their contribution is distinct and recognizable.
- People should be able to share the fruits of their creativity simply, and without unreasonable restrictions or gatekeepers.
- Communication, exchange, and collaboration should be enabled and encouraged, to foster engaged communities of interested people who can help and encourage each other. Collaboration should be at the level which participants in a project are most comfortable with, which could be in tiny bits, or substantial chunks.[16]

We could work out the implications of these points in any number of areas. Here I've picked four: in media, in education, in work, and in politics and the environment. For each one I will briefly outline a vision of the future. I'm not going for far-fetched futuristic scenarios here – these are modest developments of the world as we know it. And these are not manifestos, exactly, but rather illustrations of what this approach might mean in practice.

'Making is connecting' future scenario – media

The implications for electronic media are perhaps most obvious, and have been discussed in different chapters of this book. In the future imagined here, people have easy-to-use, intuitive electronic devices which enable the simple capture, editing, and preparation of creative material, such as text, images, and video. Because such tasks never seem *that* simple to everyone – and because some people want to work to high standards – accessible, local hands-on training is readily available to people of all ages, pitched at the right level, and never too patronizing or laborious. Participants simply learn by making the thing that they want to make, getting help where necessary. Because such sessions are not to everyone's taste, there are also lots of inspiring free booklets to get people started, working and experimenting at their own pace, and peer-support networks for the exchange of friendly mutual help and support.

The everyday creative material which people make is typically shared on user-friendly platforms, funded – but in no way controlled – by a consortium of governments who are eager to encourage creativity in their populations. Access to this material is not restricted by country, or indeed by any other variable (apart from basic restrictions on inflammatory bigoted material, and content where people or animals have been harmed in its preparation). Alternatively, users can choose other platforms, including ones where users are able to create their own distinctive personal space online, unrestricted by templates or fixed requirements (although less ambitious users are able to choose from, and adapt, a range of readymade patterns) – with no advertising – for a reasonable monthly fee. There are also free services supported by advertising.

Although much personal making and sharing activity is not motivated by money, in this future, there are some mechanisms so that producers of entertainment and information which become popular can get paid, with the money coming from grants, sponsors, and in some cases from unobtrusive advertising. (At present, funding solutions which are not based on advertising may seem unlikely. But consider that the TV Licence in the UK raises around £3.45 billion each year for the preparation and distribution of a particular haul of media content;[17] a similar annual fee used to reward producers of online material could be a powerful incentive for those who wanted to produce good quality material for a wider audience.)

In this future, incidentally, conventional professionally produced media is not dead. People still enjoy high-quality stories produced to excellent standards, so this is *not* a world where things like television and cinema have perished – but in this future people spend less time with such mass-produced media, because they find greater amounts of emotional engagement and inspiration from the home-made media made by their friends and the other amateurs they follow, and enjoy the feelings and discoveries within the sense of absorbed reflection as they make their own stuff. Professional news reporting has also survived, incidentally, as this is a particular kind of material which cannot be replaced by the kind of random ramshackle homemade content which we otherwise love.

People have not merely swapped some of their former traditional screen time for a more diverse mix of screen-based activity, however. Overall screen time has gone down, because people are using the internet to make real-world connections, and are having their interests sparked in new things – stuff you can actually *do*, rather than just other things to watch or listen to.

In short, in this future the Web has enabled people to cast off the primarily slumped, passive model of twentieth-century 'leisure time', and given them the opportunity to embrace a more social and connected life of creative exchange, which in turn leads to a greater awareness of other people, and their needs. Over time, people have come to feel more connected to the local and global environment in which they live, and have started to perceive their own role as one in which they can make a difference, rather than stand by as a detached observer.

'Making is connecting' future scenario – education

In this future, it has been realized that memorizing stuff for tests is the antithesis of real learning, which takes place through meaningful activity. This shift turned out to be somewhat easier than expected, once government policies had been changed, since most teachers had tended to doubt the value of shovelling information in pursuit of test scores.[18] In the new system, students work on learning projects, in which their teachers encourage them to ask questions and to seek out understanding for themselves. To present their learning to others, they produce exhibitions, physical performances, online presentations, and games. They are inspired by their teachers, who are no longer just the holders of the 'answer book' but are visibly also learning new knowledge and skills in their own lives.

Students are encouraged to ask difficult questions and challenge conventional assumptions, and to interpret the 'syllabus' widely and imaginatively. They are not required to regurgitate 'correct' answers which have been previously dispensed by the teacher, but are expected to research and think about a subject and then produce their own responses to it, sometimes individually and sometimes collaboratively. Some of the knowledge they develop is abstract and theoretical, but is usually connected to real-world questions and problems. In particular, a substantial part of the school experience is embedded in the surrounding environment, and genuine local issues.

This future education system recognizes the characteristics of powerful learners (as set out in the present day by educationalist Guy Claxton[19]): they are *curious* about the world, and wish to understand the how and why of things; they have *courage*, which means they are willing to take risks, and to try things out to see what happens; and they recognize that mistakes are not shameful disasters but are just events that can be learned from. They like to *explore*, *investigate*, and *experiment*. Tinkering with things is a way of learning. They have *imagination*, which is grounded by reason, thoughtfulness, and the ability to plan. They have the virtue of *sociability*, which means they know how to make use of the potent social space of learning. Finally, they are *reflective*, and are aware of their own strengths and weaknesses in the learning process.

This approach has been adopted, in this future, as the natural follow-on from other 'making is connecting' principles. As this is a society which values and makes time for everyday creativity – and one which casually *expects* that culture will come from 'ordinary people' rather than distant organizations – it naturally fosters these approaches to learning, as they stem from the same orientation to knowledge and the experience of hands-on creative action.

Conversely, in this future, people look back with some horror at the way in which a strangely passive, 'sit back and be told' population managed to drift into the kind of situation where their acceptance of the political rhetoric demanding 'standards' in schools led to relentless tests – tests of 'correct facts,' rather than assessments of real insight or intelligence – which teachers had to prepare their students for, which in turn led to the collapse of *actual* 'standards' in terms of genuine learning and creative capacity. In this story alone it is noted that 'making is connecting' is not just a warm, fuzzy, pleasant notion, but a more fundamental concept with significant social implications.

'Making is connecting' future scenario – work

In this future, the change in education corresponds with, and enables, something of a shift in the nature of work. It has been recognized that the role of the interchangeable 'knowledge worker' is unrewarding, leading to personal unhappiness as well as business inefficiency. Being unable to see any direct fruits of their labour, employees become bored and lethargic, with small attempts to disrupt the system their only form of pleasure. Therefore, in this future, work is organized as far as possible so that individuals can feel pride in performing whole tasks, of the sort that can be held in the mind all at once,[20] rather than the diffuse processing of bits of a task which can never seem to be completed and therefore admired.

The future-people have not entirely worked out how to make everyone's lives and jobs 100 per cent creative. The implication in Charles Leadbeater's *We Think* book that every working person should spend their time producing creative ideas, and collaborating to develop them with others online, turned out to be unrealistic. This was partly because society does not require tens of thousands of 'new ideas', but rather needs a few good ones, implemented thoughtfully and well. And it was partly because many jobs are about producing, fixing, and implementing versions of existing things, and not all of them can be done in cloudy networks.

Nevertheless, in this future the education system no longer produces mere drones, and students' new-found appetite for self-expression and hands-on creativity does not stop when they leave school or college. These workers expect – and are expected – to be able to make their mark on the things that they work with, to make their presence felt, and to shape their environment so that it is enriching, sustainable, and effective. Having been encouraged to be inquisitive and courageous learners in school, and having managers who are similarly curious and imaginative – and who welcome challenging questions – these employees typically seek creative solutions to their everyday tasks, and their longer-term goals, and are supported to express their own human voice in what they do.

This shift has meant that employers and managers have to *trust* the individuals in their organizations more, and subject them to auditing less. Maintaining a lighter, supportive oversight of work has led not to more shirking or laziness, as some had feared, but to a more ethical engagement with work. In this future, people are more likely to want to do good work for its own sake, as they are motivated to feel pride in what they have done themselves, rather than doing it to satisfy a management demand. (Inevitably, this is not *always* the case, but the idea of spoiling the process for everyone with endless bureaucracy and auditing, in order to avoid occasional instances of poor practice, has been rejected.)

As this model has spread the responsibility for doing things well, with creative input and leadership being distributed more widely, it has also brought an end to the 'mega-salaries' previously enjoyed by business and organizational leaders. It has been recognized that huge differences in pay contributed to everyday unhappiness, as well as visible inequalities, and greater social problems,[21] and so – although greater levels of experience, insight, and responsibility are still rewarded – there has been a move towards more equal pay and conditions. This is widely accepted as reasonable, because it reflects the way in which everyone is expected to make a thoughtful and creative difference in their own work.

'Making is connecting' future scenario – politics and the environment

These changes in creative everyday activity, and in education and work, are political shifts in themselves, of course, and they connect with other changes. In the future imagined here, people typically assume that a hands-on engagement with the processes that affect their lives is desirable, and therefore feel more inclined to connect with political processes, of both formal and informal kinds.

Having blossomed as creators of their own cultural worlds, and as participants in a culture of originality and exchange, these people want to have a meaningful and imaginative input into local and national policies – not (only) through polls and elections but through participatory events where they have genuine opportunities to influence strategies and practice. These are not talking-shops where the most articulate individuals get to pontificate, but hands-on experiences where participants build models, showing their ideas in metaphors and collaborating to build these into shared visions. This means that everyone in the room gets the opportunity to contribute, can take time to reflect, and develop their ideas and works with others to address needs and concerns that they may not have thought of. (That's not

a random idea – it's a real process, as described in my previous book *Creative Explorations*.)[22] There are also stimulating
opportunities to build creative ideas together online.

In this future, political communication has become much
more two-way. Rather than offering traditional media and
internet content which explains 'This is what we're doing',
the political actors and representatives of the future have
been compelled to create a range of meaningful forums
for the exchange of ideas, where the politicians and different stakeholders have to properly respond to each other
– and not just through an illusion of 'interactivity' – because
voters of the future are dissatisfied with candidates offering
anything less.

Aside from conventional political structures, people are
also much more enthusiastic about taking matters into their
own hands – especially because they feel encouraged and
supported to do so. They have in part been inspired by the
Transition Towns movement (as mentioned in chapter 1),
which offered a model for this kind of engagement – people
getting together to do something, using creativity and
imagination, in response to a shared concern. This did not
necessarily mean protest – certainly not only protest – but
rather working out a positive, resilient, and sustainable solution for the future. As Transition movement founder Rob
Hopkins put it in 2009:

> This is really about looking the challenges of peak oil and
> climate change square in the face, and responding with a
> creativity and an adaptability and an imagination that we
> really need. It's something which has spread incredibly fast,
> and it is something which has several characteristics. It's
> viral. It seems to spread under the radar very very quickly.
> It's open source. It's something which everybody who's
> involved with it develops and passes on as they work with

it. It's self-organizing. There is no great central organization that pushes this; people just pick up an idea and they
run with it, and they implement it where they are. It's
solutions-focused. It's very much looking at what people
can do where they are, to respond to this. It's sensitive to
place, and to scale.[23]

Having adopted this kind of approach to creative political
activity, people take up the tools developed and shared by
others, or originate their own, build on them, and then pass
them on again. They share exciting, promising, fruitful ideas
of what can be done, and are less interested in prophecies of
doom (which can be essential warnings, but don't get us anywhere in themselves). They put on events, and take a playful
making-things orientation to challenges which otherwise
could seem forbiddingly serious and difficult. And through
this they have started to make an actual difference.

This is not a complete *alternative* to the big-scale politics,
of course. As Hopkins has said in relation to the Transition
movement:

> I think it's really important to make the point that actually
> this isn't something which is going to do everything on its
> own. We need international legislation from [the United
> Nations Climate Change Conference] and so on. We need
> national responses. We need local government responses.
> But all of those things are going to be much easier if we
> have communities that are vibrant and coming up with ideas
> and leading from the front, making unelectable policies
> electable, over the next 5 to 10 years.[24]

In this future, then, people have accepted that things had to
change. When they had been living in the tail end of the
earlier period, of plentiful oil and accompanying economic

growth, they had been lucky. But they also knew that people had been able to craft interesting and rewarding lives for themselves *before* that time, and could do so again after it. And they knew that the period of plentiful oil and economic growth had also been the time in which an unanticipated dullness passed, like a shadow, over their lives. Being able to buy everything from mega-supermarkets, to consume in front of massive televisions, had been, in a sense, *too* comforting and easy. Now, with a revitalized sense of their own creative powers, and helpfully connected to ideas and people via the flourishing internet, people feel more like vibrant *agents*, rather than observers, in the world. They correspondingly feel more concerned about their local and global environments, as they are more emphatically *living* there. And, therefore, people have started to sort things out.

IN CONCLUSION

The near-future scenarios I have painted above are all part of the shift that I have described as being from the 'sit back and be told' culture which became entrenched in the twentieth century, towards the 'making and doing' culture which could flourish in the twenty-first. Although I think there is an appetite for such a change, we could hardly say that this would be an easy shift. Many people have become comfortable with the undemanding role that contemporary culture expects us to enjoy – it appears pleasant enough, allows us to consume wall-to-wall entertainments, and nothing very bad seems to happen. But at the same time, we are not left feeling very whole, or fulfilled, or creative. And bad things *are* happening – see all the evidence of social isolation, fragmented communities, environmental pollution, and climate change in particular – but we choose not to really notice them.

It doesn't seem right to suggest that people just don't know what's good for them: but the empirical research on happiness and well-being does show a clear mismatch between the things which we say help us to feel positive, alive, and connected, and the things which we actually spend most time on. It sounds illogical, but we all do it. And because modern life is often tiring and complicated, we are often likely to welcome the blessed relief of the 'sit back and be told' elements which don't require us to *do* very much. The 'making and doing' culture does require a bit more effort – but it comes with rich rewards.

Making things shows us that we are powerful, creative agents – people who can really *do* things, things that other people can see, learn from, and enjoy. Making things is about transforming materials into something new, but it is also about transforming one's own sense of self. Creativity is a gift, not in the sense of it being a talent, but in the sense that it is a way of sharing meaningful things, ideas, or wisdom, which form bridges between people and communities. Through creative activity, where making is connecting, we can increase our pleasure in everyday life, unlock innovative capacity, and build resilience in our communities, so that we can face future challenges with confidence and originality.

NOTES

Notes to chapter 1, pages 1–21

1. David Gauntlett, *Creative Explorations: New Approaches to Identities and Audiences* (London: Routledge, 2007).

2. Tim O'Reilly, 'Levels of the Game: The Hierarchy of Web 2.0 Applications', 17 July 2006, http://radar.oreilly.com/2006/07/levels-of-the-game-the-hierarc.html

3. Charles Leadbeater, *We Think: Mass Innovation not Mass Production* (London: Profile Books, 2008). Clay Shirky, *Here Comes Everybody: The Power of Organizing Without Organizations* (London: Allen Lane, 2008). Clay Shirky, *Cognitive Surplus: Creativity and Generosity in a Connected Age* (London: Allen Lane, 2010).

4. I expect Charles Leadbeater is doing some of this, implicitly if not explicitly, in some of his other work, such as his ideas on education reform – see http://www.charlesleadbeater.net

5. See coverage such as BBC News, 'Tests Scrapped for 14-Year-Olds', 14 October 2008, http://news.bbc.

co.uk/1/hi/education/7669254.stm. 'Children's Secretary Ed Balls . . . said that the decision to stop Sats tests for 14-year-olds was "not a u-turn" – and that the wider principle of the need for testing and accountability remained.'

6. The Wikipedia article 'No Child Left Behind Act' includes a lot of referenced information about the arguments of the Act's advocates and opponents.

7. Jackie Calmes, 'Obama Defends Education Program', *The New York Times*, 29 July 2010, http://www.nytimes.com/2010/07/30/education/30obama.html

8. For the latest data, see http://www.nielsen.com. Summaries of television viewing appear in 'Reports' in the 'Insights' section.

9. For the latest data, see http://www.barb.co.uk. Summaries of television viewing appear under 'Viewing figures'.

10. David Gauntlett, *Moving Experiences, Second Edition: Media Effects and Beyond*, (London: John Libbey, 2005).

11. Max Horkheimer and Theodor W. Adorno, *Dialectic of Enlightenment* (London: Verso, 1979).

12. Sigmund Freud, *'A Case of Hysteria', 'Three Essays on Sexuality' and Other Works* (London: Vintage, 2001).

13. Karl Marx, *Capital: A Critique of Political Economy, Volume 1* (London: Penguin, 2004).

14. Guy Claxton, *What's the Point of School?* (Oxford: Oneworld, 2008).

15. See data in chapter 6, pp. 147–8.

16. Victoria J. Rideout, Ulla G. Foehr and Donald F. Roberts, *Generation M²: Media in the Lives of 8- to 18-Year-Olds* (Menlo Park, California: The Henry J. Kaiser Family Foundation, 2010); available at http://www.kff.org/entmedia/8010.cfm. Note that time spent online cannot be simply subtracted from time spent with

conventional media, as an ever-growing ability to multi-
task meant that these young people managed to pack
more media use into their time than before.

17. Alastair Jamieson, 'Facebook's 500m Users Include One
in Three Britons', 22 July 2010, http://www.telegraph.
co.uk/technology/facebook/7904103/Facebooks-500m-
users-include-one-in-three-Britons.html

18. Some detailed data appear in Steph Gray and Rebecca
Jennings, 'How Are Young People Using Social
Media?', Forrester and the Department for Innovation,
Universities and Skills, September 2008, http://www.
slideshare.net/diusgovuk/how-are-young-people-using-
social-media-presentation

19. *The Guardian*'s Digital Content Blog, 'Facebook Leads
Rise in Mobile Web Use', 8 February 2010, http://www.
guardian.co.uk/media/pda/2010/feb/08/facebook-rise-
mobile-web-use

20. For instance, the resurgence of interest in craft activities
is one of the key findings of the 'Living Britain' report,
an independent study by The Future Laboratory, commissioned by Zurich, 2007, http://www.zurich.co.uk/
home/Welcome/livingbritain/. Although commercially
funded, the study draws on a wide range of data and
expertise, and Zurich has no apparent vested interests
in this kind of finding. Similarly, Joanne Turney cites
a number of statistics which suggest that significantly
increased numbers of people are taking up knitting, in
The Culture of Knitting (Oxford: Berg, 2009), p. 1.

21. This is a physical magazine, but also has a comprehen-
sive website at http://www.makezine.com

22. See note 30.

23. Mihaly Csikszentmihalyi, *Creativity: Flow and the
Psychology of Discovery and Invention* (New York: Harper
Perennial, 1997), p. 8.

24. Ibid., p. 6.
25. Ibid.
26. Gauntlett, *Creative Explorations*, p.19.
27. Charles J. Lumsden, 'Evolving Creative Minds: Stories and Mechanisms', in Robert J. Sternberg, ed., *Handbook of Creativity* (Cambridge: Cambridge University Press, 1999), p. 153.
28. Matthew Crawford, *The Case for Working with Your Hands: or Why Office Work is Bad for Us and Fixing Things Feels Good* (London: Viking, 2010). Mark Frauenfelder, *Made by Hand: Searching for Meaning in a Throwaway World* (New York: Portfolio, 2010).
29. Richard Sennett, *The Craftsman* (London: Allen Lane, 2008). And for a particular focus on doing things by hand, see Frank R. Wilson, *The Hand: How its Use Shapes the Brain, Language, and Human Culture* (New York: Vintage, 1999).
30. Rob Hopkins, *The Transition Handbook: From Oil Dependency to Local Resilience* (Totnes: Green Books, 2008). Shaun Chamberlin, *The Transition Timeline: For a Local, Resilient Future* (Totnes: Green Books, 2010). For an introduction, see Rob Hopkins' TED talk, http://www.ted.com/talks/rob_hopkins_transition_to_a_world_without_oil.html

Notes to chapter 2, pages 22–44

1. Peter Dormer, 'The Status of Craft', in Peter Dormer, ed., *The Culture of Craft* (Manchester: Manchester University Press, 1997), p. 18.
2. Richard Sennett, *The Craftsman* (London: Allen Lane, 2008), p. 7.
3. Ibid., p. 11.
4. Ellen Dissanayake, 'The Pleasure and Meaning of Making', *American Craft*, April–May 1995, quoted at the

American Craft Council website, http://www.craftcouncil. org/html/about/craft_is.shtml.

5. Dormer, 'The Status of Craft', p. 18.

6. Peter Dormer, 'Craft and the Turing Test for Practical Thinking', in Peter Dormer, ed., *The Culture of Craft* (Manchester: Manchester University Press, 1997), p. 154.

7. John Ruskin, *Selected Writings*, edited by Dinah Birch (Oxford: Oxford University Press, 2009), p. 279.

8. Clive Wilmer, 'Introduction', in John Ruskin, *Unto This Last and Other Writings* (London: Penguin, 1997), p. 24.

9. Ruskin, *Selected Writings*, p. 100.

10. A good short introduction to this context appears in Clive Wilmer's 'Introduction'.

11. By 'moral' I refer to strong ethical beliefs, but not the narrow code of 'Victorian morality'.

12. John Ruskin, 'Unto This Last: Essay IV: Ad Valorem', in *Unto This Last and Other Writings*, edited by Clive Wilmer (London: Penguin, 1997), p. 222.

13. Ibid.

14. See Wilmer, 'Introduction', p. 22.

15. William Morris, 'Preface to The Nature of Gothic', in *News from Nowhere and Other Writings*, edited by Clive Wilmer (London: Penguin, 2004), p. 367.

16. John Ruskin, 'The Nature of Gothic', in *Unto This Last and Other Writings*, edited by Clive Wilmer (London: Penguin, 1997), p. 83.

17. Ibid.

18. Ibid.

19. Ibid., p. 84.

20. Ibid.

21. Ibid., p. 85.

22. Ibid., pp. 85–6.

23. Adam Smith, *An Inquiry into the Nature and Causes of the Wealth of Nations*, available at Project Gutenberg, http://www.gutenberg.org/etext/3300. The quote is from the start of chapter one.

24. Ibid.; this quote is in Book Five, Chapter One, Part Three.

25. Karl Marx, 'Wages of Labour', in *Economic and Philosophic Manuscripts of 1844*, http://www.marxists.org/archive/marx/works/1844/manuscripts/wages.htm. These writings were not published until 1932.

26. P. D. Anthony, *John Ruskin's Labour: A Study of Ruskin's Social Theory* (Cambridge: Cambridge University Press, 1983), pp. 171–2.

27. Ruskin, 'The Nature of Gothic', p. 87.

28. Ibid., p. 90.

29. Ibid.

30. Anthony, *John Ruskin's Labour*, pp. 171–2.

31. Viscount Snowden, in his untitled contribution to *William Morris 1834–1896: Some Appreciations* (London: Walthamstow Historical Society, 2003, originally published 1934).

32. E. P. Thompson, *William Morris: Romantic to Revolutionary* (London: Merlin, 1977), p. 4.

33. Ibid., p. 28.

34. 'Interview with William Morris', *Clarion*, 19 November 1892, reprinted in Tony Pinkney, ed., *We Met Morris: Interviews with William Morris, 1885–96* (Reading: Spire Books, 2005), pp. 63–4.

35. 'The Kelmscott Press: An Illustrated Interview with Mr William Morris', *Bookselling*, Christmas 1895, reprinted in Tony Pinkney, ed., *We Met Morris*, pp. 114–15.

36. 'The Poet as Printer: An Interview with Mr William Morris', *Pall Mall Gazette*, 12 November 1891, reprinted in Tony Pinkney, ed., *We Met Morris*, p. 56.

37. As the company history on Penguin's website explains, 'Penguin paperbacks were the brainchild of Allen Lane [who] found himself on a platform at Exeter station searching its bookstall for something to read on his journey back to London, but discovered only popular magazines and reprints of Victorian novels. Appalled by the selection on offer, Lane decided that good quality contemporary fiction should be made available at an attractive price. . . .The first Penguin paperbacks appeared in the summer of 1935 and included works by Ernest Hemingway, André Maurois and Agatha Christie. They were colour coded (orange for fiction, blue for biography, green for crime) and cost just sixpence, the same price as a packet of cigarettes.' Available at: http://www.penguin.co.uk/static/cs/uk/0/aboutus/aboutpenguin_companyhistory.html
38. Pinkney, 'Introduction', in *We Met Morris*, pp. 18–19.
39. Clive Wilmer, 'Introduction', in *William Morris, News from Nowhere and Other Writings* (London: Penguin, 2004), p. xxii. My emphasis.
40. Ibid., p. xxiii.
41. Thompson, *William Morris*, p. 126.
42. William Morris, 'The Lesser Arts', in *William Morris, News from Nowhere and Other Writings* (London: Penguin, 2004), p. 252.
43. Ibid., p. 253.
44. Ibid., p. 235.
45. Ibid.
46. William Morris, 'Useful Work versus Useless Toil', in *William Morris, News from Nowhere and Other Writings* (London: Penguin, 2004), p. 288.
47. Ibid., pp. 288–9.
48. Ibid., pp. 291–2.
49. Morris, 'Preface to The Nature of Gothic', p. 369.

50. Morris, 'Art Under Plutocracy', quoted in Thompson, *William Morris*, p. 642.

51. Ibid.

52. Clay Shirky, *Here Comes Everybody: The Power of Organizing Without Organizations* (London: Allen Lane, 2008), pp. 81–108.

53. William Morris, 'The Art of the People', in *Hopes and Fears for Art*; available at http://www.marxists.org/archive/morris/works/1882/hopes/

54. Thompson, *William Morris*, p. 686.

Notes to chapter 3, pages 45–79

1. Paul Greenhalgh, 'The History of Craft', in Peter Dormer, ed., *The Culture of Craft* (Manchester: Manchester University Press, 1997), p. 22.

2. The 1785 edition is online at http://www.archive.org/details/dictionaryofengl01johnuoft

3. Greenhalgh, 'The History of Craft', p. 22.

4. Ibid., p. 23.

5. Ibid., p. 25.

6. Elizabeth Cumming and Wendy Kaplan, *The Arts and Crafts Movement* (London: Thames and Hudson, 1991).

7. Greenhalgh, 'The History of Craft', p. 35.

8. Ibid., p. 35.

9. Cumming and Kaplan, *The Arts and Crafts Movement*, p. 178.

10. I found this quote via the helpful Wikipedia article on 'Do it yourself'. A full transcript of the event is available at http://www.vallejo.to/articles/summit_pt1.htm

11. John Holt, *How Children Fail* (London: Penguin, 1990, originally published 1964). John Holt, *How Children Learn* (London: Penguin, 1991, originally published 1967).

12. See also the very good John Holt, *Instead of Education:*

Ways to Help People Do Things Better (Boulder, CO: Sentient, 2004, originally published 1976).

13. Fred Turner, *From Counterculture to Cyberculture: Stewart Brand, the Whole Earth Network, and the Rise of Digital Utopianism* (Chicago: University of Chicago Press, 2006), pp. 69-70. See also Stewart Brand, 'Photography Changes our Relationship to our Planet', http://click.si.edu/Story.aspx?story=31

14. A facsimile of the 1968 catalogue is available online at http://www.wholeearth.com. The word 'defects' is missing from the online reproduction but this seems to be a typographical error which may or may not have been in the original. It is included in Brand's discussion of this statement of purpose at http://wholeearth.com/issue/1010/article/195/we.are.as.gods

15. Amy Spencer, *DIY: The Rise of Lo-Fi Culture* (London: Marion Boyars, 2008), p. 11.

16. Ibid., p. 13.

17. David Gauntlett, 'Web Studies: A User's Guide', in David Gauntlett, ed., *Web Studies: Rewiring Media Studies for the Digital Age* (London: Arnold, 2000), p. 13.

18. Spencer, *DIY*, pp. 19–20.

19. Ibid., p. 50.

20. Betsy Greer is quoted in Spencer, *DIY*, p. 61. See also her website, http://www.craftivism.com, and her book, *Knitting for Good!: A Guide to Creating Personal, Social, and Political Change, Stitch by Stitch* (Boston: Trumpeter, 2008).

21. John Naish, *Enough: Breaking Free from the World of Excess* (London: Hodder and Stoughton, 2009), p. 4.

22. For information and links, see the Wikipedia article, 'Great Pacific Garbage Patch', and the Greenpeace report at http://www.greenpeace.org/international/campaigns/oceans/pollution/trash-vortex/

23. Anthony McCann, 'Crafting Gentleness', at http://www. craftinggentleness.org

24. Ibid.

25. Carl Honoré, *In Praise of Slow: How a Worldwide Movement is Challenging the Cult of Speed* (London: Orion, 2004).

26. This relationship was explored in the exhibition Taking Time: Craft and the Slow Revolution, developed by Helen Carnac and Andy Horn, which toured the UK from 2009 to 2011. For information see http://makingaslowrevolution.wordpress.com and for a related Twitter application see http://www.tweave.co.uk

27. Marybeth C. Stalp, *Quilting: The Fabric of Everyday Life* (Oxford: Berg, 2007), p. 9.

28. Ibid.

29. Faythe Levine, 'Preface', in Faythe Levine and Cortney Heimerl, eds, *Handmade Nation: The Rise of DIY, Art, Craft and Design* (New York: Princeton Architectural Press, 2008), pp. ix–x.

30. The internet, of course, also gives a home to more surprising interests. IKEA Hacker (http://www.ikeahacker. blogspot.com), for instance, is a community sharing ideas and instructions on how to customize and redeploy IKEA furniture in novel ways. There we can see that Martina from Austria has posted instructions on how to turn the IKEA Expedit bookcase into an elaborate hamster home; a user called Steffen shows how to build a model railway inside the IKEA Vinninga coffee table; and David Mingay from Cornwall demonstrates how to make a pinhole camera out of the IKEA Bjuron plant pot holder.

31. Garth Johnson, 'Down the Tubes: In Search of Internet Craft', in Levine and Heimerl, eds, *Handmade Nation*, pp. 30–35.

32. Illustrated in Levine and Heimerl, eds, *Handmade Nation*, p. xx.

33. Interviewed in Levine and Heimerl, eds, *Handmade Nation*, p. 26.

34. Ibid.

35. Matthew Crawford, *The Case for Working With Your Hands: or Why Office Work is Bad for Us and Fixing Things Feels Good* (London: Viking, 2010).

36. Interviewed in Levine and Heimerl, eds, *Handmade Nation*, p. 10.

37. Ibid., p. 46.

38. Ibid., p. 50.

39. Ibid., p. 94.

40. Amanda Blake Soule, *The Creative Family: How to Encourage Imagination and Nurture Family Connections* (Boston: Trumpeter, 2008), p. 7.

41. Ibid., p. 5.

42. http://www.afghansforafghans.org and http://www.fireprojects.org/dulaan

43. Rozsika Parker, *The Subversive Stitch: Embroidery and the Making of the Feminine*, new edition (London: I. B. Tauris, 2010), p. ix.

44. Ibid., p. xx.

45. Joanne Turney, *The Culture of Knitting* (Oxford: Berg, 2009), p. 217.

46. Ibid., p. 220.

47. Marybeth C. Stalp, *Quilting: The Fabric of Everyday Life* (Oxford: Berg, 2007), pp. 129–40.

48. Ibid., p. 132.

49. Richard Reynolds, *On Guerrilla Gardening: A Handbook for Gardening Without Boundaries* (London: Bloomsbury, 2008), p. 16.

50. See also Barbara Pallenberg, *Guerrilla Gardening: How to Create Gorgeous Gardens for Free* (Los Angeles:

Renaissance Books, 2001), and David Tracey, *Guerrilla Gardening: A Manualfesto* (Gabriola Island: New Society, 2007).

51. Mihaly Csikszentmihalyi, *Flow: The Classic Work on How to Achieve Happiness*, revised edition (London: Rider, 2002, first published 1990).

Notes to chapter 4, pages 80–114

1. To be fair, software did exist to support webpage and website creation in 1997, but I didn't have it. As it turned out, the early tools which created HTML on your behalf were not very good or precise anyway, so it was much better to be able to write the code yourself.

2. You will, of course, be able to find newer data online. For instance, visit the ComScore website at http://www.comscore.com, go to 'Press Releases', and search for keyword 'video'. These particular statistics come from http://www.comscore.com/Press_Events/Press_Releases/2009/9/Google_Sites_Surpasses_10_Billion_Video_Views_in_August

3. Miguel Helft, 'YouTube: We're Bigger Than You Thought', *The New York Times*, 9 October 2009, http://bits.blogs.nytimes.com/2009/10/09/youtube-were-bigger-than-you-thought/

4. YouTube, 'YouTube Fact Sheet', 2009, http://www.youtube.com/t/fact_sheet

5. I saw this video a couple of years ago, and now it is difficult to track down which one it was; but it would be one of the ones on Chris Anderson's YouTube channel for this particular hobby, at http://www.youtube.com/user/zlite or at http://diydrones.com/profile/zlitezlite

6. John Ruskin, *The Seven Lamps of Architecture* (London: Waverley, 1920), p.155; available at http://www.archive.org/details/1920sevenlampsof00ruskuoft

7. Ibid., p. 154.
8. John Ruskin, 'The Nature of Gothic', in *Unto This Last and Other Writings*, edited by Clive Wilmer (London: Penguin, 1997), p. 89.
9. Ibid.
10. Some parts of this discussion of YouTube were originally written by me as part of my contribution to Edith Ackermann, David Gauntlett and Cecilia Weckström, *Systematic Creativity in the Digital Realm* (Billund: LEGO Learning Institute, 2010).
11. See Jean Burgess and Joshua Green, *YouTube: Online Video and Participatory Culture* (Cambridge: Polity, 2009), and Pelle Snickars and Patrick Vonderau, eds, *The YouTube Reader* (Stockholm: National Library of Sweden, 2009).
12. Mark Andrejevic, 'Exploiting YouTube: Contradictions of User-Generated Labor', in Snickars and Vonderau, eds, *The YouTube Reader*.
13. Ibid., p. 421.
14. Virginia Nightingale, 'The Cameraphone and Online Image Sharing', *Continuum: Journal of Media and Cultural Studies*, vol. 21, no. 2 (2007), pp. 289–301, cited in Burgess and Green, *YouTube: Online Video and Participatory Culture*, p. 60.
15. Jean Burgess and Joshua Green, 'The Entrepreneurial Vlogger: Participatory Culture Beyond the Professional–Amateur Divide', in Snickars and Vonderau, eds, *The YouTube Reader*.
16. Patricia G. Lange, 'Videos of Affinity on YouTube', in Snickars and Vonderau, eds, *The YouTube Reader*.
17. Clay Shirky, *Here Comes Everybody: The Power of Organizing Without Organizations* (London: Penguin, 2008), p. 85.
18. Martin Creed, interviewed in *Illuminations*, eds, *Art Now:*

Interviews with Modern Artists (London: Continuum, 2002).

19. Burgess and Green, *YouTube*, pp. 38–57.
20. Machinima is a term for animations made using video games: by using game characters as puppets, recording the visual output and recording a new audio track for them.
21. Burgess and Green, *YouTube*, p. 4.
22. Jean Burgess and Joshua Green, 'The Entrepreneurial Vlogger: Participatory Culture Beyond the Professional–Amateur Divide', in Snickars and Vonderau, eds, *The YouTube Reader*.
23. Ibid., p. 101.
24. In November 2009, Oprah's YouTube channel had 64,200 subscribers, two years after its launch in November 2007.
25. Burgess and Green, 'The Entrepreneurial Vlogger', p. 105.
26. Henry Jenkins, 'What Happened Before YouTube', in Burgess and Green, *YouTube*, p. 116.
27. Ibid.
28. See Jenkins, 'What Happened Before YouTube', p. 120, and Lewis Hyde, *The Gift: How the Creative Spirit Transforms the World* (London: Canongate, 2007).
29. Leisa Reichelt, 'Ambient Intimacy', 1 March 2007, http://www.disambiguity.com/ambient-intimacy
30. Ibid.
31. Interview with David Jennings, London, 2 July 2010.
32. Ibid.
33. Amanda Blake Soule, 'Snapshots', posted on SouleMama blog, 31 March 2009, http://www.soulemama.com/soulemama/2009/03/oldest-youngest.html
34. This interesting way in which the recording of activity actually prompts *more* of that activity, as well as more

awareness of it, is discussed in a blog post by Dan Hill, who notes that he observed 'how wearing a pedometer for a week made me walk further; how using Last FM to track my listening has made me play more music, and to certainly be more aware of the music I'm playing; how using Flickr to store, organise and communicate my photos has probably made me take more photos in the first place, and again to certainly be more aware of my photos (even if it hasn't made me a better photographer).' See Dan Hill, 'The Personal Well-Tempered Environment', 15 January 2008, http://www.cityofsound. com/blog/2008/01/the-personal-we.html

35. Amanda Blake Soule, 'Snapshots'.

36. As of July 2010, there were 554 comments on this one blog post, all of them – as far as I could see – filled with appreciation.

37. Obviously this is a small, self-selected and unsystematic sample. At the time of doing this (June 2010) I had 1,238 followers on Twitter.

38. Rosanna E. Guadagno, Bradley M. Okdie and Cassie A. Eno, 'Who Blogs? Personality Predictors of Blogging', *Computers in Human Behavior*, vol. 24 (2008), pp. 1993–2004.

39. This is not a whim – discussions of research methodologies appear in a number of my books, including *Moving Experiences* (1995, 2005), *Video Critical* (1997) and *Creative Explorations* (2007).

40. Getting a university class to fill in questionnaires is, at best, a lazy way to do research, and the findings are presented in the journal abstract – and would probably be reported in newspapers – as if they cover 'people' in general. The authors' summary would lead you to assume they'd surveyed a representative sample of at least 1,000 people across the country – which would be the standard

proper way to do it – but they haven't. This seems to happen in psychology journal articles a lot – small-scale studies where the researchers have used their own students (or someone else's, a couple of doors down), and then present this as findings about the world.

41. A Google search for 'Rosanna Guadagno blogging' shows that the study has been mentioned in several places, and Google Scholar says that it has been cited in 27 other documents (as of June 2010).

42. Guadagno et al., 'Who Blogs?', p. 2001.

43. Ibid., pp. 2001–2. Punctuation slightly modified for readability.

44. Asako Miura and Kiyomi Yamashita, 'Psychological and Social Influences on Blog Writing: An Online Survey of Blog Authors in Japan', *Journal of Computer-Mediated Communication*, vol. 12, no. 4 (2007), http://jcmc.indiana.edu/vol12/issue4/miura.html

45. Ibid.

46. Ibid.

47. David R. Brake, *'As if Nobody's Reading'?: The Imagined Audience and Socio-technical Biases in Personal Blogging Practice in the UK* (PhD thesis, London School of Economics, 2009); available at http://eprints.lse.ac.uk/25535/

48. Email from David Brake, 1 July 2010.

49. Nancy K. Baym and Robert Burnett, 'Amateur Experts: International Fan Labour in Swedish Independent Music', *International Journal of Cultural Studies*, vol. 12, no. 5 (2009), pp. 433–49.

50. Ibid., p. 445.

51. Ibid., p. 443.

52. Modified from Rozsika Parker, *The Subversive Stitch: Embroidery and the Making of the Feminine*, new edition (London: I. B. Tauris, 2010), p. xx.

53. Wikipedia's article on Second Life, for instance, lists

many uses of the platform, http://en.wikipedia.org/wiki/
Second_Life

54. This quote has been slightly edited/rewritten for length.
Dougald Hine, 'How Not to Predict the Future (or
why Second Life is Like Video Calling)', 27 April 2009,
http://otherexcuses.blogspot.com/2009/04/how-not-to-
predict-future-or-why-second.html

55. Dougald Hine, 'The "Why Don't You?" Web', blog
post, 1 December 2008, http://schoolofeverything.com/
blog/why-dont-you-web

56. Ibid.

Notes to chapter 5, pages 115–127

1. Richard Layard, *Happiness: Lessons from a New Science*
(London: Penguin, 2006), p. 42.

2. Daniel Gilbert, *Stumbling on Happiness* (London: Harper
Perennial, 2007). Drake Bennett, 'Perfectly Happy',
Boston Globe, 10 May 2009, http://www.boston.com/
bostonglobe/ideas/articles/2009/05/10/perfectly_happy/

3. Layard, *Happiness*, p. 48–9. Paul Taylor, Cary Funk and
Peyton Craighill, *Are We Happy Yet?* (Washington DC:
Pew Research Center, 2006), http://pewresearch.org/
pubs/301/are-we-happy-yet

4. Taylor et al., *Are We Happy Yet?*

5. Layard, *Happiness*. Taylor et al., *Are We Happy Yet?*

6. Interviewed in Joseph T. Hallinan, *Errornomics: Why
We Make Mistakes and What We Can Do to Avoid Them*
(London: Ebury Press, 2009), pp. 201–8.

7. Ibid., p. 201.

8. David A. Schkade and Daniel Kahneman, 'Does Living
in California Make People Happy? A Focusing Illusion
in Judgments of life Satisfaction', *Psychological Science*,
vol. 9, no. 5 (1998), pp. 340–6.

9. Deborah D. Danner, David A. Snowdon and Wallace V.

Friesen 'Positive Emotions in Early Life and Longevity: Findings from the Nun Study', *Journal of Personality and Social Psychology*, vol. 80, no. 5 (2001), pp. 804–13.
10. Layard, *Happiness*, p. 63.
11. Ibid.
12. Ibid., pp. 64–5.
13. For up-to-date information on the legal status of officially recognized same-sex partnerships, Wikipedia has a detailed article titled 'Same-Sex Marriage'.
14. Layard, *Happiness*, p. 66.
15. Ibid., p. 68.
16. Taylor et al., *Are We Happy Yet?*, p. 32.
17. Bruno S. Frey and Alois Stutzer, 'Happiness, Economy and Institutions', Working Paper No. 15 (Zurich: Institute for Empirical Research in Economics, University of Zurich, 1999); available at http://www.iew.uzh.ch/wp/iewwp015.pdf. See also Bruno S. Frey and Alois Stutzer, *Happiness and Economics: How the Economy and Institutions Affect Human Well-Being* (Princeton: Princeton University Press, 2001).
18. Frey and Stutzer, 'Happiness, Economy and Institutions', pp. 11–12.
19. Layard, *Happiness*, p. 72.
20. Taylor et al., *Are We Happy Yet?*, p. 6.
21. Ibid.
22. Layard, *Happiness*, p. 73.
23. Tibor Scitovsky, *The Joyless Economy: The Psychology of Human Satisfaction* (New York: Oxford University Press, 1992).
24. Sonja Lyubomirsky, Kennon M. Sheldon and David Schkade, 'Pursuing Happiness: The Architecture of Sustainable Change', *Review of General Psychology*, vol. 9 (2005), pp. 111–31; available at http://www.faculty.ucr.edu/~sonja/papers.html

25. Kennon M. Sheldon and Sonja Lyubomirsky, 'Change Your Actions, Not Your Circumstances: An Experimental Test of the Sustainable Happiness Model', in A. K. Dutt and B. Radcliff, eds, *Happiness, Economics, and Politics: Toward a Multi-Disciplinary Approach* (New York: Edward Elgar, 2009); available at http://www.faculty. ucr.edu/~sonja/papers.html

26. Lyubomirsky et al, 'Pursuing Happiness', pp. 118-20. Julia K. Boehm and Sonja Lyubomirsky, 'The Promise of Sustainable Happiness', in S. J. Lopez, ed., *Handbook of Positive Psychology*, second edition (Oxford: Oxford University Press, 2009), pp. 671-3; available at http:// www.faculty.ucr.edu/~sonja/papers.html

27. Layard, *Happiness*, p. 234.

Notes to chapter 6, pages 128-161

1. Governments can also, of course, offer tax breaks and financial help for married couples, although this can be perceived as lifestyle discrimination and unwarranted meddling in personal lives.

2. L. J. Hanifan, 1916, quoted in Robert D. Putnam, *Bowling Alone: The Collapse and Revival of American Community* (New York: Simon and Schuster, 2001), p. 19.

3. Pierre Bourdieu, *Distinction: A Social Critique of the Judgement of Taste* (London: Routledge and Kegan Paul, 1984). Pierre Bourdieu, 'The Forms of Capital', in John G. Richardson, ed., *Handbook of Theory and Research for the Sociology of Education* (New York: Greenwood, 1986).

4. Pierre Bourdieu, in Pierre Bourdieu and Loic J. D. Wacquant, *An Invitation to Reflexive Sociology* (Chicago: University of Chicago Press, 1992), p. 119.

5. See for instance the report, 'Unleashing Aspiration: The Final Report of the Panel on Fair Access to the

Professions', commissioned by the UK Prime Minister and published in July 2009; available at http://www.cabinetoffice.gov.uk/media/227102/fair-access.pdf. Its findings are succinctly summarized in *The Guardian*'s headline: 'Britain's Closed Shop: Damning Report on Social Mobility Failings – Wealth and Private School Remain Key to Professions', 21 July 2009.

6. James S. Coleman, 'Social Capital in the Creation of Human Capital', *American Journal of Sociology*, 94, Supplement: Organizations and Institutions: Sociological and Economic Approaches to the Analysis of Social Structure (1988), pp. S95–S120.

7. Ibid., pp. 104–5.

8. Ibid., p. 109.

9. Alexis de Tocqueville, *Democracy in America, Volume II* (1840, translated by Henry Reeve, 1899), section 2, chapter 5. The text is available online in places which include: http://xroads.virginia.edu/~HYPER/DETOC/

10. Ibid.

11. Ibid.

12. Ibid., section 2, chapter 7.

13. http://www.bowlingalone.com

14. John Field, *Social Capital*, second edition (London: Routledge, 2008), p. 35.

15. Robert D. Putnam, *Bowling Alone: The Collapse and Revival of American Community* (New York: Simon and Schuster, 2001), p. 19.

16. Ibid.

17. Ibid., p. 53.

18. Ibid., p. 104.

19. Ibid., p. 114.

20. Ibid., p. 283.

21. Ibid.

22. Ibid., p. 275, p. 283.

23. Ibid., p. 283.

24. Ibid., p. 221.

25. Ibid., p. 231.

26. Ibid., p. 241.

27. Ibid., p. 215.

28. Ibid., p. 283.

29. Some of whom seemed to be behind the badly conducted 'media effects' studies that I discussed in the book *Moving Experiences* (1995, second edition 2005).

30. Putnam, *Bowling Alone*, p. 287, emphasis added.

31. Ibid., p. 311.

32. Ibid., p. 312.

33. Ibid., pp. 288–9.

34. These statistics are from http://www.internetworldstats.com and are based on data compiled by Nielsen NetRatings.

35. Literally. In November 1998, the two-minute teaser trailer for *Star Wars Episode I: The Phantom Menace* was released online. We hadn't seen the film then, obviously, and so everyone was very excited. I left my computer on all night to download this 25 mb file. The first night it crashed half way through, so I had to try again the next night. Today, downloading a 25 mb file on my home connection takes about a minute.

36. UK data from the year 2000, http://www.statistics.gov.uk/pdfdir/inter0700.pdf

37. Office for National Statistics, *Statistical Bulletin: Internet Access – Households and Individuals*, 27 August 2010, http://www.statistics.gov.uk/pdfdir/iahi0810.pdf

38. Putnam, *Bowling Alone*, pp. 169–80.

39. Ibid., p. 170.

40. Howard Rheingold, *The Virtual Community* (1993). The book is available free online at http://www.rheingold.com/vc/book/

41. Putnam, *Bowling Alone*, p. 171.
42. Ibid.
43. Ibid., p. 172.
44. Ibid., p. 173.
45. Ibid., p. 174.
46. Ibid., pp. 174–80.
47. Ibid., p. 179.
48. Jean Burgess and Joshua Green, *YouTube: Online Video and Participatory Culture* (Cambridge: Polity, 2009).
49. Putnam, *Bowling Alone*, p. 180, emphasis added.
50. Jonathan Zittrain, *The Future of the Internet And How to Stop It* (London: Penguin, 2009).
51. See Field, *Social Capital*, second edition, p. 42.
52. Putnam, *Bowling Alone*, p. 359.
53. Michael Edwards, *Civil Society* (Cambridge: Polity, 2004), p. 42.
54. Ibid., p. 86.
55. For readable introductions to the broader field, see for instance John Field, *Social Capital*; Michael Edwards, *Civil Society*; and David Halpern, *Social Capital* (Cambridge: Polity, 2005).
56. Field, *Social Capital*, second edition, p. 160. This quote is slightly edited here: Field attributes the notion of 'meso-level social structures' to a 1997 article by Bob Edwards and Michael W. Foley, and the three dimensions of social capital to a 2007 article by Sara Ferlander.
57. Field, *Social Capital*, second edition, p. 161.

Notes to chapter 7, pages 162–184

 1. Some parts of this discussion of Ivan Illich appeared previously in David Gauntlett, 'Media Studies 2.0: A Response', *Interactions: Studies in Communication and Culture*, vol. 1, no. 1 (2009).

2. Ivan Illich, *Deschooling Society* (London: Marion Boyars, 2002), pp. 2–3.

3. Ibid., p. 3.

4. Ibid., p. 72.

5. Ibid., p. 75.

6. Ibid., p. 110.

7. Ivan Illich, *Tools for Conviviality* (London: Calder and Boyars, 1973), pp. 20–1.

8. David Cayley, *Ivan Illich in Conversation* (Toronto: House of Anansi Press, 2007), p. 108.

9. Illich, *Tools for Conviviality*, p. 11.

10. Ibid.

11. Ibid.

12. Ibid., p. xi.

13. In a later work, Illich suggests that immersion in the world of a book is a powerful experience that is lost when we live in a world of short electronic fragments of information, even if the latter are more accessible. See Ivan Illich, *In the Vineyard of the Text: A Commentary to Hugh's Didascalicon* (Chicago: University of Chicago Press, 1993). On the other hand, we learn from a memoir that Illich, in the early 1990s, 'did exchange his portable typewriter for a laptop and soon became the first person I knew in Germany who had somehow gained access to an on-line library catalogue, that of Pennsylvania State University, well before the pervasive onslaught of modems and Internet sources'. See Gesine Bottomley, 'Ivan Illich at the Wissenschaftskolleg', in Lee Hoinacki and Carl Mitcham, eds, *The Challenges of Ivan Illich: A Collective Reflection* (New York: State University of New York Press), p. 56.

14. Illich, *Deschooling Society*, p. 77.

15. Ibid.

16. See the Wikipedia article on 'Community Memory'.

17. Quoted in Charles Leadbeater, *We Think: Mass Innovation not Mass Production* (London: Profile Books, 2008), pp. 42–3. See also Patrice Flichy, *The Internet Imaginaire* (Cambridge, MA: MIT Press, 2007).
18. Illich, *Tools for Conviviality*, p. 20.
19. Ibid., p. 22.
20. Ibid., p. 21.
21. Ibid., p. 75.
22. See in particular Apple's promotional 2010 video featuring a gushing Jonathan Ive, at http://www.youtube.com/watch?v=LKNNDeLNso8, and Steven Levy, 'Tabula Rasa: Why the New Generation of Tablet Computers Changes Everything', *Wired*, UK edition, May 2010, pp. 121–9.
23. Jonathan Zittrain, *The Future of the Internet And How to Stop It* (London: Penguin, 2009).
24. This particular advert is archived at http://www.macmothership.com/gallery/MiscAds2/1977IntroApple II2.jpg
25. The Commodore Vic-20, launched in 1981, was the first computer of any kind to sell over 1 million units. The young Linus Torvalds, inventor of Linux, learnt to program on it. Of course, computers become obsolete rather quickly. By the mid-1990s, the Vic-20 was laughably old and had spent many years under a bed in my parents' house. I threw it in the bin. Today, I sometimes find myself feeling sad and ashamed that I got rid of it, even though I suppose it would be unlikely to work now. In my early teens I had written dozens of games for it, the basic ideas for which were often nicked from other arcade and computer games. My best one involved the player flying a helicopter over a landscape, picking up some things and shooting some other things. Computer programs like this were recorded and stored on cassette

tape – the same as ordinary audio cassettes – remember those? – which was a wobbly way of recording precise digital data, so there's no way those would be working today anyway. Sometimes at night I wish I could see again the games I made. But I cannot. All that is solid melts into air, etc.

26. Detail on this story, and other aspects of the Apple story, can be found at Steve Weyhrich's extensive *Apple II History* at http://apple2history.org/

27. Zittrain, *The Future of the Internet*, p. 2.

28. Ibid.

29. Ibid., p. 3.

30. AppleInsider, 'Apple Says App Store Has Made Developers over $1 billion', 7 June 2010, http://www.appleinsider.com/articles/10/06/07/apple_says_app_store_has_made_developers_over_1_billion.html

31. As in the case of Mark Fiore, a political cartoonist whose app was rejected by Apple in December 2009, because it 'mocked public figures'. This decision was reversed in April 2010, following public outcry about the rejected app, after Fiore had won the Pulitzer prize. Fiore commented: 'Sure, mine might get approved, but what about someone who hasn't won a Pulitzer and who is maybe making a better political app than mine? Do you need some media frenzy to get an app approved that has political material?' See Brian Stelter, 'A Pulitzer Winner Gets Apple's Reconsideration', *The New York Times*, 16 April 2010, http://www.nytimes.com/2010/04/17/books/17cartoonist.html

32. Zittrain, *The Future of the Internet*, pp. 3–4, p. 184.

33. Tim Berners-Lee, Testimony before the United States House of Representatives Committee on Energy and Commerce, Subcommittee on Telecommunications and the Internet, at the hearing, 'Digital Future of the

United States: Part I – The Future of the World Wide Web', March 2007, http://dig.csail.mit.edu/2007/03/01-ushouse-future-of-the-web

34. Ibid.
35. Ibid.
36. Mehan Jayasuriya, 'What the Google/Verizon Deal Means for Net Neutrality – and You', 13 August 2010, http://www.guardian.co.uk/commentisfree/libertycentral/2010/aug/13/google-verizon-net-neutrality-impact

Notes to chapter 8, pages 185–216

1. This kind of argument is made by commentators such as Mark Andrejevic, Toby Miller and Natalie Fenton.
2. Chris Anderson, *Free: The Future of a Radical Price* (London: Random House Business Books, 2009).
3. Nicholas Carr, 'Web 2.0lier Than Thou', Rough Type blog post, 23 October 2006, http://www.roughtype.com/archives/2006/10/web_20ier_than.php. I am grateful to Stefan Sonvilla-Weiss, who drew my attention to this quote when he interviewed me for his book *Mashup Cultures*.
4. For detail on this, see David Gauntlett, 'Creativity, Participation and Connectedness: An Interview with David Gauntlett', in Stefan Sonvilla-Weiss, ed., *Mashup Cultures* (New York: Springer, 2010).
5. Toby Miller, 'Cybertarians of the World Unite: You Have Nothing to Lose But Your Tubes!', in Pelle Snickars and Patrick Vonderau, eds, *The YouTube Reader* (Stockholm: National Library of Sweden, 2009), p. 432.
6. See http://www.youtube.com/partners. A useful explanation is at http://techcrunch.com/2009/08/25/youtube-extends-revenue-sharing-program-to-anyone-with-a-viral-video/
7. Since Google does not publish separate figures for

YouTube, the figure of US $240 million in ad revenue for 2009 is an estimate by analysts: see http://www. businessinsider.com/is-youtube-doomed-2009-4.   The figure for the number of videos hosted on YouTube is also an estimate. Estimates published during 2009 varied between 130 and 300 million, so in mid-2010 I've picked the round figure of 200 million. This number is, of course, going up all the time.

8. YouTube's operating costs are not published separately, but are buried within overall Google figures. There are educated estimates, however, which vary between US $400 and 700 million a year (in 2009). For this rough calculation I've split the difference and assumed it's around US $550 million dollars a year. See http://ramprate.wordpress.com/2009/06/17/youtube-google%E2%80%99s-phantom-loss-leader/

9. Miller, 'Cybertarians of the World Unite', p. 425.

10. Mark Andrejevic, 'Exploiting YouTube: Contradictions of User-Generated Labor', in Pelle Snickars and Patrick Vonderau, eds, *The YouTube Reader* (Stockholm: National Library of Sweden, 2009), p. 417. Andrejevic is here quoting Nancy Holstrom's version of Marx's understanding of exploitation.

11. Ibid., p. 421.

12. Ibid.

13. For up-to-date information on this topic, search for 'government surveillance of internet' on Google News (or similar). For an outline of the UK situation, see 'Briefing on the Interception Modernisation Programme' by the Policy Engagement Network at the London School of Economics and Political Science, 2009, http://www.lse. ac.uk/collections/informationSystems/research/policy Engagement/IMP_Briefing.pdf. In the US, a well-publicized campaign in 2010 was calling for restrictions

on government access to emails and internet records: see http://www.digitaldueprocess.org

14. See the articles in the special issue of *Interactions: Studies in Communication and Culture*, vol. 1, no. 1 (2009) – in particular the one by Paul A. Taylor – which respond to the idea of 'Media Studies 2.0' as suggested by myself and William Merrin. My original short article on 'Media Studies 2.0', from February 2007, can be found online at http://www.theory.org.uk/mediastudies2.htm

15. Jaron Lanier, *You Are Not a Gadget: A Manifesto* (London: Allen Lane, 2010).

16. Ibid., pp. 68–9.

17. Ibid., p. 48.

18. Ibid., p. 5.

19. Ibid., p. 143.

20. Ibid., p. 143.

21. Kate Land et al., 'Galaxy Zoo: The Large-Scale Spin Statistics of Spiral Galaxies in the Sloan Digital Sky Survey', *Monthly Notices of the Royal Astronomical Society*, vol. 388, no. 4 (2009), pp. 1686–92.

22. Lanier, *You Are Not a Gadget*, p. 49.

23. Ibid., p. 45, p. 49.

24. Ibid., p. 26.

25. Ray Kurzweil, *The Singularity Is Near* (London: Duckworth, 2005).

26. Lanier, *You Are Not a Gadget*, p. 50.

27. Clay Shirky, *Here Comes Everybody: The Power of Organizing Without Organizations* (London: Allen Lane, 2008).

28. Charles Leadbeater, *We Think: Mass Innovation not Mass Production* (London: Profile Books, 2008).

29. Chris Anderson, *The Long Tail: How Endless Choice Is Creating Unlimited Demand* (London: Random House Business Books, 2006).

30. Chris Anderson, *Free: The Future of a Radical Price* (London: Random House Business Books, 2009), p. 81.

31. Ibid., p. 19.

32. This phenomenon is covered by Anderson, *Free*, pp. 153-8. It has also been the subject of numerous blog posts and newspaper articles – so many that it's not worth listing them here, but for example a Google search for 'music download paying t-shirts gigs site:guardian.co.uk' gave me several. One good example is 'Who Calls the Tune in the New Music Age?' by Miranda Sawyer, *The Observer*, Sunday 3 February 2008. See also http://www.guardian.co.uk/business/musicindustry

33. See Lanier, *You Are Not a Gadget*, pp. 90-1.

34. Ibid., p. 101.

35. A great deal of online video is delivered using Adobe Flash, which is a proprietary technology. Adobe currently gives away the Flash Player for free, but there is no guarantee that this would always be the case. This is seen by some commentators as a threat to the free Web. (For examples see David Baker, 'Mozilla vs King Corporate', *Wired*, UK edition, May 2010, pp. 112-19; and the Wikipedia article, 'Adobe Flash'.) Open-source alternatives, such as HTML5, avoid this problem. Adobe Flash is also said to include an unusually high number of security risks (for instance, Symantec and McAfee have both reported that Flash has vulnerabilities that are frequently attacked with malware, in 2009-10). Again, this could be dealt with more efficiently in an open-source application.

36. 'Frequently asked questions' at the Wikimedia Foundation website, http://wikimediafoundation.org/wiki/Frequently_Asked_Questions (accessed on 24 May 2010).

37. Ibid.

38. Google, 'Corporate Information: Our Philosophy: Ten Things We Know to Be True', http://www.google.com/corporate/tenthings.html (accessed on 24 May 2010).

39. Wikimedia Foundation Financial reports, http://wikimediafoundation.org/wiki/Financial_reports (accessed on 24 May 2010).

40. See http://www.ramprate.com/2009/06/youtube-googles-phantom-loss-leader/

41. Wikimedia Foundation Financial reports, http://wikimediafoundation.org/wiki/Financial_reports (accessed on 24 May 2010).

42. In the second half of 2009, the Wikimedia Foundation received donations from 226,382 'community donors' at an average donation of US $33.18. See http://wikimedia foundation.org/wiki/Financial_reports/

43. The BBC Annual Report for 2009–10 records that the BBC's total operating costs for the year ended 31 March 2010 were £4,268 million.

44. Sometimes the 'no ads' offers can be confusing. For instance, Vimeo, a popular video-sharing site, allows users to pay a monthly or annual fee for a 'Vimeo Plus' account, which offers – amongst other features – 'No ads'. However, this only applies to the user who has paid for the 'Vimeo Plus' account – *they* won't see ads on the site. But when that person's videos are viewed by other regular users, adverts will still be displayed alongside that content.

Notes to chapter 9, pages 217–245

1. For instance, upmarket newspapers in the UK, especially *The Guardian*, have tended to be relatively curious and positive about online culture, although the bigger-selling tabloids, in particular the *Daily Mail* and *Daily Express*, have generally gone for ridiculous scare stories.

The fear of the online amateur amongst media professionals is most lucidly expressed in Andrew Keen's book *The Cult of the Amateur: How Today's Internet Is Killing Our Culture and Assaulting Our Economy* (London: Nicholas Brealey, 2007).

2. Clay Shirky, *Cognitive Surplus: Creativity and Generosity in a Connected Age* (London: Allen Lane, 2010), pp. 17–20. The 'lolcat' site he picks out is http://icanhascheez burger.com

3. Facebook statistics and timeline can be found at http://www.facebook.com/press. YouTube statistics are periodically highlighted at the Official YouTube Blog, at http://youtube-global.blogspot.com. The post about exceeding 2 billion views per day ('nearly double the prime-time audience of all three major U.S. television networks combined') was from 16 May 2010.

4. Richard Layard, *Happiness: Lessons from a New Science* (London: Penguin, 2006), p. 66.

5. Ibid., p. 234, emphasis added.

6. A summary of this approach appears in the chapter on Giddens in my book *Media, Gender and Identity*, second edition (London: Routledge, 2008).

7. John Field, *Social Capital*, second edition (London: Routledge, 2008), p. 160.

8. Ivan Illich, *Tools for Conviviality* (London: Calder and Boyars, 1973), p. 21.

9. Nick Couldry, *Why Voice Matters: Culture and Politics after Neoliberalism* (London: Sage, 2010), p. vi.

10. For instance, Couldry mentions a 2006 UK survey which found that 'Most pre-school children want to be a celebrity when they are older' (Couldry, 2010, p. 81). Similarly, a 2009 survey of 3,000 UK young people aged 5–11 found that their top three career aspirations were sports star, pop star, and actor, as reported by their

parents. The parents also said what they themselves had aspired to be; the top three were teacher, banker, and doctor. Available at http://www.taylorherring.com/blog/index.php/tag/traditional-careers/ and http://www.guardian.co.uk/lifeandstyle/2010/apr/17/i-want-to-be-famous

11. Couldry, *Why Voice Matters*, pp. 16–17.

12. To find recent studies of Twitter usage, I suggest you ask Google for 'Twitter user survey' or 'Twitter user statistics'. Two studies from 2009 confirming the trends mentioned here can be found at http://www.sysomos.com/insidetwitter and http://www.pearanalytics.com/blog/wp-content/uploads/2010/05/Twitter-Study-August-2009.pdf

13. This is the more gloomy way to express the argument made by Chris Anderson in *The Long Tail: How Endless Choice Is Creating Unlimited Demand* (London: Random House Business Books, 2006). Anderson's point is that there is a very *high* demand for all these items in aggregate, even though at an individual level each one may be requested rarely.

14. Matthew Hindman, *The Myth of Digital Democracy* (Princeton: Princeton University Press, 2009).

15. I apologize that this is a mangled remix of the pebbles – boulders – beach metaphor used by Charles Leadbeater to describe the rise of amateur/online producers in the media landscape.

16. In other words, adding plants to a garden is valuable – you don't have to be doing bio-engineering on individual flowers simultaneously with 1,000 others. (That is to say: Wikipedia is a good model of collaboration, but so is YouTube.)

17. The BBC's licence fee income was £3.447 billion in the year to April 2010, and £3.494 billion in the year to April

2009. BBC, Full Financial and Governance Statements 2009/10, http://downloads.bbc.co.uk/annualreport/pdf/bbc_ar_online_2009_10.pdf

18. Remarkably, for instance, Guy Claxton reports in his book *What's the Point of School?* (Oxford: Oneworld, 2008) that of all the headteachers whom he has asked in an informal poll at conferences, almost none of them believe that the current system is preparing young people well for the future (pp. 22–3).

19. Claxton, *What's the Point of School?*, pp. 123–6.

20. This is a paraphrase of an argument made by Matthew Crawford, *The Case for Working With Your Hands: or Why Office Work is Bad for Us and Fixing Things Feels Good* (London: Viking, 2010), p. 156.

21. See Richard Wilkinson and Kate Pickett, *The Spirit Level: Why Equality is Better for Everyone* (London: Penguin, 2010).

22. David Gauntlett, *Creative Explorations: New Approaches to Identities and Audiences* (London: Routledge, 2007). The methods indicated here are those of Lego Serious Play.

23. Rob Hopkins, 'Transition to a World Without Oil', presentation at TED Global, Oxford, July 2009, http://www.ted.com/talks/rob_hopkins_transition_to_a_world_without_oil.html

24. Ibid.

INDEX